Para

Michael Huemer

Paradox Lost

Logical Solutions to Ten Puzzles of Philosophy

Michael Huemer
Philosophy Department
University of Colorado Boulder
Boulder, CO, USA

ISBN 978-3-319-90489-4   ISBN 978-3-319-90490-0   (eBook)
https://doi.org/10.1007/978-3-319-90490-0

Library of Congress Control Number: 2018942225

Cover credit: Physicx
Cover design: Fatima Jamadar

Printed on acid-free paper

This Palgrave Macmillan imprint is published by the registered company Springer International Publishing AG part of Springer Nature.
The registered company address is: Gewerbestrasse 11, 6330 Cham, Switzerland

Printed by Markono Print Media Pte Ltd

For those to whom this book is dedicated

Preface

I wrote this book because I like paradoxes … but even more than paradoxes, I like solutions. If you like such things too, then you might enjoy this book. I have offered my solutions to ten of what I found to be particularly fascinating and mind-boggling philosophical paradoxes. I hope that when you read the paradoxes, you feel puzzled and challenged, and that when you read the solutions, you feel a sense of things falling into place. In some cases, I hope you also come away with philosophically significant lessons.

I have written this book in such a way that, I hope, the generally educated reader can follow it. That is, although I assume you are generally smart and educated, I do not assume that you have read any of the literature on the paradoxes, nor any other specialized literature. Thus, I explain each paradox as if you don't know what it is. When I want to address an idea that other philosophers have advanced, I explain that idea. I have made my explanations as clear and concise as I knew how to do, hoping neither to confuse you nor to waste your time. Complications and qualifications, as well as references to the literature, appear in footnotes.

At the same time, I have tried to write something of interest to professional philosophers. In many cases, my take on a paradox is distinctive and unorthodox. (If not for this, I would not have been motivated to write the book.) This is true particularly for chapters 2, 3, 6, 8, and 10.

Academic authors routinely overestimate their audiences – whatever our topic, we tend to vastly overestimate both the number of people interested in it, and the level of background knowledge people have about it. I think we overestimate the knowledge and interest even of other academics. (This involves a certain failure of reflection – we know, or should know, that our own knowledge of almost every other subject is minimal, yet we fail to consider that almost everyone else has about the same level of knowledge of our area of specialization.) Thus, there are many books that can only be usefully read by a handful of people in the world. I wrote this book in the way that I did because I wanted to make an intellectually valuable contribution, without adding to the stock of nearly-unread academic volumes. That is why it is as complex as it is, and why it is not more complex.

Now I would like to thank several other thinkers for discussion of some of the ideas in this book, including Iskra Fileva, Randall McCutcheon, Roy Sorensen, Eddy Chen, Christian Lee, Sam Director, David Barnett, Ari Armstrong, an anonymous referee for Palgrave, and the philosophers at the University of Vermont (to whom I presented chapter 3). Without their help, this book would be worse than it is. Naturally, none of these people can be blamed for any errors that remain. In the preface to my last book, I laid the blame for any errors on my PhD advisor, Peter Klein. I now realize that this was unfair and highly inappropriate. So I want to be clear that Peter is not to blame for the errors in this book. Of course, the blame for any errors falls entirely on my research assistant, Jasmine Carter, and my former student Matt Skene. I specifically instructed them to correct all errors in the manuscript. I thank them for their comments, and I will graciously accept their apology for my mistakes.

Fortunately, however, if the sentence you are now reading is true, then there are no errors in this book.

Boulder, CO, USA   Michael Huemer

Contents

Analytical Contents

List of Figures

1

Introduction

1.1 What Is a Paradox?

First, some words about what a paradox *isn't*. Some people understand the word "paradox" to refer to a case in which reality is contradictory, that is, a situation that you would correctly describe by contradicting yourself. I do not use the word this way, because I find it inconvenient. If we use "paradox" to denote a situation containing a true contradiction, then we will have to say that, by definition, there are no paradoxes, since contradictions are necessarily false – thus apparently depriving this book of its subject matter. I should then have to say that this is a book about "*apparent* paradoxes", that the next chapter is about "the Liar Pseudo-paradox", and so on. This would be tedious. So I won't understand "paradox" that way.

Some people use "paradox" simply to refer to a contradictory statement, or apparently contradictory statement, such as "Nobody goes to that restaurant anymore because it is too crowded." That also is not what I mean by "paradox". Such statements are either false, or simply have an alternate meaning that is different from the most superficial interpretation (as in the statement, "I am nobody", which really just means "I am unimportant"). In either case, there is no real puzzle.

© The Author(s) 2018
M. Huemer, *Paradox Lost*, https://doi.org/10.1007/978-3-319-90490-0_1

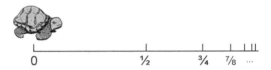

Fig. 1.1 Zeno's paradox

I understand a paradox, roughly, as a situation in which we have seemingly compelling reasoning for a contradictory or otherwise absurd conclusion.[1] We feel that we cannot accept the conclusion, but nor can we readily identify a flaw in the reasoning. For example, consider Zeno's famous paradox of motion (figure 1.1):

> In order for an object to move from point A to point B, the object must first travel half the distance. Then it will have to travel half the remaining distance. Then half the remaining distance again. And so on. This is an infinite series. An infinite series has no end; hence, it is impossible to complete an infinite series. Therefore, it is impossible for the object to reach point B. Thus, no object can move anywhere.

The conclusion is absurd, so the reasoning must be wrong. Nevertheless, the reasoning has a certain obvious, intuitive force, and it is difficult to say exactly what is wrong with it.

To count as "paradoxical", the reasoning for the absurd conclusion must have widespread appeal – that is, the reasoning must be of a sort that would seem compelling to typical human reasoners; an idiosyncratic error that I personally can't seem to shake does not qualify. Thus, if I make a calculation error in multiplying a string of numbers, which results in my deriving a logically impossible conclusion, this will not count as a paradox – not even if I personally cannot find the error after many tries.

To count as "paradoxical", a piece of erroneous reasoning must also have a certain sort of *robustness*: paradoxes bear extended contemplation and discussion. Paradoxes can have solutions and attempted solutions, but the correctness of a given solution will be a matter of debate, at least for some

---

[1] Similarly, Sainsbury (2009, p. 1) defines a paradox as "an apparently unacceptable conclusion derived by apparently acceptable reasoning from apparently acceptable premises". But see below in the text for further conditions on paradoxicality.

time, even among the experts. A paradox is not merely a problem whose solution, though known to experts, is unknown to most non-experts. Thus, for example, I do not consider the Monty Hall Problem to be a paradox. The Monty Hall Problem goes like this:

You are a contestant on the game show *Let's Make a Deal*, with host Monty Hall. You know how the game works: at a certain point in the game, Monty shows the contestant three closed doors. One of the doors has a nice prize behind it (say, a new car); the other two have goats behind them (assume that no one wants a goat). The contestant is allowed to choose one of the doors, and will be allowed to have whatever is behind it. After the contestant chooses, but before he reveals what is behind the chosen door, Monty opens one of the *other* two doors and shows the contestant a goat.[2] He never opens the door with the car behind it; he always shows the contestant a goat.[3] Monty then asks if the contestant would like to change their choice, that is, to switch to the other closed door. Thus, suppose you initially

---

[2] This is not exactly how the real game worked, but pretend the game works this way for purposes of the problem. In the real game, Monty was not required to show the contestant a goat or offer the chance to switch, and usually he did not do so (Tierney 1991).

[3] The stipulation that Monty always opens a door with a goat behind it is sometimes erroneously omitted from the statement of the problem, as in vos Savant (1990–91) (vos Savant makes the assumption in her solution, but the original problem statement did not contain it). Without this stipulation, the correct probability is ½. That is, suppose we assume that Monty, rather than deliberately avoiding the door with the prize, simply chooses randomly which door to open, from the two doors that the contestant didn't pick. Let h_1 = [The car is behind door 1], h_2 = [The car is behind door 2], h_3 = [The car is behind door 3], and e = [Monty opens door 3 and there is a goat behind it]. After you have chosen door 1 but before Monty opens door 3, you should have the following credences: $P(h_1) = P(h_2) = P(h_3) = \frac{1}{3}$; $P(e|h_1) = \frac{1}{2}$; $P(e|h_2) = \frac{1}{2}$; $P(e|h_3) = 0$. Then the probability of door 1 having the prize behind it, given that Monty opens door 3 and reveals a goat, is given by Bayes' Theorem as follows:

$$P\left(h_1|e\right) = \frac{P\left(h_1\right)P\left(e|h_1\right)}{P\left(h_1\right)P\left(e|h_1\right) + P\left(h_2\right)P\left(e|h_2\right) + P\left(h_3\right)P\left(e|h_3\right)}$$

$$= \frac{\left(1/3\right)\left(1/2\right)}{\left(1/3\right)\left(1/2\right) + \left(1/3\right)\left(1/2\right) + \left(1/3\right)\left(0\right)} = \frac{1}{2}.$$

The key is that in *this* version of the problem, $P(e|h_2) = \frac{1}{2}$. In the standard version (where Monty always avoids opening the door with the prize), $P(e|h_2) = 1$. Substituting 1 for $P(e|h_2)$ in the above equation changes the final answer to ⅓, the standard answer.

choose door #1. Monty then opens, say, door #3 and shows you a goat behind it. He then asks if you would like to change your choice from door #1 to door #2. Should you switch?

Most people have a strong intuition that it doesn't matter whether you switch to door #2 or stick with door #1; that's because most people think that the prize is now 50% likely to be behind door #1 and 50% likely to be behind door #2. The correct answer, however, is that you should definitely switch to door #2: door #1 has a 1/3 probability of having the real prize behind it, and door #2 now (after you saw the goat behind door #3) has a 2/3 probability of having the real prize.

It can be difficult to convince people of this. In fact, almost everyone, on first hearing the problem, gives the wrong answer, and persists in that answer until bludgeoned for a while with probability calculations or experiments.[4] In this case, there are compelling arguments (discussed below and in fn. 3) for a highly counter-intuitive answer. Nevertheless, I do not consider this a *paradox*. One reason is that this problem is not robust enough to bear debate among experts. The Monty Hall Problem has a well-known, objectively correct solution that can be shown to be so in a fairly brief span of time; it does not, for example, bear years of reflection.

Why does the prize have a 2/3 probability of being behind door B? This is beside my present point (which, remember, was just to define "paradox"); however, in case you can't sleep until you know, an explanation follows. (You can also do a calculation employing Bayes' Theorem, but the following is probably going to be more satisfying.)

Suppose Monty runs the game 300 times. Each time, the location of the good prize is randomly selected from among the three doors. We would expect that in about 100 of these games, the contestant's initial guess is correct, that is, the first door they pick has the prize behind it. The other 200 times, the initial guess is wrong. Therefore, if the contestants always stick with their initial guess, then 100 of the 300 will win the real prize, and 200 will receive goats. (The 200 who initially selected a goat door can't possibly improve their result by sticking with that choice!)

---

[4] See the responses to Marilyn vos Savant's famous column on the problem (vos Savant 1990–91).

Now, on the other hand, suppose that the contestants always switch doors. Then the 100 contestants who initially picked the correct door will lose, as they give up that door. But the other 200, the ones who initially picked wrong, will all switch doors. And they will all switch to the *correct* door, since the correct door will be the only remaining door, after rejecting the door they initially picked and the goat door that Monty just opened.

So the "switch doors" strategy wins 2/3 of the time, whereas the "stick with your door" strategy wins only 1/3 of the time.

Now, back to our main point: a paradox is a piece of reasoning, or a situation about which such reasoning is constructed, that has widespread and robust appeal, but that leads to a contradictory or absurd conclusion, where even experts have difficulty identifying the error in the reasoning. This account of paradoxicality makes it species-relative: perhaps a super-intelligent alien species would find our "paradoxes" so easy to see through that the aliens would not consider these puzzles paradoxical at all. Nevertheless, for humans at the present time, there are many paradoxical situations and pieces of reasoning.

1.2   What Is a Solution?

Paradoxes trade on intellectual illusions: cases in which something that is actually wrong seems correct when considered intellectually. It is characteristic of illusions that what *seems* to be the case is not necessarily what we *believe* – often, in fact, we know that things cannot be as they appear, yet this does not stop them from appearing that way. We know, for instance, that the reasoning in Zeno's Paradox is wrong, since we know that objects move. But this does not stop the reasoning from exerting its intellectual pull: each step in the reasoning still seems correct and the steps seemingly lead to the conclusion that nothing moves.

Intellectual illusions, however, are at least somewhat more tractable than sensory illusions. Sensory illusions (for example, the illusion whereby a straight stick appears bent when half-submerged in water) virtually never respond to reflection or additional evidence-gathering. No matter how much you understand about the actual situation, the half-submerged stick still *looks* bent. Intellectual illusions are not that way. Admittedly, as noted, they do not respond immediately to the knowledge that the conclusion of a piece of reasoning is wrong – the mere fact that we know that objects move does not dispel the force of Zeno's reasoning. But usually, there is some degree of understanding, of the right points, that dispels the illusion. It is often possible for someone to identify the particular point at which the fallacious reasoning goes wrong, and to explain why the mistake in question is a mistake, in such a way that it no longer even appears correct; we can then *see through* the fallacy. That is what it is to "solve" a paradox.

To illustrate, consider one of the infamous "proofs" that $2 = 1$:

1. Let b be any positive number, and let $a = b$.	
2. $a^2 = ab$.	(From 1, multiplying both sides by a.)
3. $a^2 - b^2 = ab - b^2$.	(From 2, subtracting b^2.)
4. $(a + b)(a - b) = b(a - b)$.	(From 3, factoring.)
5. $a + b = b$.	(From 4, dividing both sides by $(a - b)$.)
6. $b + b = b$.	(From 1, 5, substituting b for a since $a = b$.)
7. $2b = b$.	(From 6.)
8. $2 = 1$.	(From 7, dividing by b.)

What went wrong? This puzzle is too easy to qualify as a *paradox*; nevertheless, we can use it to illustrate what counts as a solution. We could not claim to solve this puzzle by saying, "Some step in this deduction must be wrong, since 2 does not equal 1. Since step 5 is the least obvious, it is wrong." That would not be a solution, even if it were true that step 5 somehow initially seemed less certain than the others. The solution is this: step 5 is in error because it contains a division by zero. Since $a = b$, $(a - b) = 0$. And here is why it is not valid to divide by zero: the quotient $(x \div y)$ is defined as the number such that, when multiplied by y, it yields x. So "$x \div 0$" would have to mean "the number such that, when multiplied by 0, it yields x". But if x is nonzero, then there is *no* number that when multiplied by 0 yields x. And if x is zero, then *every* number is such that, when multiplied by 0, it yields x. So the expression "$x \div 0$" is ill-defined; it does not pick out any definite number, no matter what x is.

Since inferring step 5 from step 4 requires dividing by zero, this is an invalid inference.

Notice that this explanation does not merely reject a step in the reasoning and give a reason for holding that step to be in error. It explains the error in such a way that the erroneous step no longer even looks valid. Having understood the point about division by zero, and attending to the fact that in this case $a - b$ must be zero, we can no longer see step 5 as following from step 4.

Similarly, to solve a paradox, it is not enough simply to convince the audience that a particular step is an error. This might be done, say, by pointing out that a given step is the only controversial step, or simply the least certain step, in a piece of reasoning that leads to a contradiction.[5] This is not enough to have a *solution* in my sense, because this does not suffice to dispel the erroneous appearance. One must give some explanation that enables the audience to *see* why the step is in fact erroneous.

So that is what I aim to do for each of the paradoxes discussed in the following pages. How well I succeed is for the reader to judge.

1.3   How to Seek Solutions

Is there some general account, applicable to all cases, of the origins of paradoxes? Or, whether or not they have a common origin, is there some common approach that may be used to solve any paradox? If I had such a general account and method, I should explain it here, then apply it to each paradox in turn in the following chapters. But I have no such general account or method – at least, none that is actually informative and helpful.

Why the "informative and helpful" qualifier? Well, it is simple enough to offer *some* account of the origin of paradoxes and how to solve them. Here is one: "Paradoxes originate in the tendency of the human mind to sometimes find jointly incompatible sets of propositions individually plausible. The way to solve a paradox is to identify the proposition in the

---

[5] This is essentially the approach recommended by Rescher (2001, ch. 2). But note that when discussing individual paradoxes, Rescher does not in fact rest content with rejecting the least plausible proposition. Rather, he offers explanations in each case of why the proposition to be rejected is false, explanations that would *render* the proposition much less plausible than it is initially.

set that is false, and offer an explanation in light of which it seems false or at least ceases to seem true." That is fine as far as it goes. But it is not informative enough to be useful. All the useful work would come in constructing the needed *explanations* – and these explanations would be exactly the sort of thing that everyone trying to solve paradoxes is already trying to provide. Thus, in offering the above account, I have not helped anyone.

A more useful and informative account would be one that identifies a specific sort of error that putatively leads, in the case of every paradox, to a false proposition's appearing true. This would doubtless give us substantial guidance in solving individual paradoxes. But I know of no such common source of error, and I would be extremely skeptical if someone else were to offer one. Most likely, there are many sources of error, and if one tries to fit all paradoxes under some one category of mistake, one will find oneself distorting the problems.

So I do not offer a general diagnosis or prescription for paradoxes. More generally, I do not offer a general philosophical theory that purports to solve all the paradoxes. In fact, I think that if I were to lay down such a theory here, you should be extremely suspicious from the start. The way to solve intellectual problems is not to lay down an abstract theory at the beginning, and then shoe-horn every problem into the mold created by that theory. Rather, the way to arrive at a theory is to first solve some problems, then reflect on how you solved them, and generalize from there. Of course, I can't prove that epistemological view to you here (it is a view I have arrived at by reflecting on many examples). But that is to explain why I do not offer a theory of paradoxes at the beginning of this book; at the end, however, I offer reflections on some common paradox-inducing errors.

I do, however, have some very broad philosophical commitments that I bring to the study of paradoxes. They are the same commitments I bring to every other issue. To begin with, I am committed to classical logic, including such things as the law of non-contradiction (no contradictions are true), the law of excluded middle (every proposition either is or is not the case), and bivalence (every proposition-expressing sentence is true or false). In most discussions, one does not mention "commitments" such as these, because they are considered trivial. In debating global warming, for example, one need not first discuss one's belief that global warming is man-made or not man-made, or that it isn't both man-made and not man-made. Only when philosophical paradoxes are in play do many thinkers become tempted to reject classical logic. Accordingly, some have developed alternative ("deviant") logics that reject the law of excluded middle, non-contradiction, or other key principles that you learned in logic 101.

I cannot substantively address these alternatives here, lest this book turn into a book on deviant logics. I will only briefly remark, autobiographically, on my personal reactions. The principles of classical logic, I believe, are the principles of classical logic for a reason: they are very general, fundamental, and *self-evident* truths. This is not an idiosyncratic reaction on my part. Virtually everyone, upon first considering the axioms of classical logic, finds them obvious to the point of triviality. In a sense, it is out of place to attempt to argue for classical logic, because there are no more obvious premises to which to appeal, nor are there any more secure rules of reasoning than those of classical logic. I believe, in fact, that even when one tries to adopt a deviant logic, one only does so by reasoning *classically* to figure out what one is supposed to say according to the deviant system.

So, if one sees some (classically valid) reasoning that leads to a contradiction, one should not conclude that contradictions can be true, nor should one reject some seemingly self-evident rule of inference. One should look for the mistake in the premises.

All of that is a special case of the following theoretical commitment of mine (if one wants to call such a thing a "theoretical commitment"): principles that almost everyone finds self-evident are probably not flat-out wrong. Accordingly, a satisfying solution to a paradox will not be to reject a seemingly self-evident principle that is used in generating the paradox. For example, one cannot solve Zeno's paradox by simply declaring that motion is really, contrary to appearances, impossible; nor by simply denying, on no grounds other than that this denial avoids the paradox, that in moving from point A to point B, an object must first traverse half the distance. If we have nothing better to say than that, we had better just admit that the solution eludes us.

Now, I stated that one should be very suspicious of any general theory of paradoxes laid out at the start. Why does my commitment to classical logic not incur this same suspicion – why isn't it the sort of general, abstract theory that I aim to eschew at the start of our investigation?

In reply, I am not opposed to *all* general, theoretical starting points. I am only opposed to starting from general, *substantive* theoretical assumptions that are *not self-evident*. It is *those* sorts of assumptions that must be justified by examining particular cases. The principles of classical logic, by contrast, are both self-evident and trivial. (This is compatible with the fact that some smart philosophers deny them; philosophy is a strange field.) They do not amount to a substantive philosophical theory. Rather, they simply reflect the meanings of such words as "and", "or", "not", and "true" (see discussion, section 2.3 below). If someone thinks, for example, that an object can be both "red" and "not red" at the same time, then that person has failed to grasp how "not" is used in English.

Obviously, proponents of deviant logics would not be persuaded by this. They would say that it is I who have misunderstood "not", "or", or some similar word. I am not trying to convince these philosophers here. I am only explaining, for the benefit of non-deviant readers, why I do not consider such approaches as viable options for avoiding the paradoxes.

1.4   Why Paradoxes?

Why study paradoxes? You might worry that studying paradoxical arguments is a waste of time, or at best a harmless diversion from more serious pursuits. This is because paradoxical arguments are arguments that virtually no one seriously defends. For example, virtually everyone (apart from Zeno himself, apparently) knows that Zeno's argument is wrong and that things move. So why should we spend our time discussing that argument?

Admittedly, paradoxical reasoning does not merit extended consideration for the same reason that most arguments that merit extended consideration do so – namely, for the purpose of determining whether the argument is correct and its conclusion true. But even when we know an argument is wrong and its conclusion false, we can still learn from thinking about it. Paradoxes test our understanding of a concept or subject matter. The existence of a paradox shows that we are prey to some sort of confusion, hidden false assumption, or other intellectual malfunction. Whatever the error is, it must be serious, for it leads to a contradiction or other absurdity; it must be widespread, for the paradoxical reasoning has widespread appeal; and it must be deeply held, else the error would not survive extended contemplation and discussion, as paradoxes do. That sounds like a type of error well worth correcting.

The paradoxes I shall address in the chapters to follow also bear on some matters of fundamental philosophical interest, such as the nature of meaning and truth, the basic principles of rational choice, the correct way of assigning probabilities, and the principles governing how theories are confirmed by evidence. There is reason to suspect, at the outset, that resolving the paradoxes concerning these matters will leave us with a deeper understanding of these important matters. Indeed, most of my solutions will deploy philosophical theories which, I claim, we have reason to accept in the light of how they help to resolve the paradoxes.

But to speak truthfully, none of that is the main reason why I have written a book on paradoxes; that is just how I hope to convince other philosophers to take it seriously. The main reason I have written such a book is that I find paradoxes fun, fascinating, and somehow charming. Paradoxes are like toys for the mind. It's not exactly easy to explain how a seemingly compelling argument for an obviously false conclusion is charming, or how contemplating such an argument is fun. If you don't understand what I mean by that, you probably won't like this book. If you do, then I probably need say no more.

1.5   Paradoxes Not Covered

The following chapters consider ten main paradoxes (or paradox-clusters – I treat paradoxes that are closely related to each other in the same chapter). Please accept my apologies if I have omitted your favorite paradox. Just so you know up front, I will not discuss the following sorts of paradoxes (not, that is, after the brief mentions in the immediately following list):

First, I do not consider (alleged) paradoxes that arise within a specialized science. For example, there is the Twins Paradox in the Special

Theory of Relativity: a person who travels near the speed of light according to a given reference frame will, according to that reference frame, age slower than a person who is stationary. Now imagine two twins who, as twins are wont to do, start out the same age, but one of them remains (relatively) stationary on Earth, while the other twin flies around in a spaceship at near light speed for twenty years before returning to Earth. The twin who stayed on Earth predicts that his sibling, on returning to Earth, should appear much younger than the Earth twin himself appears. But from the perspective of the space twin (the one who traveled in the spaceship), the space twin was stationary and it was the Earth twin who was moving around at near light speed; therefore, the space twin should predict (shouldn't he?) that it is the Earth Twin who will have aged less. When they meet after the long journey, which one of them will in fact appear younger?

This is the sort of puzzle I do not address in the succeeding chapters, because it turns on a theory in a specialized discipline that isn't philosophy.[6] (It also isn't a true paradox, on the criteria given above.) I only address paradoxes that are within the field of expertise of philosophers.

Second, I do not here address any of the paradoxes that appeared in my previous book, *Approaching Infinity*. That includes seventeen paradoxes that arise from thinking about the infinite. It includes, for instance, Zeno's Paradox (mentioned above); Hilbert's Hotel (if an infinite hotel is completely full, it can still accommodate infinitely many additional guests); and Thomson's Lamp (after a lamp switch is flipped infinitely many times, will the lamp end up on or off?). If you want to know the solutions to those paradoxes, see my previous book.

Third, I do not address paradoxes that arise only for a particular controversial theory. For instance, traditional theists face the question, "Can God create a stone so heavy he couldn't lift it?" (either answer seems to impugn God's omnipotence). There are also such questions as "Can God do evil?", "Can God make a mistake?", "Does God know what we will do before we do it? If so, how can we have free will?", and the ever popular, "How can God allow evil to exist?" I do not address these sorts of puzzles, mainly

---

[6] But if you want the solution, see Huemer n.d. Hint: in order for the twins to be reunited, someone has to leave their initial, inertial reference frame.

because my solutions would not be very interesting. (My solution, in almost all cases, would be to reject the theory that gives rise to the problems; for example, I would simply deny that there is an omnipotent being.)

The paradoxes I cover in the following chapters fall into three broad categories: (a) semantic paradoxes (those that concern the functioning of language), (b) paradoxes of rational choice (those that concern how a rational person would or should make decisions), and (c) paradoxes of probability (those that concern how one should assign probabilities). In each case, I will endeavor first to befuddle the reader by presenting seemingly compelling reasoning for something you know cannot be true (this may include, as a special case, presenting seemingly compelling reasoning for two contradictory conclusions). I suggest that the reader spend some time trying to think through each paradox, after reading my presentation of the paradox but before reading my solution. Spending some effort attempting to solve a paradox is the best way of preparing the mind to appreciate the eventual solution, assuming that my solutions are satisfying. It is also fun regardless.

Where appropriate, I shall try to dispose of the most common mistaken solutions to the paradoxes. Then I present what I take to be the correct solution. If all goes according to plan, your initial state of confusion will be replaced with a state of greater clarity and understanding than before you encountered the paradox. If all *doesn't* go according to plan, you will probably wind up thinking I have some crazy ideas. In some cases, both outcomes may occur at once.

References

Huemer, Michael. n.d. "Correct Resolution of the Twin Paradox", http://www.owl232.net/papers/twinparadox.pdf, accessed May 11, 2018.

Rescher, Nicholas. 2001. *Paradoxes: Their Roots, Range, and Resolution*. Chicago, IL: Open Court.

Sainsbury, Richard M. 2009. *Paradoxes*, 3rd ed. Cambridge: Cambridge University Press.

Tierney, John. 1991. "Behind Monty Hall's Doors: Puzzle, Debate and Answer?", *The New York Times*, July 21, p. 1. Available at http://www.nytimes. com/1991/07/21/us/behind-monty-hall-s-doors-puzzle-debate-and-answer. html, accessed April 30, 2017.

vos Savant, Marilyn. 1990–91. "Game Show Problem", http://marilynvossavant. com/game-show-problem/, accessed April 30, 2017.

Part I

Semantic Paradoxes

2

The Liar

2.1 The Paradox

Consider the following sentence, which I will call sentence L:

(L)   This sentence is false.

L (or something like it) is called "the liar sentence" because it says something like "I am a liar." (Actually, a liar is a person who says what he *does not believe*, which of course is different from saying something *false*. But never mind that.)

Is sentence L true or false? Well, if it is true, then it is true that the sentence is false, so it's false. But if it is false, then it is false is that the sentence is false, so it isn't false, so it's true. To state the reasoning more explicitly:

1. If a sentence says that *a* is *F*, then the sentence is true if and only if *a* is *F*. (Premise.)[1]

---

[1] Why not use the more general T-schema, " ⌜P⌝ is true if and only if P", where the second "P" may be replaced with any declarative sentence, and " ⌜P⌝ " replaced with a name for that sentence (as in Tarski 1983)? This is *usually* correct; for instance, the following is correct: "'Snow is white' is true if and only if snow is white." But the schema does not always work; consider: "'*This* is the beginning of this sentence' is true if and only if *this* is the beginning of this sentence." The formulation given in the text avoids such complications.

© The Author(s) 2018
M. Huemer, *Paradox Lost*, https://doi.org/10.1007/978-3-319-90490-0_2

2. L says that L is false. (Premise.)
3. Therefore, L is true if and only if L is false. (From 1, 2.)
4. L is either true or false. (Premise.)
5. Therefore, L is both true and false. (From 3, 4.)

The conclusion is absurd since truth and falsity are incompatible by definition. We seem to be forced into contradiction just by thinking about sentence L.

2.2   A Third Truth-Value

Maybe the mistake is (4), the assumption that "true" and "false" are the only possibilities. Suppose there is a third truth-value called being "indeterminate". By stipulation, the "indeterminate" category includes all statements that don't fit under either "true" or "false". Perhaps, then, L is indeterminate.

But consider another sentence, L':

(L')   This sentence is either false or indeterminate.

We can construct a parallel argument about L':

1'. If a sentence says that *a* is *F* or *G*, then the sentence is true if and only if *a* is *F* or *G*. (Premise.)
2'. L' says that L' is false or indeterminate. (Premise.)
3'. Therefore, L' is true if and only if L' is false or indeterminate. (From 1', 2'.)
4'. L' is either true, false, or indeterminate. (Premise.)
5'. Therefore, L' is both true *and* either false or indeterminate. (From 3', 4'.)

The conclusion is still contradictory, and now there would be no point in questioning the fourth step. So something else must be wrong with this argument. Whatever it is, presumably it is also the problem with the original argument about sentence L.

2.3   True Contradictions

Some believe that the answer is to accept that sentence L is both true and false. Now, I take it that "false" entails "not true" (note: there's no point in denying this, since I could just replace sentence L with a sentence that says of itself that it is *not true*). So this view amounts to embracing a logical contradiction, namely, that L is true and not true.

What is wrong with embracing contradictions, after all? Here is one answer: according to standard logic, if you accept a contradiction, then you can validly infer any conclusion whatsoever from it. Here is how: assume that you accept a proposition A, and you also accept its denial, ~A (read, "it is not the case that A"). Let B be any arbitrarily chosen other proposition. Then you can argue:

6. A   Premise
7. ~A   Premise
8. A or B   From 6[2]
9. B   From 7, 8

For example, let A be the proposition that the liar sentence is true, and B the proposition that blue unicorns built the Taj Mahal. If you accept that the liar sentence is both true and not true, then you'll be committed to thinking that blue unicorns built the Taj Mahal. This is generally considered to be a bad result.

Some philosophers respond by adopting alternative systems of logic ("paraconsistent logics") in which contradictions can be true but in which one *cannot* derive any arbitrary proposition from a contradiction.[3] These logics reject some of the standard rules of inference, so that the move from steps 7 and 8 above to step 9 is not allowed.

I reject this approach. My reason is not (and never was) that I'm worried about being committed to the claim that unicorns built the Taj Mahal. My reason is that the law of non-contradiction is self-evident. Indeed, I'd be hard pressed to think of anything more obvious. I think

---

[2] Unless otherwise stated, I use "or" inclusively; thus, "A or B" means "At least one of {A, B} holds, possibly both."

[3] Priest 2006a, b; Beall 2009.

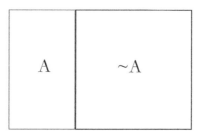

Fig. 2.1 Classical concept of negation

that if someone claims to believe that contradictions can be true, then that person has simply misunderstood the meaning of "contradiction".

Here is the classical understanding of the concepts of contradiction and negation in logic: let A be any proposition. There are certain possible situations in which A would count as true. Now, the negation of A ("~A"), *by definition*, holds in all and only the *other* situations (see figure 2.1). If you think there is a situation in which both A and ~A hold, then you're confused, because it is just part of the meaning of "not" that not-A fails in any case where A holds. The lack of overlap between A and ~A is the main point of the concept of negation. Now, a contradiction is a statement of the form (A & ~A). So, by definition, any contradiction is false.[4]

Here is a simpler way to put the point: a contradiction is a statement that entails two incompatible propositions. By definition, two propositions are "incompatible" when they can't both be true. So, by definition, contradictions can't be true.

Suppose I am wrong about this – suppose it is I who am confused about language (along with the classical logicians), and that "not" in English is actually used in such a way that the truth of "A" needn't exclude the truth of "not-A", that is, that there are situations in which both "A" and "not-A" count as being true. While we're at it, let us also allow that perhaps "A" and "not-A" don't exhaust the possibilities, that is, that there may be situations in which neither "A" nor "not-A" count as true.

This is represented in figure 2.2. The points in the diagram represent possible situations. The circle on the left represents the possible situations

---

[4]Cf. Quine 1986, p. 81: "[S]urely the notation ceased to be recognizable as negation when they took to regarding some conjunctions of the form [*p* & *~p*] as true."

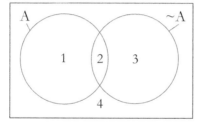

Fig. 2.2   A non-classical conception of negation

in which "A" holds; this includes regions 1 and 2. The circle on the right represents those in which "~A" holds, including regions 2 and 3. We have just supposed that regions 2 and/or 4 might be nonempty (there might be situations in which both "A" and "~A" hold, or in which neither holds).

Now I am going to introduce a new operator, which I call "not!" (with the exclamation point). I hereby stipulate that "not!" is to be used in such a way that "not!-A" includes exactly regions 3 and 4 in the diagram. That is, even if there are situations in which both "A" and "~A" hold, these situations are by definition excluded by "not!-A"; also, if there are situations in which neither "A" nor "~A" hold, these situations are by definition *included* in "not!-A".

Now you can see that any puzzle that would be avoided by adopting a non-classical interpretation of "not" can be recreated using "not!". In particular, if your solution to the Liar Paradox involves claiming that the Liar sentence and its negation are both true, or that neither of them is true, we can recreate the paradox using the strengthened liar sentence $L^!$:

(L$^!$)   This sentence is not! true.

It is not open to maintain that $L^!$ is both true and not! true, nor can we claim that it is neither true nor not! true, since both of those options are ruled out by the definition of "not!". Since $L^!$ creates the same sort of paradox originally ascribed to L, there is no point in disputing my account of the meaning of "not" or "contradiction".[5]

---

[5] Objections of this sort appear in Littman and Simmons 2004, pp. 322–4, and Sainsbury 2009, pp. 157–8.

The response for paraconsistent logicians would have to be to deny that "not!" is a legitimate concept – that is, to deny that it is even possible to refer to all and only the situations that fail to make "A" true.[6] It certainly seems that this *is* possible, and that I in fact just did it. If you understood what I said above in explaining "not!", then you, too, possess this concept that the paraconsistent logicians deny exists.

2.4   Meaninglessness

Perhaps L is meaningless in the sense that it fails to express a proposition.[7] In that case, L is neither true nor false. We saw in section 2.2 that, to avoid paradox, it is not enough to reject premise 4 ("L is either true or false"). However, if we hold that L is meaningless, then we can also reject premise 2 –

2. L says that L is false. (Premise.)

Perhaps L does not say that L is false, because L does not say anything. In that case, the paradoxical reasoning stops cold. But why might L be meaningless?

---

[6] Priest (2006b, ch. 5) and Beall (2009, pp. 48–50) take essentially this line, except that they frame the issue in terms of whether the negation operator validates *explosion* (the principle that (A & ~A) entails B, for any arbitrary B). My claim is not that the meaning of negation by definition validates explosion. My claim is that the meaning of negation *directly* rules out a sentence and its negation both being true.

Priest and Beall construct arguments that the classical notion of negation is incoherent, which I will not discuss in detail. Priest's main argument turns on shifting the burden of proof onto classical theorists to show that classical negation is coherent, and then arguing that they cannot do so without begging the question. I believe, though I will not argue the point here, that the burden is on Priest to show that "not!" is incoherent. Beall's argument, in essence, uses the Liar Paradox itself to impugn the existence of the "not!" operator. In reply, I have a solution to the paradox that does not require abandoning classical logic.

[7] This appears to be the most common view. See, e.g., Rescher 2001, pp. 196–203; Clark 2002, p. 102. Philosophers with this view disagree, however, on exactly *why* L fails to express a proposition.

2.4.1   Self-Reference

Perhaps self-referential sentences are meaningless or otherwise illegitimate. For in the case of such a sentence, a proper *part* of the sentence (e.g., the subject term) is required to stand for the *whole* sentence, and one might hold this to be impossible or otherwise illegitimate.[8] But that can't be right, for consider the following sentence:

(S)   This sentence is written in comic sans font.

S is certainly not meaningless. It is just false.

Well, perhaps it is permissible for a sentence to refer to its physical or syntactic properties, but not to its *semantic* properties. Truth and falsity are semantic properties, so a sentence may not talk about its own truth or falsity. But this doesn't suffice to avoid paradox, for consider:

(L1)   The following sentence is true.
(L2)   The preceding sentence is false.

Neither refers to *its own* semantic properties, but the pair still generates a paradox. So to avoid paradox, we would need a stronger prohibition on discussing semantic properties.

Perhaps a sentence may not refer to semantic properties in general; perhaps there is something wrong with talking about truth and falsity. But that can't be right, because the following trio of sentences is perfectly acceptable:

(L3)   The following sentence is true.
(L4)   All bears are white.
(L5)   The preceding sentence is false.

Notice that L3 and L5 are intrinsically indistinguishable from L1 and L2, respectively. And L3 and L5 are both meaningful (the former being false; the latter, true). So there is nothing internal to sentence L1 or L2 that renders either defective.

---

[8] This sort of view was taken by some medieval philosophers; see the anonymous authors discussed in Braakuis 1967 and in Spade 1975, pp. 33–4. Cf. Rescher (2001, pp. 196–7).

2.4.2 False Presupposition

Perhaps L is neither true nor false because L contains a false *presupposition*. According to some philosophers, a sentence with a false presupposition is neither true nor false.[9] In this view, it is important to distinguish what a sentence *asserts* from what it *presupposes*. For example, the question, "Have you stopped kissing squirrels yet?" does not *assert* that the addressee has been kissing squirrels; it merely *presupposes* that the addressee has been kissing squirrels. Similarly, the sentence "The King of America is foolish" does not assert that America has a king; it merely presupposes this. If one asserts that America has a king, then one speaks falsely. But when one merely presupposes that America has a king, then (some would say) what one says is neither true nor false.

Perhaps L lacks a truth-value (that is, is neither true nor false) because it contains a false presupposition. For perhaps to call a sentence false is simply to say that *the proposition expressed by the sentence* is false, and this presupposes that there is a unique proposition expressed by the sentence. L does not express a proposition, because for it to do so, there would have to be some independent way of identifying that proposition; that is, it would have to be possible to specify the proposition it expresses without first presupposing that there is such a proposition.

We need not settle whether this view about false presuppositions is correct. It doesn't matter whether L contains a false presupposition, or whether statements with false presuppositions should be considered neither true nor false, because we can simply rephrase the liar sentence to avoid the putative false presupposition. Thus, consider:

(L†)   This sentence expresses a proposition, and it is false.

L† (perhaps unlike L) does not *presuppose* that it expresses a proposition; it explicitly asserts this. In general, whatever we might think about presuppositions, if one explicitly asserts something false, then one speaks falsely (compare: "America has a king, and he's foolish" is simply false, not indeterminate). So if L† fails to express a proposition, then L† is false, not indeterminate.

---

[9] Geach 1950; Strawson 1950.

2.4.3   Lack of Communicative Use

Perhaps to be meaningful, a sentence must have a possible communicative use.[10] That is, there must be a possible situation in which the sentence could be used to convey information. But in what possible situation could the liar sentence be used to convey information? What state of affairs might it be attempting to describe? It seems that the answer to these questions is "none".

But the demand that a sentence have a possible communicative use is too strong. For a sentence to be meaningful, all that is required is that it express a proposition. There might be other reasons why it could not communicate information, for instance, that no one could believe the proposition that it expresses; this would not render it meaningless in the relevant sense.

Consider a slightly modified liar sentence,

(L")   Sentence L" is not true.

On the theory presently under consideration, L" is neither true nor false because it is meaningless. So, in particular, L" is not *true*. In other words, the following is part of this theory:

(N)   Sentence L" is not true.

Notice that L" and N are syntactically identical. N is true. So N must be meaningful. L" at least *purports* to express the same proposition that N in fact expresses. If N can be used to convey information, then why should we not say that L" can also be used to convey information – namely, the same information that N conveys?

Perhaps the liar sentence is meaningless because (unlike N), no one could seriously and sincerely assert it. But note that one *could* seriously and sincerely assert some relevantly similar sentences: I walk into my classroom and see the words "Donald Trump will make America great again!" written on the chalkboard on the west wall. I go to the chalkboard on the north wall and write, "The sentence written on the west wall of this room is false."[11] Oh wait . . . I got confused about the compass direc-

---

[10] I thank Iskra Fileva (p.c.) for this suggestion.
[11] Cf. Beall and Glanzberg 2011, section 2.3.1.

tions. Actually, the sentence about Trump was written on the south wall, and my own sentence was written on . . . the west wall. Now, what I *intended* to say with that sentence was correct. But what about what I actually said: true or false?

2.5   Putting the Blame on Truth

Some blame the paradox on the general concept of truth, claiming that a language is "inconsistent" if it contains a truth predicate applicable to every sentence in the language.[12]

To explain: There are first-order sentences, sentences that talk about ordinary things, such as squirrels and clouds. For instance, "Most squirrels are furry" is a first-order sentence. Then there are second-order sentences, which talk about first-order sentences. For instance, "The sentence 'Most squirrels are furry' is true" is a second-order sentence. Then there are third-order sentences (which talk about second-order sentences), and so on.

Now, we can define a property of first-order truth (or truth$_1$), which is had by a first-order sentence when the ordinary object that the subject term refers to really has the property the predicate ascribes to it.[13] Then there is a property of second-order truth (truth$_2$), which is had by second-order sentences that ascribe properties to first-order sentences that really have those properties. Then there is truth$_3$, truth$_4$ and so on.

According to some philosophers (notably, Alfred Tarski), the liar paradox should be avoided by rejecting any *general* notion of truth – that is, we should allow talk of truth$_1$, truth$_2$, and so on, but we should not recognize any truth predicate that applies to *all* sentences regardless of their order. If we follow these rules, the liar paradox cannot be formulated. For consider: which truth predicate is the liar sentence supposed to be using? If it is truth$_1$, then we get the following reasoning about the new liar sentence, L$_1$ (modified from the original paradoxical reasoning):

---

[12] Tarski 1944. Russell (1908) adopts a similar but more restrictive view.

[13] Of course, this only applies to simple sentences in subject-predicate form; however, if you know what this footnote means, then you probably already know how to extend the definition of truth$_1$ to other sentence forms. If you don't know what this footnote means, then you probably don't care.

(L$_1$)   This sentence is not true$_1$.

1$_1$. If a first-order sentence says that a is not F, then the sentence is true$_1$ if and only if a is not F. (Definition of truth$_1$.)

2$_1$. L$_1$ says that L$_1$ is not true$_1$. (Premise.)

3$_1$. Therefore, if L$_1$ is a first-order sentence, then L$_1$ is true$_1$ if and only if L$_1$ is not true$_1$. (From 1, 2.)

Premise 1$_1$ must include the phrase "If a *first-order* sentence says . . .", to accommodate the fact that truth$_1$ only applies to first-order sentences. Step 3$_1$ is then forced to include the same qualifier regarding "first-order" sentences. But from (3$_1$), nothing interesting follows, except that L$_1$ is not a first-order sentence. Similarly, if we try to formulate the paradox using truth$_2$, all we get is the conclusion that the liar sentence is not second-order. In general, if we try to formulate the paradox using truth$_n$, we get the conclusion that the liar sentence is not nth-order – which, after all, is correct; the liar sentence cannot be nth-order, for any n; the liar sentence has no order. So we avoid paradox.

Now, there are two ways of taking this proposal, an uninteresting way and an interesting way. The uninteresting interpretation: the solution proposes a convention whereby we simply refrain from talking about the general property of truth, so that we won't have to confront any sentences that generate paradoxes. I think this is approximately as satisfying as the following solution that could be proposed for any intellectual problem: "Suppose we change the subject." The liar sentence is in fact a sentence of English, and English appears to contain a general truth predicate. The puzzle about this sentence is hardly solved by switching attention to a possible language in which the liar sentence would not exist.

Here is the interesting interpretation: it is not merely that we can refuse to talk about truth; it is that *there is no property* of truth in general; there is only truth$_1$, truth$_2$, and so on. Thus, there is something inherently illegitimate about a general truth predicate, and any sentence that purports to ascribe generic truth must lack any determinate meaning. Why think there is no property of generic truth? Perhaps because there is no satisfactory way of defining the property without engendering paradoxes.

Note that it is not only the word "true" that creates problems. Similar paradoxes can be generated using other semantic terms, such as "refer", "ascribe", and "assert", for instance:

(R)   the smallest natural number not referred to by this expression
(A)   This sentence lacks the feature that this sentence ascribes to it.
(W)   What this sentence asserts is not the case.

We encounter paradoxes when trying to figure out what R refers to, whether A has the feature that A ascribes to itself, and whether what W asserts is the case. So we would have to reject the existence of general relations of referring, ascribing, or asserting, in addition to the general property of truth.[14]

This view seems wrong. I surely can refer to both physical objects and words, in the same sense of "refer" (indeed, I just did so). Likewise, when we think about $truth_1$, $truth_2$, and so on, there clearly is something they have in common. There clearly is a sense in which a first-order sentence and a second-order sentence can both be true. For instance, suppose a colleague says to me, "The statement 'Obama is a Muslim' is false. Obama is not a Muslim." I could then say, "Everything you just said is true." I would not then be talking nonsense or misusing the word "true", though I apply "true" to both a first-order and a second-order claim. I would be making an easily understandable and correct observation.

A partial reply: we can introduce a new truth predicate, call it "$truth_N$", where a sentence is $true_N$ provided that there is some natural number n such that the sentence is $true_n$. Then we can say that both first- and second-order sentences can be true in the same sense, namely, both may be $true_N$. This does not threaten to reintroduce the liar paradox, because we still lack any truth-predicate that could apply to sentences (such as the Liar sentence) that *have no order*.

This reply improves the theory; nevertheless, it still seems that we can understand a completely general notion of truth, namely, a sense in which

---

[14] This means that the second premise in the paradoxical reasoning, "L says that L is false", is also problematic, since it attempts to deploy a generic notion of "saying" something. If "saying" is limited to first-order saying, second-order saying, and so on, then the liar sentence does not say anything, since it does not first-order say anything, nor does it second-order say anything, and so on.

a sentence that says that *a* is *F* (regardless of the order of the sentence, or whether it has an order at all) is true if and only if *a* is *F*.

A related problem is that the proponent of this theory would be unable to claim that his own theory is true. Since the theory discusses the whole hierarchy of sentences of different orders, the theory itself does not have any particular order. Thus, no truth predicate could apply to it. By the same token, the sentences used to express the theory could not be held to *say, assert,* or *refer to* anything, nor to have any other semantic properties, since all semantic properties are subject to the same sort of restrictions as the property of truth.

2.6   A Solution

2.6.1   An Inconsistent Language

My solution to the liar paradox holds that the liar sentence fails to express a proposition due to an inconsistency built into our language. As a result, premise 2 in the paradoxical reasoning – "L says that L is false" – is false.

Consider an analogous puzzle: an (adult, male) barber in a certain village shaves all and only the men who do not shave themselves. Question: Who shaves the barber? Since the barber shaves all and only the men who do not shave themselves, it must be that the barber shaves the barber if and only if the barber doesn't shave himself. This is a contradiction parallel to that generated by the liar paradox. But few find the barber paradox very challenging. The proper response: there is no such barber.[15] There cannot be such a barber, because *the description given of him is inconsistent.* The inconsistency is a bit hidden, but the situation is essentially the same as if I had announced that there was a triangular square, and then asked you how many corners it has. You should just reject my scenario.

Something similar holds for the liar paradox: our language imposes inconsistent requirements on the proposition supposed to be expressed

---

[15] This is what everyone says about it, e.g., Rescher 2001, p. 144; Sainsbury 2009, pp. 1–2; Irvine and Deutsch 2016, section 4. The "paradox" first appears in Russell (1972, p. 101; originally published 1918), attributed to an unnamed person. Russell appears to have found it so trivial that he does not bother to state the solution.

by the liar sentence, and as a result there can be no proposition expressed by the liar sentence. What inconsistent requirements? Roughly, the rules of our language require that the liar sentence be assigned, as its meaning, the proposition that holds if and only if that very proposition does not hold. But there cannot be a proposition that holds when it doesn't hold. Hence, there is nothing to serve as the meaning of the liar sentence. Hence, the sentence cannot be either true or false.

To explain that more slowly: first, what is a proposition? Without getting overly metaphysical, let us simply say that propositions are the sort of things that one can assert, deny, believe, or doubt; they can be true or false, probable or improbable, possible or impossible.[16] Propositions are not to be confused with sentences, since more than one sentence may express the same proposition; for instance, "Squirrels are furry" expresses the same proposition (asserts the same thing) as "Les écureuils sont poilu" – two sentences, one proposition. Nor should propositions be confused with beliefs in an individual's mind, since it is possible for two different people to *believe the same thing*; that 'thing' is a proposition.

Propositions can be identified by their truth conditions. That is, given any determinate set of conditions, there is a proposition that holds (or *obtains*, or *is true*) just in case those conditions are satisfied; and for every proposition, there is a determinate set of conditions under which the proposition is true. When we speak of "the proposition that so-and-so", this refers to the proposition that holds whenever so-and-so. For instance, "the proposition that squirrels are furry" denotes the proposition that holds if and only if squirrels are furry.

Now, what does it mean to say that a sentence is false? It means that *the proposition expressed* by the sentence is false. Thus, the liar sentence,

(L) This sentence is false.

is intended to assert that the proposition expressed by L is false. That is, L is supposed to express some (unique) proposition, and it is also intended to assert that that very proposition is false. These intentions can only be

---

[16] More specifically, propositions are the *primary* bearers of truth, falsity, and so on; that is, anything else that is true, false, or the like, is so in virtue of its relation to a true or false, etc., proposition. A true sentence is one that expresses a true proposition, a true belief is a belief directed at a true proposition, and so on.

satisfied if there is a proposition that is identical to the proposition that that very proposition is false – in other words, there would have to be a proposition that holds precisely when it does not hold. But of course there is no such proposition. So L lacks any determinate meaning.

Some find the notion of an inconsistent language puzzling.[17] In what sense can a *language* be inconsistent? To clarify, note first that I am *not* saying that *the liar sentence* is inconsistent. If that were so, then the liar sentence would simply be false. But it is neither true nor false. Nor am I saying that any other sentence is inconsistent. (Some sentences *are* inconsistent, but that fact does not explain the liar paradox. Nor is a language rendered inconsistent merely because it permits one to formulate inconsistent sentences.)

Second, I am not saying that our language embodies an inconsistent *theory*.[18] Rather, the sort of inconsistency I have in mind is like the inconsistency in inconsistent *instructions*. Suppose you open the instructions for your new smart phone and you read, "Do not drop the phone into the bathtub. Also, drop the phone into the bathtub." Then you could call the instructions inconsistent. It is not that the instructions endorse a false or inconsistent theory; it is that the instructions logically could not all be followed.

How could our language embody inconsistent instructions? Not, of course, in the same way that an instruction booklet would contain inconsistent instructions, for the booklet would do so by containing certain sentences written in a natural language. Our language is not a collection of sentences. Rather, our language is constituted by a set of *conventions*, conventions that govern how linguistic expressions are supposed to be used and interpreted. These conventions can sometimes be described in words, but they may exist independent of their being linguistically formulated, simply by our having certain practices that we are disposed to conform to. Among other things, the conventions of our language dictate the meanings that should be assigned to sentences, including what proposition (if any) a given declarative sentence should be understood as expressing.

Sometimes, a set of instructions is inconsistent only when applied to certain cases. For instance, suppose that your phone instructions tell you,

---

[17] Herzberger (1967), for example, argues that it is impossible for a language to be inconsistent.
[18] As Eklund (2002) maintains.

"Hold the power button for three seconds, but do *not* hold the top button on the right side of the phone." These instructions would be fine for some models of phone. But suppose that you find that the top button on the right side of your phone is in fact the power button. Then the instructions, *as applied to this phone*, are inconsistent.

Similarly, our language implicitly contains a set of instructions for interpreting sentences, and these instructions are fine for most sentences. But *as applied to the liar sentence*, they are inconsistent, that is, they cannot be followed, because they require us to understand the liar sentence as expressing a kind of proposition that can't exist.

Lastly, note that I am not saying, as Tarski suggested, that the concept of truth is inconsistent, nor is any other particular concept or sentence relevant to this discussion inconsistent. The inconsistency at issue arises jointly from the conventions for interpreting each of the individual words in the liar sentence, the conventions for interpreting the sentence structure that the liar sentence instantiates, and the particular syntax of the liar sentence. It is all those things together that generate inconsistency – just as it was the phone instructions together with the particular configuration of your phone that generated an inconsistency in the above example.

The liar paradox, in my view, is like the following puzzle: "Consider the proposition that both holds and does not hold. Does that proposition hold?" Either answer gets you into a contradiction. But this is not a very challenging puzzle. We should just deny that there is any such proposition. The liar paradox seems more challenging only because, instead of directly *describing* a proposition that supposedly holds and does not hold, it exploits our natural disposition to follow the rules of our language to induce us to attempt to interpret a sentence as expressing a proposition that holds and does not hold.

2.6.2   Meaning Deficiency

We may be tempted to call L *meaningless*. But this would seem off: unlike "Blug trish ithong", which is really completely meaningless, "This sentence is false" seems to have some sort of meaning. After all, we can understand each word in it, we understand the way in which they are combined, and we know how to make inferences that depend on its meaning – for instance, we know that if the sentence is taken to be true, one can infer that it is false.

In general, the meaning of a sentence is established by the conventions, language usage patterns, and intentions of speakers of the language. These things provide the "instructions" for interpreting the sentence – at the least, they place constraints on how the sentence can be faithfully interpreted. In the case of "Blug trish ithong", there are no instructions since there are no relevant conventions, usage patterns, or intentions; hence, it is properly called "meaningless". A meaningful sentence is one for which there are some (more or less determinate) instructions. In the ideal case, the implicit instructions are fully *determinate* and *consistent*, in which case they determine a unique proposition; that is, the constraints rule out all but one proposition as the meaning of the sentence. But actual sentences commonly fall short of this ideal. The result is sentences that are not meaningless, but merely have a defective meaning.

There are two kinds of meaning deficiency. The first occurs when the instructions for interpreting a sentence are insufficiently determinate, that is, they rule out *too little*. In this case, there are multiple propositions that the conventions fail to rule out as interpretations of the sentence. This includes cases of ambiguity and vagueness, the latter of which will be discussed in chapter 3.

The second kind of meaning deficiency occurs when the instructions for interpreting a sentence are inconsistent, that is, they rule out *too much*. In this case, there is no proposition that can satisfy all the constraints created by the linguistic conventions (etc.). This is the case with the liar sentence and related paradoxical sentences.

2.6.3 The Truth-Teller

Compare another sentence, which I will call "the truth-teller sentence":

(T)   This sentence is true.

Reasoning about the truth-value of T does not lead to a contradiction in the way that reasoning about L seems to. (T is true if and only if T is true – nothing wrong with that.) Nevertheless, T poses a puzzle. We could *consistently* deem it either true or false, but there seems to be no basis for calling it one rather than the other. To the question, "Is it true or false?", either answer seems arbitrary. What does my view say about this case?

In my view, T fails to express a proposition and thus lacks a truth value. For T is intended to express the proposition that the proposition expressed by T is true. In other words, T is supposed to express the proposition that holds if and only if that very proposition holds. This time, the problem is not that there is no such proposition; the problem is that this is true of *every* proposition, and we are given no further guidance about what specific proposition T is supposed to express. Nor is there any proposition whose sole truth-condition is that it be true. So there is no determinate proposition singled out by T. In that sense, T is meaning-deficient.

The problem with L was that there are too many constraints on the proposition it is supposed to express. It is analogous to the description, "The man who is female", to which nothing corresponds. The problem with T is that there are *too few* constraints on the proposition it is supposed to express, so that more than one thing satisfies them. It is analogous to the description, "The man who is male," which lacks a determinate referent.

A non-deficient sentence is one for which we have just enough constraints so that a single proposition satisfies them. Such sentences are analogous to the description, "The man who wrote this book", which specifies a unique individual.

2.6.4 "The Liar Sentence Is Not True" Is True

Now consider again the following pair of sentences[19]:

(L")   Sentence L" is not true.
(N)   Sentence L" is not true.

---

[19] Previously mentioned in section 2.4.3 above.

On my view, L" fails to express a proposition; thus, in particular, it fails to express a true proposition. So it isn't true. (Nor is it false, of course.)

Now, I just asserted that L" is not true, and there was nothing wrong with that. In general, it is perfectly fine for a sentence *other than L" itself* to assert that L" is not true. For instance, sentence N, on my view, is correct. N expresses the proposition that L" is not true; yet L" does *not* express that proposition, even though L" is syntactically identical to N. Why is this? Because when we read L", we are invited to accept an inconsistent story about the proposition that it expresses; but when we read N, there is no inconsistent story about what N expresses.

Remember the analogous barber paradox. Contrast the following two stories about the barber. Story #1: There is an (adult, male) barber living in Boulder who shaves all and only the Boulder men who do not shave themselves. Who shaves the barber? Answer: There cannot be any such barber, because you gave an inconsistent description of him. Story #2: There is an (adult, male) barber living in Denver who shaves all and only the Boulder men who do not shave themselves. Who shaves the barber? Answer: It could be anyone (maybe he shaves himself, maybe someone else shaves him). Note that there is no reason why this second barber can't exist, since there is nothing inconsistent in this story.

Similarly: L" invites us to accept an inconsistent story about the proposition that it expresses (L" does not explicitly assert this story; rather, the "story" is implied by the rules of our language, the rules for how one is supposed to interpret sentences). The story is that there is a proposition that (*i*) is expressed by L", and (*ii*) holds if and only if L" doesn't express a truth. Conditions (*i*) and (*ii*) are inconsistent. Since these are the requirements for something to be the proposition expressed by L", there is no proposition expressed by L".

Matters are otherwise with sentence N. Sentence N only requires that there be a proposition that (*i*) is expressed by N, and (*ii*) holds if and only if L" fails to express a truth. Now there is no inconsistency in supposing that a proposition satisfies both (*i*) and (*ii*). So there is no obstacle to holding that N expresses such a proposition. In general, sentences express what they are supposed to express, unless there is some reason why they can't. So N expresses the proposition that holds if and only if L" fails to express a truth.

2.6.5   This Sentence Is False or Meaning-Deficient

What if we modify the liar sentence to something like LM:

(LM)   This sentence is either false or meaning-deficient.

? I have said that L is meaning-deficient. If I claim, similarly, that LM is meaning-deficient, won't it follow that LM is actually true (and therefore not meaning-deficient)?

No, it won't. LM is neither true nor false, because LM does not express any proposition. In particular, LM does not express the proposition that LM is either false or meaning-deficient; hence, LM is not made true by LM's being either false or meaning-deficient. In other words, if we consider the following reasoning –

1*.   If a sentence says that a is F or G, then the sentence is true if and only if a is F or G.
2*.   LM says that LM is false or meaning-deficient.
3*.   Therefore, LM is true if and only if LM is false or meaning-deficient.

– I reject premise 2*. Why? Because for something to be the proposition expressed by LM, it must (*i*) be expressed by LM, and (*ii*) be a proposition that holds if and only if LM is false or meaning-deficient. Nothing could satisfy both conditions. (By the definition of "true" as applied to sentences, if a proposition is expressed by LM, then that proposition is true if and only if LM is true. It could not also be the case that that proposition is true if and only if LM is false or meaning-deficient.)

2.6.6   Liar Cycles

What about series of sentences that generate paradoxes, such as this pair:

(L1)   The following sentence is true.
(L2)   The preceding sentence is false.

? Each sentence, considered by itself, seems alright; neither sentence introduces an inconsistent set of conditions for the proposition to be expressed. This is shown by the fact that if some other sentence – say, "Squirrels are furry" – were inserted between L1 and L2, then both L1 and L2 would be perfectly meaningful and would have determinate truth values.

As things stand, however, neither L1 nor L2 is either true or false. Both fail to express propositions. The reason is that the rules for determining what propositions L1 and L2 express are circular, given the actual situation (namely, that L2 immediately follows L1). Propositions are individuated by their truth conditions. The rules of our language dictate that (given the actual syntax of L1 and L2)

i) to find the truth conditions for L1, one is to first find the truth conditions for the sentence that follows it (which happens to be L2), and one is to assign L1 the same truth conditions; also,

ii) to find the truth conditions for L2, one is to first find the truth conditions for the sentence that precedes it (which happens to be L1), and one is to assign L2 the *opposite* truth conditions.

This set of instructions cannot be followed; they send us into an interminable cycle.[20]

Why not say that *one* of the two sentences is meaning-deficient, but the other fully meaningful? This would be enough to avoid paradox. Perhaps L1 expresses a proposition, since, when we read L1, we seem to understand it. If a normal sentence, such as "Squirrels are furry", appears next, then things are fine. It is only when we get to L2, finding that L2 refers us back to L1, that the breakdown occurs. So we might be tempted to say it is L2 that is meaning-deficient.

But there is no reason to single out L2 for the blame. Though we usually read from top to bottom, someone *could* start reading with L2. Thinking everything is fine so far, they proceed next to L1, and that is when the breakdown occurs. (We could also imagine a piece of paper that

---

[20] Cases like this are discussed by Sloman (1971, pp. 136, 139).

has "The sentence on the other side of this page is true" written on one side, and on the other side, "The sentence on the other side of this page is false.") Since there is no relevant difference between L1 and L2, if either of them is meaning-deficient, they both are.

Here, I have spoken of a *procedure* for *assigning* the meanings of L1 and L2, noting that this procedure would never terminate. This is loose talk; the reason L1 and L2 lack meaning is not that *a human being cannot determine* their truth-conditions. (There could be a sentence whose meaning cannot be determined by a human being – say, because the sentence is too complicated for a human being to grasp – but it need not therefore be meaning-deficient.) The reason L1 and L2 lack meaning is that the rules of the English language, together with certain features of the actual situation (notably, the fact that L2 immediately follows L1 on the page) fail to pick out a unique set of truth conditions for the two sentences. These rules and features require that L1 express a proposition that holds if and only if the proposition expressed by L2 is true, and that L2 express a proposition that holds if and only if the proposition expressed by L1 is false. But no pair of propositions can satisfy these conditions. So L1 and L2 fail to express propositions.

What if "false" in L2 were replaced with "true", to remove the contradiction? Then the problem would change from inconsistency to indeterminacy: the rules of the language, given the factual situation, would dictate only that L1 and L2 must be assigned propositions with the same truth value. This meagre constraint fails to pick out a unique pair of propositions.

2.6.7   Prohibiting Liars

As noted earlier (section 2.5), some philosophers believe that natural languages such as English are defective since they allow sentences like the liar sentence to be constructed. On their view, we should have a language in which the grammatical rules for forming sentences do not allow the liar sentence, or other paradoxical sentences or sets of sentences, to be formulated in the first place.

While it may be in some sense a defect of English that it allows the liar sentence to be formulated, I think this is not an important defect, and the project of formulating rules whereby one could declare the liar sentence "ungrammatical" or syntactically ill-formed is not a useful project.[21]

Why? Compare another social construction: the law. There are undoubtedly many inconsistencies in the body of law governing, say, the United States. In addition, many legal doctrines are sufficiently vague or ambiguous that there are many possible cases in which it is indeterminate whether an action is legal or not. How serious of a problem is this? The answer depends on how often we in fact run into inconsistencies or cases of indeterminate legality. If we can easily, unequivocally classify almost all actual actions as legal or not, then the law may serve its functions well enough – at least, it won't be prevented from doing so by the mere possibility of cases in which we cannot say what is legal. Note that the existence of inconsistencies in the body of law does not mean, for example, that murder is legal, or that we don't know whether it is legal, or that it is both legal and illegal. It is unequivocally illegal.

Similarly, our language is not prevented from serving its function by the mere possibility of a grammatical sentence that fails to express a proposition. The purpose of language is to communicate, which we do well enough in normal circumstances. We do not have a persistent problem where people fail to communicate due to their having unwittingly (or wittingly) uttered liar-like sentences. There are some possible grammatical sentences that fail to express propositions due to inconsistency in the rules for interpreting them, but these sentences are hardly ever used (due precisely to the fact that they fail to express propositions). The fact that contradictions can be derived if we take certain sentences to express propositions does not prevent us from assigning consistent, unequivocal interpretations to *most* sentences. Hence, liar sentences do not pose a significant obstacle to the functioning of language.

Nor is there any reason to expect that there must be some purely *syntactic* rule whereby all and only the paradox-generating sentences of English can be excluded. I would, however, be happy to provide a non-syntactic rule for

---

[21] Sloman (1971, pp. 142–3) takes a similar view.

identifying meaning-deficient sentences: if the rules of our language, when combined with the actual relevant facts (about, e.g., the circumstances in which a sentence is uttered), entail contradictory claims about the proposition expressed by a given sentence, or if they fail to single out a unique proposition as the one expressed by the sentence, then the sentence fails to express a proposition. In short: the meaning-deficient sentences include the ones for which there exists paradoxical reasoning (as in the case of sentences L, L1, L2, and the like), plus the ones for which there is nothing that would make them true or false (as in the case of sentence T). It is precisely the paradoxical reasoning about L that tells us that L is meaning-deficient.

2.7   Curry's Paradox

Sometimes philosophy students ask for advice on how to get a job after graduation. Fortunately, I have discovered a logically foolproof method. When you apply for the job that you desire, just include the following sentence in your cover letter:

C Either this sentence is false, or you will hire me.[22]

This guarantees that you will be hired. For suppose C is false. In that case, the first disjunct is true. But if the first disjunct is true, then the whole disjunction is true. So actually, C cannot be false.

So now suppose C is true. In that case, the first disjunct is false. Since the whole sentence is true while its first disjunct is false, it must be that the second disjunct is true. So you will be hired. It doesn't matter what your qualifications are, who recommended you, or how good you are in interviews; the hiring committee will simply be logically compelled to choose you, on pain of contradiction.

Here is a more explicit statement of the reasoning:

1. If a sentence says that p or q, then the sentence is true if and only if either p or q. (Premise.)
2. Sentence C says that C is false or you will be hired. (Premise.)

---

3. C is true if and only if either C is false or you will be hired. (From 1, 2.)
4. If C is false, then C is true. (From 3.)
5. C is true. (From 4.)
6. Either C is false or you will be hired. (From 3, 5.)
7. You will be hired. (From 5, 6.)

My solution to this puzzle parallels my solution to the Liar Paradox: premise 2 is false, because sentence C fails to express a proposition. The reason is that the rules for determining what proposition C expresses are inconsistent: they require that C be assigned, as its meaning, the proposition that holds if and only if either that very proposition *fails* to hold, or you will get the job. This would be a proposition that would be made true by its own failure to be true. But there cannot be a proposition that would be made true by its own failure to be true. So C does not express a proposition.

2.8   The Paradox of Non-Self-Applicability

Here is another paradox cut from the same cloth as the Liar.[23] Some properties apply to themselves. For instance, the property of being a property is itself a property; hence, it applies to itself (or possesses itself, or instantiates itself). The property of abstractness, I suppose, is abstract. Hence, abstractness is also self-applicable. On the other hand, most properties fail to apply to themselves. For instance, the property of being a cat is not itself a cat. Therefore, cathood is not self-applicable. The property of being happy is not itself happy (only people can be happy, not properties). So happiness, too, is non-self-applicable.

Now consider the property of non-self-applicability (the property of failing to apply to oneself): does this property apply to itself? Well, it applies to itself if and only if it does not apply to itself. Contradiction.

My solution: there is no such property as non-self-applicability, because it has an inconsistent definition. Non-self-applicability is defined to be the property that applies to each thing, x, if and only if x does not apply

---

[23] This paradox derives from Russell (1902, 1903, p. 102). Grelling and Nelson (1908) restate the paradox in slightly different words, which somehow has led some to call it "Grelling's Paradox" or "the Grelling-Nelson Paradox" (as in Clark 2002, pp. 80–81).

to *x*. That definition yields a contradiction when "non-self-applicability" is plugged in for *x*. So there is no such property.

You might protest: it certainly seems as if there is such a property. When I say that cathood does not apply to itself, and happiness does not apply to itself, it seems that I am in each case saying something sensible (and true). It seems that I am pointing out something that *cathood* and *happiness* have in common.

I think this intuition can be captured by acknowledging the existence of properties that are very similar to the supposed property of non-self-applicability. Here are two of them:

Non-self-applicability[+]: The property that applies to each thing, other than non-self-applicability[+] itself, if and only if that thing does not apply to itself, and which also applies to itself.

Non-self-applicability[−]: The property that applies to each thing, other than non-self-applicability[−] itself, if and only if that thing does not apply to itself, and which does not apply to itself.

Thus, the intuition that cathood is non-self-applicable may be replaced, say, with the judgment that cathood is non-self-applicable[+].

2.9   Russell's Paradox

It used to be thought that, for any well-defined predicate, there is a set containing all and only the things to which the predicate applies. For instance, corresponding to the predicate "is red", there is the set of all red things – that is, the set such that for any *x*, *x* belongs to the set if and only if *x* is red.

This idea runs into paradox when we consider the predicate "is not a member of itself". The corresponding set would be the set of all things that are not members of themselves. Call this "the Russell set" (after its inventor, Bertrand Russell).[24] Is the Russell set a member of itself or not? For any *x*, the Russell set contains *x* if and only if *x* isn't a member of

---

[24] Russell 1902, 1903, p. 102.

itself; that's the definition of the Russell set. If we substitute the Russell set itself for "x", we see that the Russell set contains the Russell set, if and only if the Russell set isn't a member of itself. That is a contradiction: $R \in R \leftrightarrow R \notin R$.

The standard solution: The Russell set does not exist. Everyone agrees on that, though there are several different accounts of exactly why the Russell set does not exist. There are, that is, a variety of proposed principles describing what sorts of sets exist; each proposed set of principles, to be considered adequate, must exclude the Russell set.

I don't have a comprehensive theory of what sets exist.[25] But I know this much: a putative set does not exist if it has an inconsistent definition. "The set that has exactly three members and has exactly two members" does not denote anything. Nor does "the set that contains itself if and only if it does not do so". Nor, for the same reason, does "the set that contains all and only the things that don't contain themselves".

References

Beall, J.C. 2009. *Spandrels of Truth*. Oxford: Oxford University Press.

Beall, J.C. and Michael Glanzberg. 2011. "Liar Paradox", *Stanford Encyclopedia of Philosophy*, http://plato.stanford.edu/entries/liar-paradox/, accessed April 30, 2017.

Braakuis, H.A.G. 1967. "The Second Tract on Insolubilia Found in Paris, B.N. Lat. 16.617. An Edition of the Text with an Analysis of Its Contents," *Vivarium* 5 (1967): 111–45.

Clark, Michael. 2002. *Paradoxes from A to Z*. London: Routledge.

Curry, Haskell B. 1942. "The Inconsistency of Certain Formal Logics", *Journal of Symbolic Logic* 7: 115–117.

Eklund, Matti. 2002. "Inconsistent Languages", *Philosophy and Phenomenological Research* 64: 251–75.

Geach, Peter. 1950. "Russell's Theory of Descriptions", *Analysis* 10: 84–8.

Grelling, Kurt and Leonhard Nelson. 1908. "Bemerkungen zu den Paradoxien von Russell und Burali-Forti" ("Remarks on the Paradoxes of Russell and Burali-Forti"), *Abhandlungen der Fries'schen Schule n.s.* 2: 301–34.

---

[25] Except that perhaps *no* sets exist; see my 2016, ch. 8.

Herzberger, Hans G. 1967. "The Truth-Conditional Consistency of Natural Language", *Journal of Philosophy* 64: 29–35.

Huemer, Michael. 2016. *Approaching Infinity.* New York: Palgrave Macmillan.

Irvine, Andrew David and Harry Deutsch. 2016. "Russell's Paradox", *The Stanford Encyclopedia of Philosophy*, ed. Edward N. Zalta, https://plato.stanford.edu/archives/win2016/entries/russell-paradox/, accessed May 28, 2017.

Littmann, Greg and Keith Simmons. 2004. "A Critique of Dialetheism", pp. 314–35 in *The Law of Non-Contradiction*, ed. Graham Priest, J.C. Beall, and Bradley Armour-Garb. Oxford: Oxford University Press.

Priest, Graham. 2006a. *In Contradiction: A Study of the Transconsistent*, expanded ed. Oxford: Clarendon.

Priest, Graham. 2006b. *Doubt Truth to Be a Liar.* Oxford: Clarendon.

Prior, Arthur N. 1955. "Curry's Paradox and 3-valued Logic", *Australasian Journal of Philosophy* 33: 177–82.

Quine, Willard van Orman. 1986. *Philosophy of Logic*, second ed. Cambridge, MA: Harvard University Press.

Rescher, Nicholas. 2001. *Paradoxes: Their Roots, Range, and Resolution.* Chicago, IL: Open Court.

Russell, Bertrand. 1902. Letter to Frege dated 16 June, 1902, reprinted on pp. 124–5 in Jean van Heijenoort, ed. *From Frege to Gödel: A Source Book in Mathematical Logic, 1879–1931.* Cambridge, MA: Harvard University Press, 1967.

Russell, Bertrand. 1903. *The Principles of Mathematics.* Cambridge: Cambridge University Press.

Russell, Bertrand. 1908. "Mathematical Logic as Based on the Theory of Types", *American Journal of Mathematics* 30: 222–62.

Russell, Bertrand. 1972. "The Philosophy of Logical Atomism", pp. 1–125 in *The Philosophy of Logical Atomism.* London: Routledge.

Sainsbury, Richard M. 2009. *Paradoxes*, 3rd ed. Cambridge: Cambridge University Press.

Sloman, Aaron. 1971. "Tarski, Frege and the Liar Paradox", *Philosophy* 46: 133–147.

Spade, Paul Vincent. 1975. *The Mediaeval Liar: A Catalogue of the Insolubilia-Literature.* Toronto, Canada: Pontifical Institute of Mediaeval Studies.

Strawson, Peter F. 1950. "On Referring", *Mind* 59: 320–44.

Tarski, Alfred. 1944. "The Semantic Conception of Truth: And the Foundations of Semantics", *Philosophy and Phenomenological Research* 4: 341–76.

Tarski, Alfred. 1983. "The Concept of Truth in Formalized Languages", pp. 152–278 in *Logic, Semantics, Metamathematics: Papers from 1923 to 1938*, 2nd ed., ed. John Corcoran, tr. Joseph Henry Woodger. Indianapolis: Hackett.

3

The Sorites

3.1 The Paradox

How many grains of sand must one have in order to have a "heap" of sand? I don't know. But let's assume that a million grains (suitably arranged) would constitute a paradigmatic heap, that is, a clear case of a heap. It seems plausible that removing one grain from a heap of sand does not destroy the heap – if you had a heap before, then you still have a heap after subtracting one grain. But these premises entail that a single grain of sand may constitute a heap:

1. If n grains of sand constitute a heap, then $n-1$ grains of sand constitute a heap. (Premise.)
2. 1,000,000 grains of sand constitute a heap. (Premise.)
3. Therefore, 999,999 grains of sand constitute a heap. (From 1, 2.)
4. Therefore, 999,998 grains of sand constitute a heap. (From 1, 3.)
. . .

1,000,001. Therefore, 1 grain of sand constitutes a heap. (From 1, 1,000,000.)

© The Author(s) 2018
M. Huemer, *Paradox Lost*, https://doi.org/10.1007/978-3-319-90490-0_3

This is an example of a *sorites argument* (the name comes from the Greek word "soros", meaning "heap", but similar arguments can be constructed for "bald", "large", and many other terms). The full argument has a million and one steps; I trust the reader will forgive me for not writing them all out. Every step after (2) is just a logical deduction from (1) and the step immediately above it. But the conclusion is obviously false.

It looks as though there are three views one could take: deny premise (1), deny premise (2), or embrace the conclusion.[1] There would be no point in protesting that a million grains is not enough for a heap and that one instead needs, say, a billion, since the same sort of reasoning could still be constructed to get to the same conclusion, only with more steps. So if one is going to reject (2), one will presumably hold that *no* finite number of grains of sand make a heap; that is, there are no heaps. On the other hand, if one embraces the conclusion of the sorites argument, then one will hold that *any* number of grains of sand constitute a heap.

We should not claim that there are no heaps. Why not? First, because there obviously are heaps. Second, because similar reasoning can be constructed using a vast array of properties, including baldness, largeness, redness, and so on. (The starting premises in these cases would be: "Adding one hair to the head of a bald person does not make him non-bald", "Subtracting 1 cubic micron from the size of a large person does not make him no longer large", and "Increasing the wavelength of a light ray by one angstrom does convert red light into non-red light.") If one responds similarly to all similar arguments, one will have to say, for example, that no one is ever bald (but nor is anyone hairy), nor is anything ever large, red, etc.[2]

We also should not claim that just any number of grains of sand may make a heap. (By the way, the above argument could be extended to step 1,000,002, "0 grains of sand constitutes a heap" (from steps 1 and 1,000,001).) This is also absurd, and would also lead us into absurd claims involving a host of other terms – for instance, that everything with a size is large, everyone is bald, every colored thing is red, and so on.

---

[1] These aren't really the only possibilities; more below.
[2] Unger (1979a, b) and Wheeler (1979) hold this view.

So it seems obvious that premise (1) is to blame. Why would anyone believe (1)?

(1) is supposed to be established by reflection on the vagueness of the word "heap". Note: "vague" in this discussion is not used in the common sense of "insufficiently specific"; rather, a vague term is a term that has borderline cases of its applicability. For example, there are borderline cases of heaps, so "heap" is vague.

Imagine a philosopher announcing that he has discovered the cutoff for heapness: it is 546,798 grains.[3] "If you have 546,798 grains of sand, you have a heap; if you have 546,797, no heap." Something would be wrong with this view. It isn't that 546,798 was the wrong number and that the philosopher should have picked a different number. There is something wrong with picking any specific number – if you think there is any specific number such that having a "heap" means having at least *that* number of grains, then you have misunderstood the concept of a heap. The concept is inherently vague – part of the *point* of using concepts like "heap" is to avoid precision. So it seems contrary to the meaning of "heap" to hold that there is a precise cutoff point for being a heap. To deny (1) would be to claim that there is some number n for which n grains of sand are a heap, but $n - 1$ grains are not. So it seems that we cannot plausibly deny (1).

3.2   Deviant Logic

Some piles of sand are clearly heaps, others are clearly not heaps, and others, as we say, are borderline cases. In cases of the last sort, philosophers say, "It is vague whether the pile is a heap." What should we say about the borderline cases? Many are tempted to say that if B is a borderline case of a heap, then B is neither a heap nor not a heap. This entails a violation of the law of excluded middle, the logical axiom that for any proposition, either that proposition or its negation holds (A ∨ ~A). Likewise, maybe the sentence "B is a heap" is neither true nor false, in violation of the

---

[3] Some philosophers (Hart 1992, p. 3; Krkač 2012, pp. 90–91) have suggested that the cutoff is *four* grains, but I judge this implausibly low.

principle of bivalence, the principle that every (proposition-asserting) sentence is either true or false.

A *deviant* logic is a system of logical rules that rejects at least one of the traditional principles of logic, such as the law of non-contradiction, the law of excluded middle, or bivalence.[4] The phenomenon of vagueness is one of the chief things that tempts philosophers toward deviant logics – for instance, logics on which there are three truth values ("true", "false", and "indeterminate"), or even infinitely many truth-values (which can be thought of as "degrees of truth").[5] If we adopt a three-valued logic, we can say that statements ascribing heapness to borderline cases are indeterminate. If we adopt a degree-of-truth theory, we can say that, within the range of borderline-heaps, "x is a heap" becomes *truer* (by just a little bit) as you add individual grains of sand to x.

My main problem with this class of approaches is that the traditional laws of logic seem to me self-evident, necessary truths. For example, I think the law of non-contradiction is self-evident, given the meaning of "not" and "and".[6] And here is one reason why I believe the law of excluded middle: suppose that neither A nor the negation of A holds. That means that A isn't the case, and ~A also isn't the case. That is, it's not the case that A, and it's also not the case that it's not the case that A. That is an explicit contradiction (~A & ~~A). So the starting assumption must be impossible: it cannot be that neither A nor ~A holds. That is, either A or ~A must hold.

What about sentences: must every sentence be either true or false? Clearly not: the sentence "Please pass the Cholula", for example, is neither true nor false. That is because it does not assert a proposition. Likewise, "The redness substantiates dog" is neither true nor false, because it is (though grammatical) meaningless. So the only principle of bivalence worth talking about would have to be something like this: any sentence

---

[4] The term derives from Quine (1986, pp. 80–81). As I use the term "logic", a logic includes not only inference rules and logical axioms, but also some general metatheory about truth, in particular, a theory as to how many truth-values there are and how truth-values of simpler sentences relate to truth-values of compound sentences.

[5] On three-valued logic, see Tye 1994; on degrees of truth, see Zadeh 1965; Goguen 1969; Smith 2008. Rescher (2001, p. 82) also appears to endorse a multiple-truth-value theory.

[6] See discussion above, Sect. 2.3.

that asserts a proposition is either true or false.[7] Now, here is why I believe bivalence, so understood: I think that it is part of the meaning of "true" that if a sentence asserts that A, then if A, then the sentence is true. It is part of the meaning of "false" that if a sentence asserts that A, then if ~A, then the sentence is false. As discussed above, either A or ~A must be the case. Therefore, if a sentence asserts that A, then the sentence is either true or false. That is, any proposition-asserting sentence is true or false.[8]

Degrees-of-truth theories claim that A might be partially true, that is, true to some (non-extreme) degree, rather than fully true or fully false. For instance, "*x* is a heap" might be true only to some degree. I, unfortunately, do not understand what it means for a thing to be true to a degree (nor what it means to be a heap to a degree). Granted, *some* properties come in degrees: a thing can be heavy to a degree, because weight is a quantitative concept. But TRUTH is not that kind of concept, nor is HEAP.[9]

It is important here not to confuse being *more F* (for some possible feature F) with being *closer to being F*.[10] For example, suppose that Sue is in Philadelphia, whereas Groot is on Mars. In that case, Sue is *closer* to New York than Groot is. But it is not the case that Sue is *more* in New York than Groot is, or that Sue is *in New York to a greater degree* than Groot is. Both Sue and Groot are simply not in New York. Similarly, a pile of five grains of sand is (slightly) closer to being a heap than is a pile of only four grains of sand. But the five grains are not more a heap than the four; they are not a heap to a greater degree. Both piles are simply not heaps. Accordingly, if we compare the two sentences:

H_4 A pile of four grains of sand is a heap.
H_5 A pile of five grains of sand is a heap.

---

[7] Cf. Williamson 1994b, p. 187. More precisely, we might say: if a sentence is used on a given occasion to assert a proposition, then the utterance on that occasion is either true or false. But this is needlessly tedious for the main text.

[8] Williamson (1994b, pp. 187–9) gives this defense of excluded middle and bivalence.

[9] I use small caps to denote concepts.

[10] Clark (2002, pp. 72–3) and Sainsbury (2009, pp. 57–8) appear to conflate these. Smith (2008, p. 210) wisely rejects such conflation.

H_5 is *closer to being* true than H_4 is, but it is not true to a greater degree; both are just false. Just as someone can come closer to New York without being in New York to any degree, sentences can come closer to being true without being true to any degree.

These remarks do not prove that there are no degrees of truth; they merely clear away one confusion that might have made you think you understood the notion of degrees of truth.

There is something odd about the degrees-of-truth theory. The problem with vague terms, one might have thought, is that their meanings are insufficiently determinate; that is, our conventions for their use are not precise enough to determine exactly which things they apply to and which they do not apply to. Now, the degrees-of-truth theorist proposes to replace the qualitative categories "true" and "false" with a continuum of infinitely many degrees of truth. But if our conventions fail to specify precise boundaries for the application of "heap", surely these same conventions do not go so far as to supply precise *degrees* of applicability of "heap" for each object to which the word might be applied. If one starts with the intuition that it may be indeterminate whether x is a heap, surely one should just as much doubt that there is always a determinate degree to which x is a heap.

One might respond to this problem by proposing that, rather than having a unique degree of truth, a statement of the form "x is a heap" may have a *range* of admissible degrees of truth, none of which is determinately the correct one.[11] But the problem iterates: if we at first thought the degree of truth indeterminate, then once ranges are introduced, shouldn't we also think the *range* indeterminate? If our conventions fail to determine whether "x is a heap" is true, and they fail to determine the precise degree to which it is true, surely they will also fail to determine the precise range of degrees to which it might be said to be true.

(Aside: By my lights, the best response for a degrees-of-truth theorist is simply to take an epistemicist line [see section 3.4 below], namely, that it merely appears to us that there is no fact of the matter as to a statement's precise degree of truth because it is very difficult or impossible for us to

---

[11] This is Smith's (2008, ch. 6) view.

know that degree. I reject this chiefly because I believe that "true", in English, simply does not express a degree concept.)

A related problem for all theories that introduce extra truth-values is the problem of *second-order vagueness*. First-order vagueness occurs when it is vague whether A. Second-order vagueness occurs when it is vague whether it is vague whether A. For example, not only may it be unclear whether *x* is a heap, but it may also be unclear *whether it is clear* that *x* is a heap ("clear" is itself a vague term).

The sorites paradox begins when we consider some such question as "What is the minimum number of grains of sand required for a heap?" It is hard to believe that there is a specific number that is the correct answer to that question. Now suppose we try to avoid the question by claiming that for some values of *n*, it is indeterminate whether *n* grains of sand constitute a heap. Then we could be asked: "What is the minimum number *n* for which *it is indeterminate whether n* grains of sand constitute a heap?" In other words, what is the cutoff point between something that is clearly not a heap, and something that is a borderline case of a heap? Once again, it seems hard to believe that there is a precise number that is the correct answer to this question. The degrees-of-truth theory faces a similar conundrum: "What is the minimum number of grains of sand such that it is *to some degree true* that that many grains constitute a heap?" Since this is the same sort of puzzle that originally confronted us, it appears that theories of indeterminacy or degrees of truth would not yet have provided a satisfying solution, even if they were otherwise plausible.[12]

One might reply that the same treatment can be applied to second-order vagueness as to first-order vagueness. For instance, just as there are some *n* for which it is indeterminate whether *n* grains of sand are a heap, there also are some *n* for which it is indeterminate whether it is indeterminate whether *n* grains of sand are a heap, and for which it is neither true nor false that it is neither true nor false that *n* grains of sand are a heap. At this point, however, I confess to having lost my sense of understanding what all this means.

---

[12] Similar objections appear in Unger 1979a, pp. 128–9; Tye 1994, p. 191; Williamson 1994b, pp. 127–8.

3.3   Supervaluationism

Sometimes, it makes sense to precisify a vague term – that is, to stipulate a precise cutoff point for a word that, in ordinary usage, lacks any precise cutoff. For instance, suppose we have agreed that only adults should be permitted to vote in elections. In ordinary usage, "adult" is vague – there is no precise moment at which one becomes an adult.[13] But for practical purposes, we need a precise cutoff. So we might stipulate that one becomes an adult at the moment exactly 18 years after one's time of birth. This is a reasonable enough way of precisifying "adult" for the present purpose. It does not conflict with established usage in any clear cases, or so I assume. Notice that matters would be otherwise if we stipulated that the cutoff for adulthood was to be ten years of age – that would be an unacceptable precisification of "adult", in the sense that it would get certain clear cases wrong: a ten-year-old is *clearly not* an adult in the ordinary sense of the word. Similarly, it would be unacceptable to stipulate that the cutoff for adulthood should be 40 years of age. This would be unacceptable since 39-year-olds are clearly adults in the ordinary sense of the term.

Let us say that an *acceptable* precisification of a vague term is one that agrees with our current actual usage in all clear cases; an *unacceptable* precisification, by contrast, is one that misclassifies certain clear cases. And let us define a "supertrue" statement as one that comes out true on *every acceptable precisification* of the vague terms in the statement. A "superfalse" statement is one that comes out false on every acceptable precisification. For example, it is supertrue that a 40-year-old is an adult; it is superfalse that a 10-year-old is an adult.[14] For a 17-year-old, it is neither supertrue nor superfalse.

We can now formulate what may be the most popular contemporary theory of vagueness, supervaluationism: supervaluationists hold that truth is supertruth, and falsity is superfalsity.[15] Thus, if a statement is true

---

[13] Clark (2002, pp. 74–5) gives this example.

[14] I am leaving aside weird cases, such as that of a person with abnormally accelerated or retarded aging. Assume that we are only considering individuals with normal physiological processes.

[15] Fine 1975; Lewis 1988.

on all acceptable precisifications, then it is true simply; if it is false on all acceptable precisifications, it is false. If it is true on some acceptable precisifications and false on others, then it is neither true nor false. (The theory thus requires a deviant logic.)

On this account, premise 1 of the sorites argument –

1. If n grains of sand constitute a heap, then $n - 1$ grains of sand constitute a heap.

– is false. In every acceptable precisification, there is a precise cutoff point for heapness, a number of grains from which removing one grain converts a heap to a non-heap. (1) not only fails to be supertrue; it is superfalse. Thus do we avoid the sorites paradox.

This theory also preserves the law of excluded middle, *in a sense*: the law of excluded middle is true, because it is true on any acceptable precisification. For instance, suppose B is a borderline case of a heap. The sentence, "Either B is a heap or B is not a heap", comes out true on every acceptable precisification, so it's true. *However*, "B is a heap" is not true (because not supertrue). Nor is "B is not a heap" (also not supertrue). Thus, the theory enables us to count a disjunction as true when neither disjunct is true. This is odd; you might have thought that to say a disjunction is true just *means* that at least one disjunct is true.

This problem is related to the supervaluationist's need to reject the T-schema.[16] The T-schema says that, in general, if a sentence asserts p, then the sentence is true if and only if p (in symbols: $T\ulcorner p\urcorner \leftrightarrow p$).[17] The supervaluationist holds that, if B is a borderline case of a heap, then "B is a heap" is not true, and "B is not a heap" is not true. Given the T-schema (and given that "B is a heap" asserts that B is a heap and "B is not a heap" asserts that B is not a heap), this implies that B is not a heap, and it is not the case that B is not a heap. But that is an explicit contradiction, a state-

---

[16] As noted also by Fine (1975, p. 297); Williamson (1994b, p. 162); Braun and Sider (2007, pp. 147–8).

[17] Actually, this is a principle, not a *schema*. But it's a principle that is closely-enough related to the T-schema that it would be pedantic to worry about the distinction, especially in the main text. The T-schema, technically, is a class of sentences, namely, those sentences that can be formed by taking the expression "'A' is true if and only if A" and replacing both occurrences of "A" with the same English declarative sentence.

ment of the form "*p* and not-*p*".[18] To avoid this, the supervaluationist would have to reject the T-schema. The T-schema, however, seems to be a fundamental principle (perhaps *the* fundamental principle) about the meaning of "true" in English. We should therefore reject supervaluationism rather than reject the T-schema.

In addition, this theory, again, has a problem with second-order vagueness. The intuition that there is no precise cutoff point for being a heap is supposed to be captured by the theory's declaration that, for some values of *n*, it is neither true nor false that *n* grains of sand constitute a heap. However, if we doubt that there is a precise cutoff point between heaps and non-heaps, we should probably also doubt that there is a precise cutoff point between things of which "that is a heap" is true and things of which "that is a heap" is neither true nor false. The theory has replaced a single vague boundary (between the true and the false) with two vague boundaries (one between the true and the neither-true-nor-false, and another between the neither-true-nor-false and the false). We may reasonably question whether this constitutes progress.[19]

Finally, perhaps the most troubling aspect of the theory is that supervaluationism appears to imply (given obvious background assumptions) that supervaluationism itself is false. We know that the term "heap" is vague, not precise. However, *on any acceptable precisification* of "heap", the term is precise; in particular, it has a unique, precise cutoff point. That's what "precisification" means. So the sentence "'Heap' is precise" is supertrue, and hence (according to supervaluationism) true. Similarly, "'Heap' is vague" is superfalse, and so false. But supervaluationists themselves think that terms such as "heap" are vague. Thus, the theory judges a statement expressing part of the theorist's own view to be false.

---

[18] To represent the problem formally, let *b* be the proposition that some borderline case is a heap, and read " ⌜φ⌝ " in general as denoting the sentence that expresses φ. We have: (1) T⌜*b*⌝ ↔ *b* (premise). (2) ~T⌜*b*⌝ & ~T⌜~*b*⌝ (supervaluationist view). (3) ~*b* & ~~*b* (from 1, 2). Since (3) is a contradiction, the supervaluationist must reject (1).

[19] For similar objections, see Tye 1994, pp. 192–3; Williamson 1994b, pp. 156–61.

3.4   Epistemicism

Epistemicists hold that vague terms really have precise cutoffs; it only seems otherwise to us because we do not *know* where these cutoff points are. For instance, there is a particular number of grains of sand that constitutes the smallest possible heap, although no one is in a position to know what this number is. The argument for this view is simple:

1'. One grain of sand is not a heap. (Premise.)
2'. One million grains of sand are a heap. (Premise.)
3'. Therefore, for some n, n grains of sand are not a heap, but $n+1$ grains of sand are a heap. (From 1', 2'.)

(3') deductively follows from (1') and (2'). (To see this, note that the negation of (3') would be the claim that for all n, if n grains of sand are not a heap, then $n+1$ grains of sand are also not a heap. This entails that if one grain of sand is not a heap, then one million grains of sand are not a heap.) So there is a sharp cutoff for being a heap. But obviously if there is, we do not know where this cutoff is.

Now to clear away some potential distractions: I have spoken as if what determines whether a pile of sand is a heap is solely the number of grains of sand in it. Of course, other factors also matter, such as the size and arrangement of the grains. But these complications are irrelevant to our issue: the possibility of variation along these other dimensions does not help to identify a cutoff point for "heap", nor does it eliminate the need for a cutoff; it merely creates additional dimensions along which the cutoff for being a heap is vague. We can therefore assume a fixed size, shape, arrangement, and so on, for the grains of sand. The question is: at what point does adding another grain onto the pile convert it from a non-heap to a heap?

What counts as a heap can also vary with conversational context and the speaker's purposes. For instance, in one context, we are working on a large construction project, and we need a heap of sand for landscaping purposes. In another context, we are cleaning the kitchen, and someone complains that one of the children just dumped a heap of sand on the floor. In the first context, the standards for "heap" are higher than in the second – a lot more sand is required to have a heap. But this complication, too, is irrelevant; taking account of context-sensitivity does not resolve the philosophical problem. We can simply assume a fixed context; the word "heap" will still be vague, and there will still be the above argument that there must be a precise cutoff (in the particular context).[20]

Now, why can't we know the cutoff for a vague term? Timothy Williamson offers one explanation. In general, he says, for you to count as *knowing* that x is F, it must be true not only that x is F, but also that objects that are very close to x along the dimensions that determine Fness (so close that we couldn't distinguish them from x) are also F. Now suppose that n is actually the minimum number of grains of sand required for the English word "heap" to apply. A situation in which the cutoff had instead been $n - 1$ grains would be very similar to the actual situation (so close that we couldn't distinguish it from the actual situation), but of course it would be a situation in which the cutoff was not n. Therefore, we do not satisfy the above stated requirement for *knowing* that our current situation is one in which the cutoff is n.[21]

Roy Sorensen offers another explanation for why we cannot know the cutoff for a vague term: to know where the cutoff is, we would have to be aware of the facts in the world that *make* that particular cutoff point the correct one. But, on Sorensen's view, there *are no* facts that make a particular cutoff the right one; a particular cutoff *just is* the correct one, but with nothing that explains why it is.[22]

Like most people, I find epistemicism hard to swallow. It seems to me that if there is to be a sharp boundary for the application of a word, there must be something that makes a particular boundary the correct one, presumably something having to do with where words get their meanings in the first place. Words do not have meanings intrinsically, like magical

---

[20] On one account (Raffman 1996), the meaning of "heap" shifts as one proceeds through steps 1 through 1,000,001 of the original sorites argument. The shifts occur in such a way that, for any particular n, when one is thinking about a pile of n grains, "heap" always either applies to both that pile and the pile of $n - 1$ grains, or applies to neither. However, even on this view, no change in the meaning of "heap" need occur in the brief argument comprised by steps 1'-3' in the text. So 3' must be true, for whatever sense of "heap" was in play in 1' and 2'.
[21] Williamson 1994b, pp. 226–34.
[22] See Sorensen 2001, ch. 11, esp. pp. 175–7.

connections to objects; words get whatever meanings they have from such things as conventions, usage patterns, and speakers' intentions. But our conventions, usage patterns, and intentions do not settle the exact number of grains of sand that constitute the smallest heap. We simply have not decided on an exact cutoff point for "heap". So there is no way for the word to have acquired one.

Perhaps, one might think, this is mistaken: perhaps our usage patterns *do* settle the exact cutoff point for "heap", although we are normally unaware of this. For perhaps, unbeknownst to us, there is a unique precisification of the word "heap" that best matches the total usage pattern of "heap" among English speakers. For illustrative purposes, imagine that, if forced to classify piles as heaps or non-heaps, a narrow majority of people (50.001%) would call 546,798 grains of sand a heap, while a narrow minority (49.999%) would call 546,797 grains a heap. Perhaps something like this could make it the case that, unbeknownst to typical English speakers, 546,798 grains of sand is in fact the cutoff point for a heap of sand, because that cutoff best coheres with our dispositions to apply the word. Of course, this is a simplification – the facts about our classificatory dispositions are more complex than this example indicates, and the facts that determine meaning are more complex than our classificatory dispositions. Nevertheless, this illustrates how there might be, unbeknownst to us, an objective fact about which precisification of "heap" best matches our usage. (Aside: though most epistemicists say we *cannot* know the cutoff for a vague term, the present suggestion explains how we might in principle be able to discover the cutoff point, though we have not in fact done so.)

I don't think this is a crazy idea; at least it is less counterintuitive than a rejection of classical logic. Nevertheless, it seems false. For, as noted, the facts about our dispositions, conventions, and intentions are more complex than the above example indicates. For one thing, our classificatory behavior may vary depending on the conditions in which we are asked to classify. Perhaps people are very slightly more (or less) willing to apply the word "heap" during the daytime than they are at night; even so, intuitively, the meaning of "heap" should not therefore be taken as changing with time of day. Different groups of people also might give slightly different patterns of answers without, intuitively, being taken as either misusing the word or employing a different sense (but if the patterns differ by too much, *then* they will count as misusing or using a different sense). So to have a precise cutoff for "heap", we would need to have a precise, privileged type of observer and set of conditions. Even if we had such a privileged observer and set of conditions, there would be different ways of construing the best cutoff point. Perhaps the cutoff for "heap" should be the average number that privileged observers would name when asked "What is the smallest possible heap?" Or perhaps it should be the midpoint between the point where most privileged observers first start to call something a borderline case of a heap, and the point where most stop calling something a borderline case. And so on.

The problem is that there is no uniquely correct way of construing the notion of the "best match" to our linguistic conventions, dispositions, and intentions. Nor can one reasonably claim, in epistemicist fashion, that there is a unique best interpretation of "best match" and we merely do not know what it is. For the existence of a correct precisification of vague terms in general depends upon there already being a privileged way of construing the "best match" to our conventions. On pain of circularity, we cannot suppose that the privileged construal of "best match" itself determines the correct precisification of "best match". So there just isn't anything to settle the precise cutoff points for vague terms in general.

Why not say that there is a property of heaphood out there, existing independently of our minds, and it is the objective nature of that property, rather than any thoughts or conventions of ours, that determines the cutoff for "heap"?

I have no objection to positing properties and other abstract objects existing independent of us. But if there is one such property, then there are many. If there is a property that a pile of sand has when it contains at least 500,000 grains, then there is another property that a pile has when it contains at least 500,001 grains, another for 500,002 grains, and so on. Each of these properties, I am happy to agree, exist completely independent of our thoughts and conventions. What is not independent of our thoughts and conventions is the *mapping* from our language to the objectively existing properties. Thoughts and conventions must determine *which* of the many objectively existing properties the word "heap" is to express, if indeed there is one that it expresses.

3.5   A Moderate Nihilist Solution

A solution to the sorites paradox should explain what vagueness is and why it exists. That explanation should provide a basis for diagnosing where the sorites argument goes wrong, as well as for answering such questions as "Is there a precise cutoff point for being a heap?", "Are some statements neither true nor false?", and "Why is there second-order vagueness?"

Before explaining the nature of vagueness, we will first need to reflect on the contents of thoughts, and on how the meanings of our sentences relate to the contents of our thoughts.

3.5.1   Fit Determines Content

According to a standard view in the philosophy of mind and language, mental states such as beliefs, desires, and hopes have propositional contents – that is, particular propositions that the mental states are directed at. A mental state either fits or fails to fit the world, depending on whether the proposition in question is true.[23] A desire that fits the world is said to be "satisfied"; a belief that fits the world is said to be "true" or "correct". Thus, suppose I desire a kale salad. This is normally taken to be elliptical for "I desire that I have a kale salad", so the content of my desire is the proposition, [I have a kale salad]. If this proposition is or becomes true, then my desire thereby counts as satisfied. Otherwise, it is frustrated. Similarly, if I believe that I have a kale salad, then my belief will count as correct if and only if the proposition [I have a kale salad] is true. Since, in my view, propositions are always either true or false, all this would mean that beliefs and desires always either fit or fail to fit the world. Since, as I claim, truth does not come in degrees, fit could not come in degrees either.

But this last implication is false: fit *does* come in degrees. This is easiest to see in the case of desires, which may be more or less satisfied, rather than merely satisfied or unsatisfied. Suppose I have a certain gastronomic desire, which I might attempt to express with the words, "I want a kale salad" (but

---

[23] Searle 1983, ch. 1.

note that it is an open question whether these words adequately capture the desire's full character). The underlying fact is that there are a variety of possible food items that would satisfy my craving to varying degrees. Among these, a typical kale salad would do a very good job of satisfying me, which is (at least part of) what makes it appropriate for me to comment on my conative state using the words "I want a kale salad." But some possible kale salads (not necessarily the more paradigmatic kale salads) would do a better job than others of satisfying my desire, and some non-kale salads (for example, a good spinach salad) would do a better job than some kale salads (for example, a rotten kale salad) of satisfying the desire.

You might be tempted to say that this just shows that [I have a kale salad] is a misdescription of the desire's content – the desire's true content is some much more complex proposition, perhaps with a long series of conjunctions and disjunctions. But what needs to be accommodated here is not merely the fact that some kale salads would fail to satisfy and some non-kale salads would satisfy; what needs to be accommodated is the varying *degrees* of satisfaction that can occur for what intuitively seems like a single desire state. A kale salad that is too small, for example, will ill satisfy my desire; the desire will be better satisfied as the salad approaches some optimum size. Some quinoa and nuts added to the salad would improve my satisfaction level still further, and so on. If we start from the simple idea that the desire is directed at some particular proposition, we cannot then explain this phenomenon of degrees of satisfaction – however complex the proposition may be.

Here is an alternate picture. The basic phenomenon is the degrees of fit (satisfaction) or clash between a mental state and a possible state of the world. I do not attempt to explain "fit"; I treat that as primitive. My point here concerns the order of explanation: the traditional view takes propositional content as basic, and explains satisfaction in terms of that. My view takes satisfaction as basic, and explains (purported) propositional content in terms of satisfaction.

Only certain kinds of objects or situations will be relevant to a given desire. For my gastronomic desire, the relevant items are food items (more precisely, situations in which I receive food items) – these are the things that may do better or worse at satisfying that particular desire. Other situations – for instance, peace in the Middle East – may be relevant to (and thus may satisfy or frustrate to varying degrees) some of my *other* desires, but not this particular desire.

There will in general be some function from characteristics of possible, relevant objects or situations to degrees of fit. The intrinsic character of my gastronomic desire determines some function from food characteristics to degrees of satisfaction. In figure 3.1, the horizontal axis represents the range of foods I might get (food items really vary along many dimensions, but for ease of visualization, let's pretend they just vary along one dimension). The vertical axis represents degrees of satisfaction, and the curved line shows the degree to which my desire ("for a kale salad") would be satisfied as a function of the character of the food I receive.

A proposition is a range of possibilities, that is, a range of ways the world might be. For any given (maximally specific) possibility, any given proposition is either true or false in that possibility, depending on whether the range includes that particular possibility or not. For the present example, propositions correspond to specific *ranges* along the x-axis in figure 3.1. If I receive a meal falling within a given range, then the corresponding proposition (the proposition that I receive a meal of the given kind) is true; otherwise, it is false.

Propositional contents are imputed to mental states based on their satisfaction profiles. In the present example, we would ascribe to my desire a propositional content based on the conditions under which the desire would be pretty well satisfied. We say that my desire has the content p when the desire would be well satisfied provided that p obtains. But

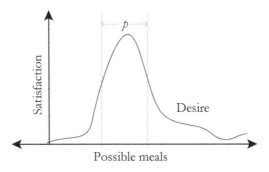

Fig. 3.1 Satisfaction profile of a desire

when we describe a desire in this way, we greatly simplify matters. We draw semi-arbitrary boundaries, and we throw away a good deal of information. We treat the desire, whose real nature is represented by something like figure 3.1, as if it were like the desire represented in figure 3.2, a desire that is either fully satisfied or fully unsatisfied at every point. Talk of a desire's propositional content is thus a kind of loose talk.

What holds for desires, I claim, holds in principle for belief states as well (though perhaps beliefs are more likely to come close to matching figure 3.2 than desires are). As of this writing, for example, I have a vague mass of expectations about the 2020 U.S. elections, which I might partially report by saying, "I think things will go well for the Democrats in 2020." It is not that the expectation at which I am gesturing here will simply be satisfied or unsatisfied. Rather, there is a range of things that might happen, which would fulfill my relevant expectation to greater or lesser degrees. This would be reflected in the different levels of surprise or vindication I might feel upon witnessing various possible courses of events. My expectation thus has a satisfaction profile, analogous to the satisfaction profile for the desire depicted in figure 3.1. A propositional content can be imputed to my belief state based on the range of possibilities that would pretty well satisfy my expectation, but this ascription would merely give a rough approximation to the belief's meaning. No proposition adequately captures my belief, because my belief has varying degrees of satisfaction across possible situations, whereas propositions do not have degrees of truth; they just obtain or fail to obtain in each possible situation.

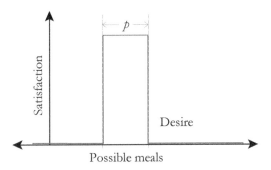

Fig. 3.2 Simplified desire profile

3.5.2   When Thoughts Are Vague

Vagueness is the natural result of our attempt to translate a continuous reality into discrete categories.

There are, at least for a wide range of possible mental states, no "joints" in the satisfaction profile – no uniquely natural places to draw the boundaries for the proposition we are to impute as the mental state's content. Some ways of drawing these boundaries make more sense than others, but there is no particular way of drawing the boundaries that has a claim to being "the correct way". Above, I spoke of the range of possibilities in which a mental state is "pretty well satisfied". You might be tempted to ask what are the precise criteria for being "pretty well" satisfied. But of course there aren't any such precise criteria, and the use of such expressions is a kind of loose talk. The underlying reality is the continuously variable satisfaction profile for the given mental state. The propositional content of the state is, at least in most cases, a kind of fiction that requires ignoring the state's vagueness. On this view, the common philosopher's term "propositional attitude" (as applied to beliefs, desires, and related mental states) is perhaps a misnomer; nevertheless, I shall continue to use this term.

The vague belief "that H is a heap", directed at some particular sand pile H, might have a satisfaction profile like that represented in figure 3.3. (I use scare quotes around "that H is a heap" because this way of speaking reflects the pretense that the belief state in question has a specific propo-

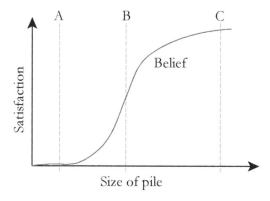

Fig. 3.3 Profile of belief that H is a heap

sitional content.) If H's actual size is close to point A in the diagram, then normal speakers of English would say that H is a clear case of a non-heap, and thus that the belief is "clearly false"; if H is near point C, then we call it a clear heap and thus call the belief "clearly true"; and if H is near point B, we say that H is a borderline case of a heap, and thus many will be tempted to say the belief is indeterminate, or "neither true nor false". This belief counts as vague because it has a range of intermediate degrees of satisfaction.

Not all propositional attitudes are vague; some are precise. A precise propositional attitude is one with a satisfaction profile like figure 3.2, that is, a state that is fully satisfied or fully unsatisfied in every possible situation. The "propositional content of" the state is just the range of cases in which it is fully satisfied (or, the proposition that obtains in that range of cases).[24]

The domain of mathematics provides perhaps the best examples of precision. My belief that the interior angles of a triangle sum to two right angles is fully precise: it is definitely true in every possible situation. The hope that the Continuum Hypothesis should be true is equally precise; it is either fully satisfied in all possible situations, or fully unsatisfied in all possible situations. (The CH is a famous undecided mathematical proposition. It is either necessarily true or necessarily false, but no one knows which.) Our lack of *knowledge* of the CH's truth value does not affect this point; attitudes directed at the CH are fully precise regardless. Nevertheless, fully precise thoughts are scarce – so much so that it is difficult to think of examples outside of mathematics and formal logic.[25]

Among vague thoughts, some are vaguer than others. This, too, can be explained in terms of the shapes of their satisfaction profiles. A fully precise thought is one whose satisfaction level is extreme (either 0% or 100%) in all cases. A *nearly* precise thought, then, is one whose satisfac-

---

[24] Throughout this discussion, I ignore distinctions between logically equivalent propositions. Perhaps there can be distinct propositions that are nonetheless logically equivalent; if so, I do not know how to explain what makes them distinct. I leave this tangential matter aside. The central point is that the satisfaction profile of a vague mental state fails to pick out a unique range of possibilities. If you think propositions are individuated even more finely than ranges of possibilities, then a fortiori, the satisfaction profile fails to pick out a determinate *proposition*.

[25] Russell (1923) goes so far as to claim that *all* sentences are vague.

tion level approximates being extreme in all cases. The further the satisfaction level is from the extremes, and the wider the range of cases for which it differs from one of the extremes, the vaguer the thought is.[26]

3.5.3   Uncertainty About Vagueness

Human beings lack perfect access to our own minds. This would be true even without vagueness; for example, any pain has some precise degree of intensity, but the sufferer cannot specify that precise degree. (For more discussion, see chapter 4 below.) This is true despite that pains are not representational states and thus cannot themselves be either vague or precise in the sense that beliefs and desires can be. What is true of pains is true also of representational mental states. Thus, we cannot, purely on the basis of introspection, produce the precise satisfaction profile for a given one of our mental states. We typically can have only a rough idea of what the satisfaction profile looks like (this rough idea being, itself, another mental state with its own, possibly vague, satisfaction profile). Nevertheless, there always *is* a fully determinate satisfaction profile, since mental states and their degrees of satisfaction are part of reality, and reality is never indeterminate.

This limited access to our own minds also means that we can find ourselves unable to tell whether or to what degree one of our mental states is vague. For example, I do not know whether the ethical concept of *permissibility* is vague. One can describe what look like sorites series involving permissibility – series of actions of gradually increasing acceptability, leading from a clearly impermissible to a clearly permissible act, where we cannot say which is the first permissible act in the series – but this need

---

[26] For a mathematical representation: let $s(p)$ be the satisfaction level of a given mental state, as a function of the possibility, p, that is realized (letting s range from 0 to 1, and again pretending that possibilities vary along a single dimension). Assume the range of possibilities has a width of 1. Then the degree of vagueness of a mental state could be represented by $V = 1 - \int_{p=0}^{1} |1 - 2s| \, dp$. This gives the result that the most precise mental state (vagueness degree 0) is one that is at each point satisfied to degree 0 or 1, and the vaguest state (vagueness degree 1) is one that is always halfway satisfied.

not be interpreted in terms of vagueness; it might just be moral igno-rance.[27] Compare the concept of being at least 5 meters long: it is possible to produce a series of physical objects of gradually increasing length, where it is difficult to tell, due to measurement error, which object in the series is the first to be at least 5 meters long. Nevertheless, the concept "at least 5 meters" is not vague; it specifies a precise threshold which any given object either passes or fails to pass, whether we know it or not. Does "permissible" similarly specify a precise threshold, despite our (even greater) difficulty in telling whether it applies in some cases? I am not sure; accordingly, I am unsure whether "permissible" is vague or precise.

In this context, "vague" means "at least to some degree vague"; "pre-cise" means "maximally precise". The concept of being precise is thus precise; nevertheless, it can be *uncertain* whether "precise" applies in a given case, because any precise mental state is very similar to a mental state that is merely *almost* precise. On the other hand, many vague mental states are nowhere close to precise; hence, in these cases it is easy to know that the state is vague.

3.5.4   Vague Thoughts Make for Vague Language, and Vice Versa

So far, I have been speaking of the vagueness of our thoughts. But most discussion of vagueness concerns the vagueness of *words*, such as the word "heap". How are these two related? The answer is that the vagueness of language derives in part from the vagueness of our thoughts, but that additional sources of vagueness are introduced when we move to consid-ering linguistic meaning.

Words derive their meanings mainly from the thoughts of speakers of the language.[28] For instance, the meaning of "know" in English is deter-

---

[27] I thank Ben Kultgen for discussion of this point.
[28] Here, I leave aside the theory of natural kinds (Putnam 1975; Kripke 1980), whose discussion would lead us too far afield. Briefly, I believe that intuitions about how natural kinds affect linguis-tic meaning can be accommodated by theories that appeal to speakers' meaning-relevant states, provided that (as is true) language speakers have mental states that themselves are sensitive to natu-ral kindhood. However, natural kinds do not plausibly help us draw the boundaries for most vague terms; hence, they are not useful to the present discussion.

mined by the sorts of thoughts that English speakers typically intend to express when they say things like "Groot knows what time it is", what sort of thoughts they typically interpret each other as expressing with such words, and the range of situations in which they are disposed to find the application of the word "know" appropriate. I shall refer to these kinds of states as "meaning-relevant mental states" or just "meaning-relevant states".[29]

For illustration, take the following example, often invoked in epistemology:

> Groot wants to know what time it is. He consults the perfectly innocent-looking clock on the wall, which reads 3:00, whereupon he believes that it is 3:00. Unbeknownst to Groot, the clock is stopped, but coincidentally, it is in fact 3:00 at the time Groot is looking at the clock.[30] Does Groot *know* what time it is?

Most speakers of English are disposed, upon considering this example, to experience an intuitive sense of the inappropriateness of applying the word "know" here. If we were to say that Groot "knows" the time, we would be expressing (and would generally be interpreted by others as expressing) a kind of belief about Groot that would not be satisfied by a situation in which Groot acquired his belief about the time by consulting a stopped clock. These sorts of dispositions are precisely the sorts of things that determine what "know" means in English. Because we have these dispositions, "knowledge" cannot merely mean "justified, true belief" (Groot has a justified, true belief about the time, but he lacks knowledge of it). If typical English speakers had the opposite reactions – if, say, they regularly had the sense that it was perfectly appropriate to call Groot's belief "knowledge" – then "know" would have a different meaning from its actual meaning (perhaps it would then mean "justified, true belief").

---

[29] Earlier (esp. Sect. 2.6.2), I described linguistic meaning as deriving from "conventions, language usage patterns, and intentions". How do meaning-relevant mental states relate to conventions and usage patterns? The existence of a convention is partly constituted by a certain pattern of meaning-relevant mental states in the linguistic community. There are other conditions required for a convention to exist, so the meaning-relevant states do not *suffice*. Nevertheless, they are the aspect I want to focus on in this discussion. Usage patterns, too, must be explained by appropriate meaning-relevant mental states in order to affect linguistic meaning.

[30] This example (without the Groot allusion) is from Russell (1948, p. 98).

The "determination" relation here is constitutive, not causal: it is not that our meaning-relevant mental states *cause* a word to acquire a particular meaning. Facts about meaning just *consist of* facts about our meaning-relevant states. For a word to have a given meaning is just (roughly) for it to conventionally express an idea with the given meaning. If our meaning-relevant states are vague, they will confer vague meanings on our words. The vagueness of the *thoughts* that we typically intend to express when we say things of the form "S knows that *p*" guarantees that such statements must be vague.

Language is in worse shape than thought, as far as precision goes. For a sentence of English is supposed to be assigned a propositional content, not merely on the basis of a vague thought, but on the basis of a range of distinct vague thoughts that different speakers might be disposed in different circumstances to use the sentence to express. Just as each thought may have a fit profile without natural joints, the *range* of thoughts may lack natural joints. Some cases that seem to you like cases of "knowledge" may not seem so to me, or we may have linguistic intuitions of differing strengths. In addition, some individuals may be considered more authoritative than others, where this authority is created by the conventions of the society and may come in degrees. For instance, when it comes to determining what "fruit" means, the tendency of botanists to call tomatoes "fruits" counts for more than the unreflective tendency of lay people to call them "vegetables". So there is a complex total pattern of meaning-relevant states across a linguistic community that goes into determining what we consider the conventional meaning of a word in a given language. This complex pattern need not, and typically will not, have precise, natural joints that would determine a uniquely appropriate object to serve as "the meaning" of a given expression.

To complicate (and vaguefy) matters further, the vagueness of language feeds back into thought. Our thoughts are strongly influenced by the language that we speak. We frequently (usually?) have thoughts that we would not or could not have if we did not know the particular words used to formulate them. When we formulate our thoughts inwardly using words, we normally implicitly intend to use these words in accordance with the conventions of our language. Thus, the conventional meanings of the words impact the satisfaction-conditions of those thoughts. This has the effect of introducing into many of our thoughts the sources of vagueness that apply to language.

3.5.5 An Argument that Vague Statements Do Not Express Propositions

Most treatments of the sorites paradox treat the sentences in the paradoxical argument as expressing genuine propositions and having genuine truth values (whether "true", "false", or some intermediate degree of truth). I think that is the mistake. I think none of the sentences of the form "x is a heap" express propositions, none of them have truth values, and thus there is no first member of the series that is false.[31] The theoretical account of this: a proposition is a determinate range of possibilities; "x is a heap" does not pick out any determinate range of possibilities; so it does not express a proposition. Compound sentences formed from "x is a heap" also fail to express propositions and so lack truth-values, including those of the form "If x is a heap then y is a heap" and "x is a heap or x is not a heap."

This is a radical view. One argument for it is that it solves the sorites paradox: we need not identify the false step in the sorites argument, since none of the steps has a truth value. Nor need we revise our logic, since logic only applies to sentences that express propositions. But you may not be greatly impressed with this argument on its own; you might think there must be some better, less radical solution.

Here is a more substantial argument:

1. Vague sentences either express precise propositions, or express vague propositions, or fail to express propositions.
2. Vague sentences do not express precise propositions.
3. Vague sentences do not express vague propositions.
4. Therefore, vague sentences fail to express propositions.

---

[31] Braun and Sider (2007) defend this view, which they call "semantic nihilism". It is from this that the title of Sect. 3.5 derives; however, I think the name misleading, as the view does not deny that vague sentences are meaningful. Frege (2013, vol. 2, section 56; first published 1903) appears to be the first to endorse the view in print.

Premise 1 looks like an analytic truth. Premise 2 also looks nearly analytic. Wouldn't expressing a precise proposition *ipso facto* make a sentence precise? Suppose we held that the putatively vague sentence "*H* is a heap of sand" actually expressed the precise proposition that *H* is a pile of at least 546,798 grains of sand. Wouldn't this mean that the sentence is not really vague after all? (See our above objections to epistemicism, section 3.4.)

Now why accept premise 3? The orthodox view of vagueness among philosophers holds that vagueness is a purely semantic, not a metaphysical (nor an epistemic) phenomenon; that is, indeterminacy resides solely in the mapping from our language (or our thoughts) to the world, and not at all in the world in itself.[32] As David Lewis puts it, "Vagueness is semantic indecision."[33] This common view seems to imply that there are no vague properties, only vague predicates; no vague objects, only vague terms. If so, then presumably there also are no vague propositions, only vague sentences.

To clarify: a vague object would be an object with indeterminate boundaries (there would be certain putative parts that the object neither includes nor fails to include). There could not be such an object, since the notion of such an object is contradictory. What there may be, instead, is a collection of objects with slightly different boundaries, together with some term whose reference has not been precisely decided. For instance, it is vague exactly where Mount Everest begins. This is not because there is an object, Mount Everest, with indeterminate boundaries. Rather, there is a large (possibly infinite) number of things we *could mean* by the expression "Mount Everest", corresponding to all the different precise ways of drawing boundaries around "the" mountain, and we haven't decided exactly which of these things we want the word to mean.

Similarly, a vague property would be a property with indeterminate application conditions, such that it would be possible for a particular object to neither have nor lack the property. There could not be such a property, since the notion of such a property is contradictory. What there

---

[32] Russell 1923; Evans 1978; Lewis 1988; Sainsbury 2009, p. 64. But for a defense of metaphysical vagueness, see Barnes and Williams 2009. Here, I simply assume there is no metaphysical vagueness.

[33] Lewis 1986, p. 212.

may be, instead, is a collection of different possible properties, together with some predicate whose reference has not been precisely decided. For instance, it is vague whether certain particular reddish/orangish color shades count as red. This is not because there is a property, redness, that has indeterminate boundaries. It is because there is a large number of things we could mean by the word "red", corresponding to different precise ranges of the color spectrum (or regions of the color cone), and we have not decided exactly which of these things we want the word to mean. There is no one and nothing else to determine what the word should mean, so it lacks a determinate reference.[34]

As I say, all of that is a pretty orthodox view of vagueness. If you accept the above, then I think you should also agree that there are no vague propositions. Propositions are ways the world might be; they correspond to sentences in the way that (possible) objects correspond to terms and properties correspond to predicates. If the world can contain only precise objects with precise properties, then it seems that there are only precise ways for the world to be. For instance, if there is no vague property for the predicate "is a heap" to ascribe, then sentences of the form "*x* is a heap" fail to ascribe a property and therefore, it would seem, fail to express propositions. Moreover, the same considerations that rule out vague objects and properties directly rule out vague propositions: if the notion of a vague object or property is contradictory, so too is the notion of a vague proposition – which presumably would be a proposition capable of neither obtaining nor failing to obtain in certain circumstances.

But if there are no vague propositions, then a vague proposition cannot serve as the content of any sentence. Since we have already rejected the notion that a *precise* proposition might serve as the content of a vague sentence, the only remaining option is that a vague sentence has no propositional content.

---

[34] Peter Unger (1979a, b) and Sam Wheeler (1979) draw from this the conclusion that there are no heaps, clouds, people, red things, and so on. Unger (1979a, p. 147), however, allows that one might instead hold that vague sentences fail to "make any clear sense at all", which he takes to be at least in the same spirit as his own view. The difference between Unger and myself is that Unger regards "heap" as having an inconsistent meaning, whereas I regard it as merely having an indeterminate meaning.

Objection: perhaps a vague sentence does not express a unique, precise proposition, but it instead expresses many precise propositions, or a certain *range* of precise propositions. A supervaluationist might say this. But then we could ask: does the sentence express a *precise* range of propositions, or a vague range? If it expresses a perfectly precise range, then it appears, again, that the sentence is in a certain sense precise, rather than vague. The same considerations that made us doubt that the sentence could pick out a unique, precise proposition should equally make us doubt that it could pick out a unique, precise range of propositions. But if, on the other hand, we say that the sentence expresses a *vague* range of propositions, then there will have to be such things as "vague ranges", contrary to the supposition that vagueness is not in the world.

To generalize: if there is to be a semantic object of a vague sentence – something that the sentence expresses – this thing must be either vague or precise. If vagueness is purely semantic, not metaphysical, then this thing cannot be vague, because there are no vague objects. But nor can it plausibly be precise, since the very semantic indecision that made us call the sentence vague in the first place prevents it from picking out any determinate, precise object. The only alternative is that a vague sentence lacks a semantic object: it fails to express anything.

3.5.6   Arguments by Analogy

If you remain unconvinced, it may help to compare other cases of semantic indecision. Out of the blue, I announce, "He has arrived." You ask, "Who do you mean? Arrived where?" I reply, "Oh, I didn't really have in mind anyone in particular, nor any place in particular." Question: is my statement, "He has arrived", true or false?

In this case, we have little difficulty concluding that my statement fails to express a proposition. We are not tempted to postulate a special, indeterminate sort of proposition that obtains when some unspecified male being arrives at some unspecified location. (Nor did I express the proposition that someone has arrived somewhere, for the term "he" in English does not mean merely "someone". It is supposed to refer to a specific person made salient by the context.) The indeterminacy in my intentions deprives my statement of meaning and thus prevents it from being either true or false. The statement is not completely meaningless; it is merely meaning-deficient, since there is not *enough* meaning there to pick out a unique proposition.

That is an extreme case. But we can imagine a range of less extreme cases. In one, I announce that Sue is "at the bank", but I have not decided whether I mean she is at the side of the local river or at the local financial institution that holds her money. In another case, I am talking to colleagues at a conference when I mention that "Iskra is also here" – but I have not decided whether I mean she is here in town, here at the conference, or here in the very room where we are speaking. In these cases, it remains plausible that I fail to express a proposition because my communicative intentions are not sufficiently determinate to pick out any particular proposition as the one I am asserting.

If I am right about the nature of vagueness, vague sentences suffer a qualitatively similar problem; they merely involve less extreme semantic indecision than the preceding examples. When we apply a vague predicate to something, our intentions and other meaning-relevant states fail to pick out a unique property as the one we are ascribing, or a unique class of objects as the one to which we are assigning the subject. We have not decided precisely what we mean, so there isn't anything, precisely, that we mean. So there isn't any specific proposition that we are asserting.

Consider the character Chewbacca from the Star Wars universe. When is his birthday? The answer to this is indeterminate, that is, there is no particular day that can correctly be described as Chewbacca's birthday. The reason is that the *Star Wars* stories (the movies, books, computer games, and so on) simply do not give us enough information to identify the beloved Wookiee's birthday; he is thus condemned to be without any definite birthday.

We can think of the meaning-relevant mental states of our linguistic community as analogous to the Star Wars stories: they tell a story, so to speak, about the propositions expressed by various sentences in our language. If the story for a given sentence is inconsistent, or if it simply does not contain enough information to identify a particular proposition, then – just as no particular date is Chewie's birthday – no particular proposition will be the content of the relevant sentence.

3.5.7   Logic Is Classical

Epistemicists posit sharp boundaries for all terms because they think (*i*) that classical logic is self-evident, and (*ii*) that classical logic (with other obvious background assumptions) requires us to posit sharp boundaries.[35] They are right about (*i*), but wrong about (*ii*). My view preserves classical logic, without the sharp boundaries.

There is no *metaphysical indeterminacy* in my account – no objects that lack precise natures, no propositions that are neither true nor false. There is, however, *semantic indeterminacy* in my account: there are mental states and statements that fail to represent any determinate properties and thus fail to be either true or false. This is no violation of logic. Granted, if an object were to lack any particular, precise nature, this would violate classical logic – this is logically impossible. But if a representation merely fails to represent any particular precise nature, this is no violation of logic – it is far from impossible that there should be such a representation. (Compare: it is contradictory to say that there is someone who has a birthday but that no specific birthday is his; it is *not* contradictory to say that there is a story that represents that someone has a birthday but fails to represent any specific birthday as his.) And the semantic indeterminacy in my account arises naturally from the underlying, completely determinate characteristics of our mental states and language.

My view preserves the law of excluded middle, which affirms that any proposition either obtains or fails to obtain; this principle is not threatened by the news that certain sentences fail to express propositions. "Blug" fails to express a proposition; as a result, "Blug or not blug" also fails to express a proposition. When I utter "He has arrived" without having any particular person or place in mind, I again fail to express a proposition, despite that in this case I am using a grammatical English sentence. As a result, "Either he has arrived or he has not arrived" fails to express a proposition and so fails to be true.[36] These are not counterexamples to the

---

[35] Sorensen 1988, p. 215; 2001, p. 1; cf. Williamson 1994a. Both authors at some point recognize the possibility of the type of view suggested here but seem to regard it as worth little notice.

[36] Fine (1975, p. 286) disagrees with me on this. Fortunately, I have Tye (1989, pp. 142–3) and Lewis (1982, p. 438) on my side.

law of excluded middle, properly understood. Similarly, if "That is a heap" fails to express a proposition, then so does "That is a heap or not a heap", but this is not a counterexample to excluded middle.

The view also preserves bivalence, properly understood. The principle of bivalence holds that every *proposition-expressing* sentence is either true or false; this is not threatened by the news that some class of sentences fail to express propositions. The failure of "He has arrived" to be true or false when no person or place has been specified is not, properly understood, a counterexample to bivalence.

Classical logic is a correct theory of propositions and proposition-expressing sentences. It of course cannot be a correct theory about all sentences (including sentences that fail to express propositions), but that is old news. What is new in my account is merely that the class of proposition-expressing sentences has been shrunk by quite a bit, relative to more orthodox views.

You might worry that I am taking away with one hand what I give with the other: sure, my account nominally preserves classical logic, but only at the cost of restricting its *scope* so much that it hardly ever applies to any actual statement.[37] Does this really count as preserving classical logic?

In reply, we must clarify why we wanted to preserve classical logic. If the reason is simply that we find (as I do) that the principles of classical logic seem obviously, necessarily true, then we should bear in mind that limiting the *scope* of these principles is a revision of a different order from revising their *content*. We can appeal to the obviousness of the traditional laws of logic to reject theories of vagueness that employ deviant logics. But we cannot appeal to the obviousness of these laws to show that vague sentences express genuine propositions. The latter claim is a semantic hypothesis, not a self-evident axiom.

Perhaps the concern is more practical: classical logic seems to be appropriately used in evaluating all sorts of arguments formulated in natural language. It would be most unfortunate were we forced to give all that up. I will address this in section 3.5.10 below, after we have discussed the appropriate use of approximations.

---

[37] Sorensen (2001, pp. 181–4) worries about such scope restrictions.

3.5.8 How to Almost Say Something

You may find my view crazy. Given the pervasiveness of vagueness, it implies that almost none of the sentences that are typically taken to express propositions actually do so. "A single grain of sand is a heap" and "A pile of a billion grains of sand is a heap" both fail to express propositions. "There is a heap of sand in the yard, or there isn't" fails to express a proposition and so, strictly speaking, fails to be true (but see further discussion below, section 3.5.11). Indeed, probably most of the sentences in this book fail to express propositions.

If that were the end of the story – and in particular, if there were no way to distinguish sentences like "There is a heap of sand in the yard" from inscriptions like "Blug trish ithong" – then the view would indeed be too crazy. Obviously, there is something that we are doing when we say "There is a heap of sand in the yard" that is different from uttering meaningless sounds like "Blug trish ithong", something that we typically call "asserting a proposition". If "There is a heap of sand in the yard" does not really assert a proposition, we still need to say something about how it, unlike "Blug trish ithong", does something *like* asserting a proposition.

In fact, it is easy to see how this is so. A vague mental state, on my account, fails to express a proposition; nevertheless, it may come *close* to expressing a proposition (as explained in section 3.5.2 above). Figure 3.4 shows satisfaction profiles for two possible beliefs, B1 and B2. In an obvious sense, B1 comes closer to expressing a proposition (e.g., it comes close to expressing p) than B2 does.

A similar point holds for sentences. We know what it would take for a sentence to have a perfectly precise meaning. (The linguistic community would have to be unanimously, unequivocally, and in all conditions disposed to use the sentence to express a particular, fully precise mental state.) Sentences that are in a situation *close* to that can be said to come close to expressing propositions.

Note that I am not saying that a vague sentence expresses something *like* a proposition – that is, I am not postulating some other sort of object that is similar to a proposition, where vague sentences are related to this other object in the same way that precise sentences are related to proposi-

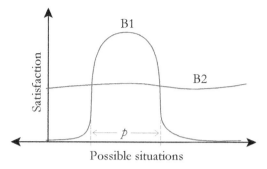

Fig. 3.4 Degrees of vagueness

tions. There are no relevant non-linguistic objects for sentences to assert, other than propositions.[38] So vague sentences don't come close to expressing propositions by expressing things similar to propositions. Rather, they come close to expressing propositions by having associated meaning-relevant states that are intrinsically similar to the meaning-relevant states that would make the sentences actually express propositions.

Granted, some vague sentences are relatively far from being precise and in that sense far from expressing propositions. Nevertheless, almost all sentences of English that are actually used, including vague ones, are closer to expressing propositions than they are to being meaningless. Despite its high level of vagueness, "There is a heap of sand in the yard" comes much closer to expressing a proposition than, say, "He has arrived" (uttered with no person or place in mind) or the really meaningless "Blug trish ithong".

3.5.9　Almost Is Good Enough

Approximation is ubiquitous and well-tolerated in ordinary speech. I may say that my wine glass is "empty" even though there remain two

---

[38] Braun and Sider (2007, p. 4), for example, posit a "cloud of propositions" corresponding to all the legitimate disambiguations of a vague sentence. One could (though they do not) call this cloud "the content" of the vague sentence. But, again, this is not my view. I think that ascribing a cloud as the content would itself give only an approximate characterization of the sentence's meaning. We would then need to posit a cloud of clouds, since no unique, precise cloud would fully capture the meaning.

drops' worth of wine distributed across the sides and bottom.[39] My statement will be accepted without comment by typical listeners, since the glass is empty enough for practical purposes and it would be tedious of me to instead say, "My glass is empty enough for practical purposes."

Similarly, we can aptly describe a sentence as expressing a proposition when it comes close enough to expressing a proposition for practical purposes. What are these practical purposes? We use language mainly to influence each other's thoughts, attitudes, and behavior. In the ideal case, we make a statement asserting a unique proposition, and the audience takes up our statement by believing precisely that proposition. In the more complex and more common case, we issue a statement that comes close to asserting a proposition, and the audience takes it up by modifying their mental state in a manner that comes close to believing a proposition. The audience's other attitudes and behavior may also be influenced in a manner very similar to how they would be influenced if the speaker had expressed a unique proposition. For instance, when one reports that there is a heap of sand in the yard, most people's reactions in most circumstances will be almost the same as they would have been if "heap" had a precise cutoff point. It is in that sense that the sentence comes close enough to expressing a proposition for practical purposes. Only annoying children or finicky philosophers will protest that the wine glass isn't really empty, or that "there is a heap of sand in the yard" doesn't really express a proposition.

When we accept approximations, we engage in a kind of pretense; we agree to ignore small inaccuracies. In employing vague language, we agree to ignore undecided cases and pretend that there are specific properties (objects, etc.) that we are referring to.[40]

But any sort of pretense has limits. When your child pretends to be conversing with her doll, you should not protest that the doll has no vocal

---

[39] Dretske (1981, p. 366, 370) holds that "empty" means "devoid of any objects *of the relevant kind*", rather than "devoid of any objects whatsoever". This explains why you can truthfully report that your refrigerator is empty when it contains shelves and air molecules but no food. It does not, however, accommodate the wine glass example, for wine is surely a relevant kind for assessing emptiness of wine glasses; if there were more of it, we would not call the glass "empty". The reason the glass is aptly called empty really seems to be just that it is approximately empty.

[40] Cf. Braun and Sider 2007, pp. 135–7.

chords, is just filled with cotton, and so cannot possibly talk. When you watch *Star Trek*, you should not protest that no one knows what will happen in the twenty-fourth century, so the stories must all be lies. If you push on the pretense in such ways, it dissolves; we cease being able to pretend.

The pretense involved in vague language is more robust than these cases; it conflicts with our beliefs more subtly and breaks down in fewer conditions. In most contexts, it does not matter that "heap" lacks definite boundaries and so does not actually pick out any particular property. This does not matter since most statements and reasoning about heaps of sand do not concern borderline cases. Still, the pretense of having identified a property using a vague term has its limits. Engaging in sorites reasoning is pushing on the pretense in precisely the manner that makes it break down. It is like arguing that your daughter is lying about her doll because dolls can't talk.

The pretense involved in vague language is different from that involved in fiction in an interesting way: almost everyone realizes that fictional stories are untrue, but few realize that vague sentences don't really express propositions. The use of vague language might thus be called a "sincere pretense" – a practice in which we pretend that something is the case, and we don't quite realize that we are only pretending. I say only that we don't *quite* realize this, rather than that we do not realize it *at all*, because I think the core elements of my account are hardly surprising. It isn't as if we actually believe that we have picked out a precise boundary for "heap", nor is it our considered opinion that there are vague properties in the world. It is rather that most of us engage in the pretense of vague language unreflectively; most never think about the implications of our having indeterminate semantic dispositions.

3.5.10   Applying Logic to Vague Sentences

You might wonder: if sentences about heaps don't express propositions, does this mean that the principles of logic fail to apply to them? If so, does that mean that we cannot engage in reasoning using such sentences, that we cannot identify valid or invalid arguments involving them? This would be an untoward result, for it certainly seems that we *can* identify valid or invalid deductions involving vague sentences. For instance, the following seems like a valid argument:

H1. There is a heap of sand in the yard.
H2. All heaps of sand weigh more than one gram. Therefore,
H3. There is more than one gram's worth of sand in the yard.

and the following, by contrast, an invalid argument:

H3. There is more than one gram's worth of sand in the yard.
H2. All heaps of sand weigh more than one gram. Therefore,
H1. There is a heap of sand in the yard.

In reply: yes, strictly speaking, the principles of logic fail to apply to vague sentences, since logical theories are theories about propositions or proposition-expressing sentences. So, strictly speaking, there are no valid or invalid arguments involving vague sentences.[41]

There are, however, inferences or inference-like transitions involving vague sentences that are *close enough for practical purposes* to being valid or invalid. When we reason using vague sentences, we adopt a pretense that there is a specific proposition expressed by each vague sentence, and we thereupon apply the logical rules that apply to propositions. Compare the following piece of "reasoning":

A1. Jon is a blug.
A2. All blugs are trish.
A3. Therefore, Jon is trish.

"Blug" and "trish" are nonsense words; no conventions have been established associating either word with any property or class of objects. Thus, A1, A2, and A3 all fail to express propositions, none of them can be either true or false, and the above is not, strictly speaking, an example of a valid argument. But this does not prevent us from applying our logical faculties to the above "argument". If we pretend that there is a class of objects called "blugs" and a property called being "trish", then our logical

---

[41] Similarly, Russell (1923, pp. 88–9) denies that logic applies to any actual sentences, on the ground that all actual sentences are vague. But for reasons that remain unclear to me, he does not deny that vague sentences have truth values or express propositions.

faculties tell us that, within this pretense, the above is a valid argument. Similarly, then, we can apply our logical faculties to reason (or "reason") with vague sentences just as if they expressed propositions.

The above quasi-inference using "blug" and "trish" is, of course, both practically and epistemically useless. Why isn't reasoning using vague sentences similarly useless? Because most vague sentences, unlike A1–A3 above, come close enough for practical purposes to expressing propositions. And when we start from sentences that are close enough for practical purposes to being true, and we apply our deductive reasoning faculties to them, we generally arrive at other sentences that are also close enough for practical purposes to being true.

This is not *always* the case. Valid rules of deduction necessarily preserve strict truth (if applied to true premises, they must deliver true conclusions), but they do not necessarily preserve the property of *being close enough to true for practical purposes*. There are particular inference patterns that are designed to exploit the gap between the true and the almost true, to derive conclusions that are very far from being true, from premises that are almost true. The sorites reasoning is precisely that sort of reasoning.

3.5.11   Interpreting 'Truth': Strict Truth vs. Loose Truth

The time has come for taking back some of what I said about truth above. I have been assuming that a sentence or belief is true just in case it expresses a true proposition, and false just in case it expresses a false proposition. Call this interpretation of truth and falsity "strict truth" and "strict falsity". On this interpretation, vague beliefs and sentences could not be either true or false, since they do not express propositions.

But another interpretation of "truth" is possible. Perhaps a sentence or belief is true just in case it is close enough to true for practical purposes – that is, it fits reality well enough given the particular situation in which it occurs and the purposes that are relevant in that situation.[42] Similarly, we might say a sentence or belief is false just in case it is close enough to false

---

[42] Braun and Sider (2007, p. 4) adopt a notion of "approximate truth", which serves much the same purpose. They, however, define this notion in terms of truth under every acceptable disambiguation (see above discussion of supertruth, but note that they deny that supertruth = truth).

for practical purposes, that is, it has a sufficiently low degree of satisfaction by the world. We can call this interpretation of truth and falsity "approximate truth/falsity", or (for added color) "truthiness" (adjective: "truthy") and "falsiness" (adjective: "falsy").[43] On this interpretation, "truth" is vague; thus, the belief that some belief is true would itself fail to express a proposition but might nonetheless be true (that is, truthy).

Which interpretation is better: does "true" in English mean "strictly true" or "truthy"? There are arguments on both sides. In favor of truthiness: truthiness best accounts for our usage in particular cases. As we have seen, almost all of the sentences that competent English speakers typically call "true" are sentences that are truthy but not strictly true, and almost every sentence normally called "false" is falsy but not strictly false. For instance, "There is a heap of sand" (said while pointing to a large pile of sand) may come *close enough* to expressing a true proposition for practical purposes (see section 3.5.9 above), but it does not succeed in expressing a proposition and so is not strictly true. Since the meaning of "true" in English is determined by how competent English speakers *use* the word, one might argue, strict truth is simply a misinterpretation of the meaning of "true" in English.

On the other hand, strict truth satisfies intuitive general principles about truth, such as:

T1 If a sentence is true, then it expresses a proposition.

T2 If a sentence can be true or false, then it is either true or false in any given, precise circumstance.

T3 If an argument has only true premises and follows only valid inference rules (such as modus ponens, disjunctive syllogism, or constructive dilemma), then the conclusion must be true.

All these principles seem correct. But if "true" is read as "truthy", then all three apparently fail: T1 fails since vague sentences can be truthy but fail

---

[43] I stole the word "truthiness" from Stephen Colbert (2005). What is worse, I am using it in a completely different sense from his.

to express propositions. T2 fails since statements applying vague predicates in borderline cases are neither truthy nor falsy. And T3 apparently fails since sorites arguments would be counterexamples.[44] We could preserve T3 by declaring that certain inferences held to be valid in classical logic are in fact invalid. But if we find ourselves denying the validity of modus ponens (from "A" and "if A then B", infer "B"), that is not exactly a happy consequence.[45]

Plausibly, ordinary English speakers intend to use "true" (as applied to thoughts and sentences) in a manner such that T1–T3 are all true *and* statements like "A pile of a million grains of sand is a heap" are true. These intentions cannot all be satisfied. What happens when the speakers of a language have inconsistent intentions regarding the meaning of some term? If the inconsistency is sufficiently serious, then the term becomes empty – it fails to refer to anything or to ascribe any property (example: "the set of all sets that don't contain themselves"). If the inconsistency is comparatively minor, then the term refers to whatever comes closest to satisfying the speakers' intentions – what satisfies most of the intentions, or the most important intentions, etc.

All of that is, in general, vague – it is vague when an inconsistency is sufficiently serious, and it is vague what counts as the best match to an inconsistent set of intentions. So, in such cases, it is vague what the expression in question means. In this case, therefore, it is vague what "true" means in English.

As with most semantic disputes, there is little insight to be gained by attempting to settle on a single sense of "true". Even if we should con-

---

[44] The induction premise in the sorites argument, "For all n, if n grains make a heap, then $n - 1$ grains make a heap", might not be truthy. But we could reformulate the sorites argument to instead use the premises "if 1,000,000 grains make a heap, then 999,999 grains make a heap", "if 999,999 grains make a heap, then 999,998 grains make a heap", and so on. The new argument would contain only truthy premises (albeit a great number of them) and would use only the inference pattern modus ponens.

[45] Machina (1976, pp. 69–75) denies the validity of modus ponens, based on a degree-of-truth theory. My original formulation of the sorites argument also uses universal instantiation (∀ elimination), but I assume no one would reject that.

Besides rejecting modus ponens, we would also need to deny the validity of conjunction introduction. Otherwise, we could conjoin "1,000,000 grains make a heap" with "if 1,000,000 grains make a heap, then 999,999 grains make a heap", "if 999,999 grains make a heap, then 999,998 grains make a heap", and so on. But that conjunction would not be truthy.

clude that one interpretation better fits the most common use of "true" in English, this fact will be philosophically unimportant. Thus, I will simply say this: if we read "true" as "expresses a proposition that is true", then sentences containing vague terms are never true. If we read "true" as "comes close enough for practical purposes to expressing a true proposition", then sentences containing vague terms are very often true. Either use of "true" is reasonable, and neither appears to be clearly the uniquely correct English usage.

Return now to the sorites argument with which this chapter began:

1. If n grains of sand are a heap, then n-1 grains of sand are a heap.
2. 1,000,000 grains of sand are a heap.

. . .

1,000,001. Therefore, 1 grain of sand is a heap.

Strictly speaking, none of the sentences in the argument is true since they all fail to express propositions. The inference pattern (modus ponens) necessarily preserves strict truth, but since the starting premises are not strictly true, it is no surprise that the conclusion 1,000,001 is not strictly true either.

On the other hand, premises 1 and 2 are close enough to true for practical purposes in most contexts (but perhaps not in the context where we are evaluating the sorites argument itself). But the modus ponens inference pattern does not necessarily preserve *approximate* truth. So it is unsurprising that conclusion 1,000,001 is not approximately true.

3.5.12   Why Is There Second-Order Vagueness?

How can it be vague whether it is vague whether P? The explanation for this, as we should expect, is essentially the same as the explanation for why there is vagueness in general. Both first- and second-order vagueness arise from semantic indecision: it can be vague whether x is a heap because we have not decided precisely where the boundary for the category "heap" should lie; and it can be vague whether it is *clear* that x is a heap, because we have not decided precisely where the boundary for the category "clear

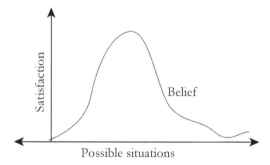

Fig. 3.5   A vague belief

heap" should lie. By definition, it is vague whether x is a heap, if and only if x is neither clearly a heap nor clearly not a heap. So it can be vague whether it is vague whether x is a heap.

Figure 3.5 depicts the satisfaction profile of a possible belief. If that is the underlying reality, then in exactly what range of situations should we say that the belief counts as *close enough* to true? There is no objective basis for a precise answer, since there are no natural joints in the phenomenon. So the answer would have to be produced by some human decision. But we have not in fact made that decision, so there is not in fact an answer.

Notice that the same is true if we ask the question "In what range of possibilities is the belief *clearly* truthy?" Or "In what range of possibilities is the belief clearly clearly truthy?" None of these has a precise answer any more than the first question did, because, again, there are no natural joints in the objective phenomenon, and we have not made stipulations or otherwise decided exactly where the boundaries should lie.

3.6   Conclusion

The sorites argument goes like this:

1. For any n, if n grains make a heap, then $n - 1$ grains make a heap.
2. A million grains make a heap. Therefore,
3. One grain makes a heap.

3 follows from 1 and 2 in classical logic (by 999,999 applications of modus ponens). What can we say about this argument? There are very few options. We could:

(a) Accept the conclusion. (This is crazy.)
(b) Reject premise 2; claim that there are no heaps. Then we will presumably also wind up denying that there are tables, red things, people, and so on. (Also crazy.)
(c) Reject premise 1. This leads us, given classical logic, to epistemicism: there are sharp cutoffs for every vague term, though we don't know where they lie. (Most people find this pretty crazy too.)

If this were any normal modus ponens argument, the above would be the only options considered. But in this case, these three options are all so unpalatable that we are driven to consider two more options[46]:

(d) Reject classical logic. (Again, pretty crazy.)
(e) Deny content: claim that one or more of the sentences in the sorites argument fail to express propositions.

These, again, are the only possible views. If statements 1, 2, and 3 express propositions, and classical logic is correct, then 3 follows from 1 and 2, in which case either 1 is false, or 2 is false, or 3 is true. Some theories may embrace more than one of the above five options; supervaluationism, for instance, rejects premise 1 *and* rejects classical logic. But any theory that addresses the issue must take up *at least* one of the five options. No other options will ever be devised.

(a)–(d) are all crazy. (e) is less crazy, so we should go with (e). There is a very natural explanation for (e). Mental representations are not simply satisfied or unsatisfied by the world; they have degrees of satisfaction. A mental state's profile of degrees of satisfaction, as a function of the state of the world, may lack natural joints. To assign a propositional content to such a representation is to give at best an approximate characteriza-

---

[46] The first four options are commonly considered, while (e) is usually neglected, perhaps due to oversight; e.g., Sainsbury (2009, p. 47) lists the options as accepting the conclusion, rejecting a premise, and rejecting the reasoning.

tion of its meaning; strictly speaking, no particular proposition captures the meaning of the mental state. Language, in turn, inherits its vagueness from thought: because many thoughts lack propositional contents, many sentences lack propositional contents. They are not meaningless; they merely have a kind of meaning that fails to single out a definite proposition.

Thoughts and statements without propositional content cannot be true or false in the strictest sense of "true" and "false". They can, however, be satisfied to a high degree, and in most contexts, this suffices to make them appropriate. In most contexts, we may even call them "true", using a loose notion of truth. But when we encounter sorites arguments, we must insist on the distinction between strict truth and mere approximate truth. The sorites argument exploits the gap between the two to derive an absurdity, applying the logical laws for strict truths to mere approximate truths.

References

Barnes, Elizabeth and John Robert Gareth Williams. 2009. "Vague Parts and Vague Identity", *Pacific Philosophical Quarterly* 90: 176–87.

Braun, David and Theodore Sider. 2007. "Vague, So Untrue", *Noûs* 41: 133–56.

Clark, Michael. 2002. *Paradoxes from A to Z*. London: Routledge.

Colbert, Stephen. 2005. "The Word – Truthiness", *The Colbert Report*, October 17, http://www.cc.com/video-clips/63ite2/the-colbert-report-the-word---truthiness, accessed May 26, 2017.

Dretske, Fred. 1981. "The Pragmatic Dimension of Knowledge", *Philosophical Studies* 40: 363–78.

Evans, Gareth. 1978. "Can There Be Vague Objects?", *Analysis* 38: 208.

Fine, Kit. 1975. "Vagueness, Truth and Logic", *Synthese* 30: 265–300.

Frege, Gottlob. 2013. *Basic Laws of Arithmetic*, tr. and ed. Philip Ebert, Marcus Rossberg, and Crispin Wright. Oxford: Oxford University Press. Originally published in two volumes, 1893 and 1903.

Goguen, Joseph A. 1969. "The Logic of Inexact Concepts", *Synthese* 19: 325–73.

Hart, Wilbur D. 1992. "Hat-Tricks and Heaps", *Philosophical Studies* (Dublin) 33: 1–24.

Kripke, Saul. 1980. *Naming and Necessity*. Oxford: Basil Blackwell.

Krkač, Kristijan. 2012. *A Custodian of Grammar: Essays on Wiggenstein's Philosophical Morphology*. Lanham, MD: Rowman & Littlefield.

Lewis, David. 1982. "Logic for Equivocators", *Noûs* 16: 431–41.

Lewis, David. 1986. *On the Plurality of Worlds*. Oxford: Blackwell.

Lewis, David. 1988. "Vague Identity: Evans Misunderstood", *Analysis* 48: 128–30.

Machina, Kenton F. 1976. "Truth, Belief, and Vagueness", *Journal of Philosophical Logic* 5: 47–78.

Putnam, Hilary. 1975. "The Meaning of 'Meaning'", *Minnesota Studies in the Philosophy of Science* 7: 215–71.

Quine, Willard van Orman. 1986. *Philosophy of Logic*, 2nd ed. Cambridge, MA: Harvard University Press.

Raffman, Diana. 1996. "Vagueness and Context-sensitivity", *Philosophical Studies* 81: 175–92.

Rescher, Nicholas. 2001. *Paradoxes: Their Roots, Range, and Resolution*. Chicago, IL: Open Court.

Russell, Bertrand. 1923. "Vagueness", *Australasian Journal of Philosophy and Psychology* 1: 84–92.

Russell, Bertrand. 1948. *Human Knowledge: Its Scope and its Limits*. London: Allen & Unwin.

Sainsbury, Richard M. 2009. *Paradoxes*, 3rd ed. Cambridge: Cambridge University Press.

Searle, John R. 1983. *Intentionality*. Cambridge: Cambridge University Press.

Smith, Nicholas J. J. 2008. *Vagueness and Degrees of Truth*. Oxford: Oxford University Press.

Sorensen, Roy. 1988. *Blindspots*. Oxford: Clarendon.

Sorensen, Roy. 2001. *Vagueness and Contradiction*. Oxford: Clarendon.

Tye, Michael. 1989. "Supervaluationism and the Law of Excluded Middle", *Analysis* 49: 141–3.

Tye, Michael. 1994. "Sorites Paradoxes and the Semantics of Vagueness", *Philosophical Perspectives* 8: *Logic and Language*, pp. 189–206.

Unger, Peter. 1979a. "There Are No Ordinary Things", *Synthese* 41: 117–54.

Unger, Peter. 1979b. "Why There Are No People", *Midwest Studies in Philosophy* 4: 177–222.

Wheeler, Samuel C. 1979. "On That Which Is Not", *Synthese* 41: 155–73.

Williamson, Timothy. 1994a. "Definiteness and Knowability", *Southern Journal of Philosophy* 33, Supplement: 171–91.

Williamson, Timothy. 1994b. *Vagueness*. London: Routledge.

Zadeh, Lotfi A. 1965. "Fuzzy Sets", *Information and Control* 8: 338–53.

Part II

Paradoxes of Rational Choice

4

The Self-Torturer

4.1 The Paradox

You have been fitted with an unobtrusive torture device, which will be attached to you for the rest of your life.[1] It has a thousand and one settings, labeled from 0 up to 1,000. At setting 0, the device is off, so you feel no suffering caused by the device. At setting 1, the device applies a very slight electric current to the pain center in your brain. It is so slight that you wouldn't even notice it. At setting 2, it applies a very slightly higher electric current. And so on. For any setting n, the setting $n+1$ applies a very slightly higher current than n, with the increase being so small that you cannot introspectively tell the difference between being at setting n and being at $n+1$. However, by the time you get up to setting 1,000, you are in severe pain.

Imagine that you are offered a series of choices over the next thousand days: at the beginning of each day, you may either turn the dial up by one, or leave the device alone. If you turn it up by one, you will be given $10,000. You can never turn the dial down (not even if you give back the money!). Should you turn the dial up on day one? You might reason as

[1] This paradox discussed in this chapter derives from Warren Quinn (1990). I have altered the scenario in minor ways here.

follows: "If I turn the dial up just one setting, I won't even notice the difference. However, I will have an additional $10,000, which is a significant and very noticeable benefit. A significant benefit outweighs an unnoticeable cost (if indeed an unnoticeable 'cost' counts as a cost at all). So I should turn the dial."

This seems reasonable. And the same reasoning applies every day. So it looks as if it is rational to turn the dial up each time. The result: at the end of 1,000 days, you have made $10 million, and you are condemned to spend the rest of your life in agony. It seems, however, that the $10 million, as nice as it may be, would not adequately compensate for the harm of spending the rest of your days in severe pain.

Something must have gone wrong. But it seems that you made the correct (rational, self-interested) choice at each stage. How is it possible that by making the correct choice at every stage, you predictably wind up much worse off than when you started (when you had the option of keeping your starting situation)? This case might also be taken to illustrate how the "better than" relation can be intransitive. *Transitivity* is the principle that if x is better than y, and y is better than z, then x is better than z. The self-torturer case seemingly violates this principle: for each n, it is better to go to setting $n+1$ than to remain at n, yet it is not better to go to setting 1,000 than to stay at 0 – or so one might argue.[2]

This scenario resembles some real-life situations.[3] Suppose you have a large supply of potato chips on hand. You like potato chips, but you do not want to become overweight. You pick up chip #1 and consider whether to eat it. If you eat it, you will experience a noticeable pleasure attributable to that particular chip. And surely that one chip will not affect your waistline. So it seems that it makes sense to eat it. You do so. Next you consider chip #2, which will also cause a noticeable pleasure without itself causing any noticeable change in your waistline. You eat that one too. Next, chip #3. And so on. Before long, you've eaten the whole bag. As this happens to you every day for several months, you eventually come to regret your chip-eating habit.

---

[2] Quinn (1990, pp. 79–80) assumes that "better-than" is transitive, so he says only that the self-torturer has intransitive preferences. Andreou (2006, 2016) also accepts the rationality of holding intransitive preferences in this case.

[3] Quinn 1990, p. 79.

What could we expect of a solution to this paradox? First, many find the intransitivity of betterness or of rational preference paradoxical – that is, it seems paradoxical that one's situation could be repeatedly getting better at each of a series of stages (or that one's rational preferences could be repeatedly getting satisfied) and yet that the end result be decidedly worse for one than the starting situation (or rationally dispreferred to the starting situation). So it would be nice to have a solution that explains why this scenario does not truly exhibit intransitivity of betterness or rational preferences. Second, it would be nice to have a theory of rational choice that can explain why a rational chooser would not in fact wind up turning the dial all the way up to 1,000, and what the rational chooser would do instead.

4.2   Quinn's Solution

In the original discussion of the paradox, Warren Quinn proposes that the self-torturer should try focusing his attention on some proper *subset* of all the settings of the device – for example, instead of thinking about all the settings 0, 1, 2, . . . , 1000, the self-torturer might just think about the six settings numbered 0, 200, 400, 600, 800, and 1000.[4] He should take a subset such that (*i*) his preferences over this subset are transitive, and (*ii*) there is at least one setting in the series that he prefers over his original state (setting 0). He should employ the most refined set of which conditions (*i*) and (*ii*) hold, within some systematic scheme for generating such subsets. The self-torturer should form a plan to proceed to whatever is his most preferred setting from that subset. He should then in fact proceed to that setting and stop. For instance, perhaps from the set {0, 200, 400, 600, 800, 1000}, his favorite setting would be 200, since going to 200 would earn him two million dollars while only subjecting him to mild pain that would be compensated for by the money; perhaps the additional pain resulting from proceeding up to 400 would not be worth the additional two million dollars. In that case, the self-torturer should turn the dial up every day for 200 days, and thereafter leave the dial alone.

---

[4] Andreou (2016) takes a similar strategy, which depends upon dividing up options into evaluatively described, qualitative categories, such as "terrible", "poor", "acceptable", and the like.

What happens when the self-torturer reaches day 201, and he is offered the chance to turn the dial up just one more time, in exchange for another $10,000? In Quinn's view, the self-torturer should rationally decline the offer, on the grounds that accepting the offer would involve departing from his earlier-formed rational plan, and no new information has appeared to justify changing the plan. Quoth Quinn: "He should be stopped by the principle that a reasonable strategy that correctly antici-pated all later facts . . . still binds."[5]

There are two plausible principles of rational choice in play here, which I will call "Preference Consistency" and "Strategy Consistency"; intui-tively, the idea is that one's choices should be consistent with one's ratio-nal preferences and with one's rationally chosen strategies, respectively:

Preference Consistency: If one has a choice between A and B, and one rationally prefers A to B, it is rational to choose A.
Strategy Consistency: If an agent has adopted a rational strategy that cor-rectly anticipated all later facts, then the agent is rationally required to follow through on that strategy.

Strategy Consistency is Quinn's principle of rational choice. Quinn holds that we should reject Preference Consistency because, in the case of the self-torturer on day 201, Preference Consistency conflicts with Strategy Consistency.[6] This conflict exists, allegedly, because the self-torturer rationally prefers being at setting 201 with an extra $10,000 to being at setting 200; yet his rationally chosen strategy requires him to stop at setting 200.

I find this reasoning unpersuasive, for two reasons. First, I think Preference Consistency is a self-evident principle about rational choice – indeed, it is perhaps the most straightforward, obvious principle of rational choice. I am tempted to call Preference Consistency "true by defi-

---

[5] Quinn 1990, p. 87.
[6] More precisely, Quinn (1990, p. 85) says that we should reject the "Principle of Strategic Readjustment", which holds that "Strategies continue to have authority only if they continue to offer him what he prefers overall. Otherwise, they should be changed." The Principle of Strategic Readjustment, so described, is a special case of Preference Consistency.

nition". So if Strategy Consistency conflicts with Preference Consistency, I think one should reject the former.

Second, it is possible to develop a plausible view on which Preference Consistency and Strategy Consistency are both true. Since both principles are plausible, such a view is to be preferred over one that renounces Preference Consistency. This view will be described presently.

4.3 An Orthodox Solution

4.3.1 In Defense of Undetectable Changes

It is plausible that there could be a device that works like the above-described torture device – in particular, that there could be no introspectively detectable difference between (the experiences caused by) adjacent settings, but a large and very detectable difference between the first and the last setting. This shows that it is possible for there to be changes in a person's conscious experience too small to be introspectively detected. For instance, there could be two pains so similar to each other that one could not tell by introspection which of the two, if either, was more intense; nevertheless, one might in fact be more intense than the other.

Something analogous is certainly true of observable physical properties. There could be two objects so similar to each other that one could not tell which was larger, which was warmer, or which was heavier; nevertheless, one might in fact be larger, warmer, or heavier than the other. But some philosophers would say that what is true of physical properties is not true of pains: unlike physical properties, pains are conscious experiences whose entire nature is exhausted by how they feel to us. Therefore, one might claim, if two pain sensations *feel to us* the same, then *ipso facto* they *are* exactly the same. Therefore, if one cannot tell the difference between the pains caused by settings n and $n+1$ on the torture device, then those pains are the same.

This argument cannot be correct; it seeks to defend a logically incoherent account of the case. Let "Q_n" denote the qualitative character of the conscious experience one has when one has the torture device at setting

n. By stipulation, any other experience has Q_n if and only if it is precisely, qualitatively identical to the experience one has at setting n (including having the identical pain intensity). Now suppose we accept the reasoning of the preceding paragraph, that is, we accept that for each n, setting n on the torture device feels exactly the same as setting $n+1$. For instance, setting 0 feels the same as setting 1. When at setting 0, one experiences qualitative feel Q_0. When at setting 1, one experiences Q_1. On the present view, these experiences are qualitatively identical, so $Q_0=Q_1$. The "=" sign there is the identity symbol: "Q_0" and "Q_1" are two names for one and the same qualitative character. By the same reasoning, $Q_1=Q_2$, and then $Q_2=Q_3$, and so on. By transitivity of identity, $Q_0=Q_{1000}$. But that is absurd; Q_0 definitely is not Q_{1000}. Therefore, we must reject the assumption that for each n, $Q_n=Q_{n+1}$; therefore, we must also reject the assumption that if two experiences cannot be introspectively distinguished, then they are qualitatively identical.

Notice what is not an appropriate reply here: it would not be appropriate to object that I have falsely assumed that introspective indistinguishability is transitive. I have not assumed that; I assumed precisely the opposite. Here is another way of putting my argument:

1. Introspective indistinguishability is not transitive.
2. Qualitative identity is transitive.
3. Therefore, introspective indistinguishability does not entail qualitative identity.

Premise 1 is uncontroversial. Settings 0 and 1 are indistinguishable, as are settings 1 and 2, settings 2 and 3, and so on. But settings 0 and 1000 are not indistinguishable. So indistinguishability is not transitive.

Premise 2 is a truth of logic. Two things are qualitatively identical just in case they share all their qualitative properties.[7] If x and y possess the same set of qualitative properties, and y and z possess the same set of qualitative properties, then x and z must possess that same set of qualitative properties. It does not matter whether we are talking about mental or physical phenomena. No insight about the nature of the mind can enable

---

[7] I say "*qualitative* properties" to exclude such things as haecceities or "the property of being this particular individual".

minds to defy the laws of logic. Whatever else is true of mental states, they cannot both have and lack a property, or neither have nor fail to have a property, or do anything else that is self-contradictory.

Finally, conclusion 3 logically follows from premises 1 and 2. Premise 1 entails that there can be an x, y, and z such that x and y are indistinguishable, y and z are indistinguishable, and yet x and z are *distinguishable*. If indistinguishability entailed qualitative identity, then x and y and y and z would have to be qualitatively identical. Given premise 2, x and z would then have to be qualitatively identical. But since x and z are distinguishable, they cannot be qualitatively identical.

So the original description of the self-torturer scenario just *entails* that there can be undetectable but real differences in one's experiences.

Note that we are not here positing unconscious pains. I am not saying that turning up the dial on the device by one setting causes one to have an *unconscious* pain added onto the conscious pain one already had. There is only ever one pain, which (at least past a certain point) is conscious, and that pain becomes slightly more intense when one turns up the dial – but so slightly that the subject cannot *know*, by introspection alone, that the pain has intensified.

4.3.2   Indeterminacy

How would Quinn respond to my reasoning? He would object to my assumption that there is such a thing as the precise qualitative character of one's experience: "But the measure of the self-torturer's discomfort," says Quinn, "is indeterminate. There is no fact of the matter about exactly how bad he feels at any setting."[8] (Quinn does not elaborate; that quotation is the entire discussion of indeterminacy.)

I think this is an incoherent view. If you think Quinn has a coherent view here, it may be because you think he is saying one of the following things that he is not, in fact, saying:

---

[8] Quinn 1990, p. 81.

i)   He is not positing mere semantic indeterminacy. He is not saying merely that it is indeterminate whether some word applies to some object. He is proposing that there are pains that fail to have any specific intensity. (Perhaps he would say this is true of *all* pains, since every pain could be part of a series analogous to the pains in the self-torturer case.) In this way, the case is not like cases of vagueness.

ii)   He is not saying that the notion of intensity simply fails to apply to pains. The pain the self-torturer experiences at setting 1,000 is definitely more intense than the pain he experiences at setting 100, and Quinn would accept this. His view would have to be that pains have intensity, but they do not have any *specific* intensity.

iii)   He is not merely saying that pain intensities only come in a limited number of possible values rather than infinitely many values. For that would not avoid the transitivity argument. For instance, suppose that there are only three intensities of pain: 1, 2, and 3. Still, the relation "has the same intensity as" would be transitive.

iv)   He could not be proposing that pain intensity should be modeled by a *range* of numbers, rather than a specific number, for that view, again, fails to avoid the transitivity argument. If x and y have the same *range* of numbers associated with them, and y and z likewise have the same range, then x and z must have the same range. Thus, "has the same intensity as" would still be transitive.[9]

v)   He is not merely saying that pain intensities are qualitative properties rather than quantities. Suppose there is a series of qualitative properties, $\{q_1, q_2, . . .\}$, which are the possible intensities of a pain. Still, "same intensity as" would be transitive. If x and y have the same one of those properties, and y and z also have the same one, then x and z must have the same one. It doesn't matter that they aren't quantitative. What exactly *does* matter? Nothing except that there are intensities, and pains have them.

---

[9] What if we say that x and y "have the same intensity" provided that they have *overlapping* ranges? Then "having the same intensity" will not entail being equally bad: one pain might be worse than another in virtue of having a higher upper boundary and/or a higher lower boundary, even though the two pains have overlapping ranges.

I leave aside the question of what these ranges might mean, since the proposal in any case fails to avoid my argument for the existence of undetectable changes in the badness of a pain.

So what could Quinn be saying? I think he is saying that for any given pain, there are certain intensities such that it is *neither true nor false* that the pain has them. Of the possible intensities, there is no specific one that the pain has, because there is a range for which the pain neither has them nor fails to have them.

This is a contradiction. To say that x neither has nor fails to have q, where q is some property, is to say: it's not the case that x has q, and it is also not the case that x doesn't have q. This is an explicit contradiction; it is of the form "~A & ~~A". *If* one grants that a pain has intensity, then to say "of the possible intensities, there is no specific one that the pain has" is to say that none of the possibilities is realized. This is, by definition, impossible.

Similarly, to say that it is *neither true nor false* that x has q is to say that "x has q" isn't true and "x has q" isn't false. But "x has q" is true if and only if x has q, and "x has q" is false if and only if x doesn't have q. So, for it to be neither true nor false requires that x neither has nor doesn't have q. Which, we have already remarked, is a contradiction.

4.3.3   In Defense of an Optimal Setting

How bad is the undetectable increment in pain that results from turning the dial on the torture device up by one setting?

One might be tempted to say that, since one cannot detect the change, it is not bad at all. But this would be wrong, for reasons analogous to the error just diagnosed above. Let "B_n" denote the degree of *badness* of the experience one has when the device is at setting n. If in general, increasing from setting n to setting $n+1$ does not make things worse, then $B_n = B_{n+1}$. In that case, $B_0 = B_1 = B_2 = \ldots = B_{1000}$. But obviously B_0 does not equal B_{1000}. So it cannot be that turning up the dial never makes things worse. (This argument assumes that "is worse" means "has a higher degree of badness".)

It is logically coherent to hold that turning up the dial only *sometimes* makes things worse. But there is no reason to believe this. The self-torturer has no reason to think that any particular turning of the dial is worse than any other. Therefore, he should assign the same expected disvalue to each turning of the dial. Thus, for each n, the self-torturer should assume that turning up the dial from n to $n+1$ is one thousandth as bad (in terms of pain) as turning the dial from 0 to 1000. That is, the expected value of turning the dial up one setting is $(0.001)(B_{1000})$. (Note: if you have some reason for thinking that some increments are worse than others – e.g., perhaps the early increments are worse than the later ones – this would complicate the reasoning to follow, but the important conclusion will remain, namely, that there is an optimal stopping point for the self-torturer.)

What about the value of the $10,000 that the self-torturer gets paid each time he turns the dial up? Unlike pleasure and pain, money has *diminishing marginal value*. This is a fancy way of saying: the more money you already have, the less an additional $10,000 is worth to you. If you have no money, then getting $10,000 is terrific. If you are already a millionaire, then getting $10,000 makes much *less* difference to your well-being than it would for a person who starts with no money.

On any given day, the self-torturer should decide what to do based on his own self-interest: he should turn the dial up if and only if the marginal value of $10,000 (the increase to his well-being that ten thousand additional dollars would bring about) is greater than the disvalue of the increment in pain, which, as noted above, is $(0.001)(B_{1000})$. The marginal value of $10,000 decreases each day as the self-torturer grows richer, until eventually it is less than $(0.001)(B_{1000})$. At that point, the self-torturer should stop turning the dial. That is the optimal setting (see figure 4.1).

If the self-torturer follows this approach, how much benefit will he derive? The benefit he gets from the money he makes is represented in figure 4.1 by the area under the "Money" curve, between the y-axis and the stopping point.[10] The harm he suffers due to pain equals the area under the "Pain" curve between the y-axis and the stopping point. His net benefit is the area between the two curves, that is, the shaded region in figure 4.1. This is the maximum obtainable benefit.

---

[10] Why is this true? The marginal value of money, by definition, is the *rate* at which wellbeing increases with increases in one's wealth – in technical terms, the derivative of wellbeing with respect to wealth. The integral of this, say, from 0 to n, is the total increase in wellbeing obtained as one goes from 0 to n, which is the area under the marginal value curve. The same applies to the marginal disvalue of pain. Here, as an approximation, I treat the marginal value curve as continuous.

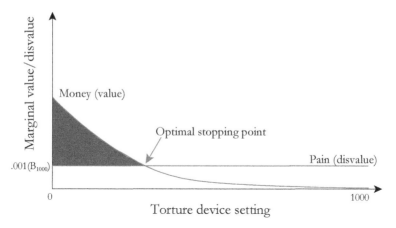

Fig. 4.1 Optimal stopping point for the self-torturer

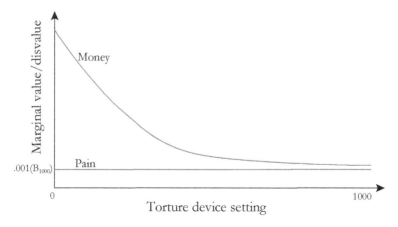

Fig. 4.2 A case with constant disvalue of pain and no optimal stopping point

How do I know that the correct graph looks like figure 4.1, rather than, say, figure 4.2 or 4.3? In figure 4.2, pain has constant marginal disvalue, and money has diminishing marginal value, but the value of an extra $10,000 always remains greater than the disvalue of an extra increment of pain. In figure 4.3, money has diminishing marginal value and pain also has diminishing marginal disvalue (perhaps as you get used to it, further increments of pain cease to be as bad as they were at the begin-

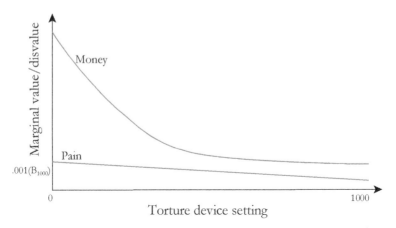

Fig. 4.3 A case with diminishing disvalue of pain and no optimal stopping point

ning?), though the *average* disvalue of an increment of pain is still (0.001) (B_{1000}). Again, the marginal value of the money always remains above that of the pain. If the correct graph is like figure 4.2 or 4.3, then the self-torturer would have to keep turning up the dial, all the way to the end. In this case, my proposed solution fails.

Here is how I know that neither figure 4.2 nor figure 4.3 is correct: because it follows from the initial description of the scenario that those graphs are not correct. By stipulation, the harm of going all the way to setting 1000 is greater than the benefit of $10 million. So the area under the Money curve, between 0 and 1000 on the x-axis, has to be less than the area under the Pain curve between those same limits. Furthermore, assuming that it is at least beneficial to turn the dial the first time, the marginal value of money has to start out greater than the marginal disvalue of pain; that is, the Money curve must start out higher than the Pain curve. The only way to draw the graph so that these things are true is to have the Money curve decline until it crosses the Pain curve, and continue going down after that, as in figure 4.1. That gives us an optimal stopping point, namely, the point where those two curves intersect. Figures 4.2 and 4.3 are both wrong because they both portray the total value of the money, as one goes all the way to setting 1000, as being greater than the total disvalue of the pain.

Admittedly, it may be difficult to know precisely where the optimal stopping point is, since the self-torturer may have trouble quantifying either the badness of pain or the value of money. What he should do, therefore, is simply to make his best estimate of where the optimal stopping point is. However rough that estimate may be, it nevertheless provides sufficient means for avoiding disaster (namely, the result where he winds up at setting 1,000), for certainly his best guess as to the optimal stopping point will be something much less than setting 1,000.

Let's suppose that his best guess as to the optimal stopping point is setting 200. (He need not believe outright that 200 is the optimum; he need only be equally uncertain as to whether the optimum is above 200 or below 200.) He turns the dial up every day for 200 days. What then happens on day 201, when he is offered the chance to turn the dial up one more time, in exchange for another $10,000?

He should decline. This would not be, as Quinn maintains, because of some sort of prudential duty to be faithful to his past intentions. It would be because at this point he has rational grounds for thinking that turning the dial up again would render him worse off, or at least no better off. Since 200 was his best estimate of the optimal stopping point, and he has obtained no new information, he (still) rationally believes that the disvalue of the additional pain he would receive from turning the dial up again would be at least as great as the value of the additional money he would receive. Or, more precisely, he regards it as at least as likely that the pain disvalue would be greater than the monetary value as that it would be less. Or, even more precisely, the *expected disvalue* of the pain, based on his subjective probability distribution, is at least as great as the expected value of the money based on that same distribution.

4.3.4   Detectable and Undetectable Values

Now it may seem that this neat solution fails to address a major part of the reasoning that got the initial paradox going: $10,000 is a significant and very noticeable benefit, and it remains such even as one's wealth expands, all the way up to $10 million. Even if we allow that there can be an undetectable increase in pain, and even if we allow that an undetectable pain increment has *some* nonzero disvalue, surely that disvalue must be very small. How could this undetectable increase in pain outweigh a very significant and noticeable benefit, such as $10,000?

I have two replies: first, I am not at all convinced that the benefit of $10,000 remains significant or even noticeable as one's wealth expands up to $10 million. Of course, one can easily notice such an increase in one's *wealth*, since one can look, say, at one's bank account balance. But noticing the *benefit* produced by that wealth is another matter. It is not obvious that a person with $5,010,000 would be happier than a person with only $5,000,000 (what would you buy if you had $5,010,000 that you would not buy if you only had $5,000,000?) – or that one could introspectively notice the difference in happiness if indeed there would be one.[11]

Second, there are in fact perfectly understandable reasons why a larger quantity might be less easily detectable than a smaller quantity. The human ability to detect a quantity is not always proportioned to the magnitude of the quantity. Imagine a very thin but very long string, one micron thick but a thousand light years long. And compare this object to a rubber ball one centimeter in radius. The string would be invisible to the human eye, whereas the ball would be very easily visible. Nevertheless, the string would be trillions of times greater in volume than the ball.

Or imagine a swimming pool in which one teaspoon of salt is dissolved. And compare this to a cup of water in which just a tenth of a teaspoon of salt is dissolved. The salt in the swimming pool would be undetectable to the human tongue, while the salt in the cup of water would be very easily detectable, even though there would be ten times as much *total* salt in the former as in the latter.

These examples illustrate that large quantities can be rendered undetectable by being spread very thinly, where a smaller but more concentrated quantity would be detectable. In the case of the self-torturer, the harm resulting from turning up the dial one notch will be spread out over the rest of the individual's life, whereas the benefit of $10,000 can be temporally concentrated: one can buy some particular good, which one

---

[11] According to Kahneman and Deaton (2010), money income increases one's happiness, up to about $75,000 per year, after which it makes no discernible difference.

can enjoy in a period much shorter than a lifetime. Thus, it is understandable that the harm might be undetectable but the benefit detectable, even if the harm is the greater quantity.

4.3.5 Advantages of This Solution

This treatment of the self-torturer puzzle is better than the treatment proposed by Quinn, because my solution lets us keep three seemingly self-evident principles that Quinn gives up.

i)   My treatment, though faithful to the factual (non-evaluative) stipulations of the scenario, does not involve any intransitivity, either of the better-than relation, or of rational preferences. My view explains why it might be *understandable* for the self-torturer to have intransitive preferences, due to the undetectability of certain harms, though this would be a mistake on his part. This is a theoretical advantage, since the transitivity of "better than" and "rationally preferred to" is among the most intuitive and widely accepted normative principles philosophers have ever articulated.

ii)   My treatment of the case does not violate classical logic. In particular, it does not require anything to be metaphysically indeterminate.

iii) My treatment of the case maintains standard principles of decision theory, including the axiom that, when given a choice between two options, one of which is rationally preferred to the other, one ought to take the preferred option. At the same time, there is no need to deny the principle that one ought to follow through on any rational plan that correctly anticipated all relevant facts. The rational plan for the self-torturer to adopt at the start is to proceed to the device setting that he estimates to be the optimal point, and then stop. When he reaches that point, it will be rational for him to follow through on his plan by declining all further offers to raise the setting on the device, since he will rationally expect any further increases to make him worse off.

The only objection to this approach appears to be that it implies that there can be unnoticeable facts about the qualitative character of conscious mental states.[12] But this does not strike me as a particularly problematic implication. It would indeed be odd, even contradictory, to maintain that there could be a conscious mental state that was introspectively unnoticeable. But the solution to the self-torturer puzzle posits no such thing. It posits only that there could be an unnoticeable fact about the relationship between two conscious mental states, namely, that the one was very slightly more intense than the other. This is not contradictory or even especially implausible. We should not abandon classical logic or standard decision theory to avoid this.

References

Andreou, Chrisoula. 2006. "Environmental Damage and the Puzzle of the Self-Torturer", *Philosophy and Public Affairs* 34: 95–108.

Andreou, Chrisoula. 2016. "The Real Puzzle of the Self-Torturer: Uncovering a New Dimension of Instrumental Rationality", *Canadian Journal of Philosophy* 45: 562–75.

Kahneman, Daniel and Angus Deaton. 2010. "High Income Improves Evaluation of Life but Not Emotional Well-being," *Proceedings of the National Academy of Sciences* 107: 16489–16493.

Quinn, Warren S. 1990. "The Puzzle of the Self-Torturer", *Philosophical Studies: An International Journal for Philosophy in the Analytic Tradition* 59: 79–90.

Williamson, Timothy. 2000. *Knowledge and Its Limits*. Oxford: Oxford University Press.

---

[12] For a general argument that almost any psychological state can be undetectable (that is, there can be a case in which one cannot know whether one is in the state), see Williamson 2000, ch. 4.

5

Newcomb's Problem

5.1 The Paradox

Scientists have just invented a wonderful device for predicting human behavior.[1] Here is how it works. First, scientists scan a person's brain with a state-of-the-art brain scanner, which records the configuration of all the dendrites, axons, neurotransmitters, and such. They feed this information into a powerful computer, along with a precise description of a possible situation that a person could be in. The computer takes this information, does some ridiculously complicated calculations, and figures out what a person with the specified brain configuration would most likely do in the specified situation. Based on extensive testing with a wide variety of subjects, the prediction system has been found to be 90% reliable: 90% of the time, if the person whose brain was scanned is placed in the relevant situation, the person does what the machine predicted.

Yesterday, your brain was scanned, so that you might participate in an experiment involving the prediction machine. You are placed in front of two boxes, box A and box B. Box A definitely has $1000 in it. Box B contains *either* $1 million *or* nothing. You are offered a choice: you may

---

[1] This chapter's paradox is based on the discussion of Robert Nozick (1969), who credits the physicist William Newcomb.

© The Author(s) 2018
M. Huemer, *Paradox Lost*, https://doi.org/10.1007/978-3-319-90490-0_5

take either box B, or *both* A and B. So far, this might seem like an easy choice: if you take both boxes, you get $1000 more than if you take only B.

Wait, there is one more piece of information to consider. Yesterday, after scanning your brain, the scientists gave the computer a description of the choice you are presently facing (including the information you are now being presented with) and asked it to predict what you would do. If the machine predicted that you would take only box B, then the scientists put $1 million in box B. (They have a lot of funding.) If the machine predicted that you would take both boxes, then (just to mess with you) they put nothing in box B. With all that in mind, how should you choose?

There are two plausible answers. First answer: Take both boxes. Box B contains either $0 or $1 million. If it contains $0, then you are in effect choosing between $0 and $1000. If it contains $1 million, then you are choosing between $1,000,000 and $1,001,000. Either way, the optimal choice is the same. $1000 is better than $0, and $1,001,000 is (slightly) better than $1,000,000, so either way, two boxes are better than one.

Second answer: Take only B. The correct choice is the one that maximizes your *expected gain*. Expected gain is a mathematical construction found by adding up the possible amounts that you stand to gain from a given course of action, weighted by the probability of each possibility. For simplicity, assume that you only care about money, and that your wellbeing increases linearly with your wealth (so, ignore the diminishing marginal value of money). If you take only B, there is a 90% chance that the machine would have correctly predicted this, so that there will be $1 million in box B. There is only a 10% chance that the machine will have made an error, in which case you will get $0. So your expected gain from taking only box B is:

(The probability that B will contain $1 million if you choose only B) (Your profit if it contains $1 million) + (The probability that B will contain $0 if you choose only B)(Your profit if it contains $0) = (0.9)(1,000,000) + (0.1)(0) = 900,000.

If, on the other hand, you take both boxes, then there is a 90% chance that the machine would have correctly predicted this, so box B will prove empty, and you will get only $1000. There is a 10% chance that the machine will have made an error, and there will be $1 million in box B, in which case you will get $1,001,000. So your expected gain from taking both boxes is:

(The probability that B will contain $1 million if you take both boxes) (Your profit if it contains $1 million) + (The probability that B will contain $0 if you take both boxes)(Your profit if it contains $0) = (0.1)(1,001,000) + (0.9)(1000) = 101,000.

900,000 is much greater than 101,000, so take only box B.

It seems, then, that we have a conflict between two widely accepted principles of rational choice:

The Dominance Principle: Suppose you are given a choice between x and y. Suppose you know that for every possible current state of the world, s, if s obtains, then x is better than y. In that case, the rational choice is x.

Expected Utility Maximization: The rational choice in any situation is the one with the highest expected utility, where this is calculated by multiplying, for each possible outcome, the probability that the outcome will occur if you take that choice by the benefit you will receive if that outcome occurs, and then summing these products for all outcomes. Thus, for example, a 10% chance of getting ten units of good is exactly as good as a 100% chance of getting one unit.

The Dominance Principle supports taking both boxes. Expected Utility Maximization supports taking only box B.[2]

---

[2] This was Nozick's (1969) original understanding of the problem.

5.2   Objections to the Scenario

Some consider this scenario unrealistic. Human beings are complicated creatures; furthermore, we have free will, which (arguably) means that our actions are not fully determined by causes occurring prior to the moment of choice. It is unlikely that scientists could create a prediction machine that was 90% reliable. And, however reliable the prediction machine might be, it is also unrealistic that there would be a *single* number representing its reliability across all conditions, regardless of whom the machine was applied to, what the choice situation was, or how many options the agent had available to them. There are some who are bothered by such unrealism and who have an aversion to contemplating such scenarios or answering questions about what would occur in them. If you are among them, this section is for you.

One way of replying to the concern would be to insist that it does not matter if the scenario is unrealistic, because there can still be an answer to what one should do in a highly unrealistic situation. That would be the standard philosophical response, but if you needed a response in the first place, you probably won't like that one.

Here is a more satisfying response: Let's make the scenario more realistic. Let's grant that people have free will, and thus that it is never possible to predict human behavior with perfect accuracy. Nevertheless, free will certainly does not imply that people are *maximally unpredictable* – it does not mean that in any given circumstance, you are *equally* likely to do *anything* that you're capable of doing. (If that were so, life would be crazy.)

So the scientists have made a computer algorithm. It looks at a variety of pieces of information, including such things as neurotransmitter levels, past behavior, and scores on personality tests. Different bits of this information are relevant to different choice scenarios, and the scientists have done a great deal of experimentation to fine tune the algorithm, adjusting the weights for different situations, and so on. The algorithm has been found to be between 53% and 75% reliable at predicting human choices, across a wide variety of situations in which it has been tested out. These situations include the Newcomb scenario – the scientists have already given the Newcomb problem to a random sample of 1000 other people, and the machine correctly predicted most of those people's choices. The algorithm's reliability also varies according to characteristics of the person whose choices it is used to predict, including the person's age, IQ, personality type, and so on.

After thoroughly reviewing all the experimental evidence, you estimate that the machine should be about 60% reliable at predicting the choices of people like you, give or take a few percentage points, in circumstances like the one you are now in.

Now you sit down to do your expected utility calculation. If you take one box, there is about a 60% chance that the prediction algorithm will have correctly predicted this, and you'll get $1 million. If you take both boxes, there is about a 60% chance that the algorithm will have correctly predicted that, and you'll get $1,000. You thus calculate the expected values as follows:

Given 60% reliability:

Expected utility of taking one box: $(.6)(1,000,000) + (.4)(0) = 600,000$
Expected utility of taking two boxes: $(.6)(1,000) + (.4)(1,001,000) =$ 401,000

So it looks like your expected utility is higher if you take one box.

But since you're still not sure of your reliability estimate, you decide to calculate the break-even point – the level of reliability such that "one-boxing" (taking one box) and "two-boxing" (taking both boxes) would have equal expected utility. It turns out that this point is 50.05%:

Given 50.05% reliability:

Expected utility of taking one box: $(.5005)(1,000,000) + (.4995)(0) =$ 500,500
Expected utility of taking two boxes: $(.5005)(1,000) + (.4995)$ $(1,001,000) = 500,500$

If the prediction algorithm is *more* than 50.05% reliable, then you get more expected utility by taking one box. If it is *less* than 50.05% reliable, then you get more expected utility by taking two boxes. Having looked at the research on the device, you are extremely confident that the algorithm is more than 50.05% reliable for cases relevantly like yours. I take it that now no one will claim that this is an unrealistic supposition.

But at the same time, the old dominance reasoning still applies: if you take both boxes, you get whatever is in box A (which was already determined yesterday) plus $1000.

5.3 The Right Expected Utility Principle

5.3.1 The Right Way to Make Good Things More Likely

In his original discussion, Nozick presented the problem, as I have above, as a conflict between the Dominance Principle and the principle of Expected Utility Maximization. If those two principles are really in conflict, then we have a serious intellectual problem, since both principles seem correct; more precisely, both clearly seem to capture a certain type of rationality, instrumental rationality. The best solution to the paradox would be one that somehow reconciles the two principles of rational choice, showing how Expected Utility Maximization really recommends the same course of action as Dominance reasoning.

This can in fact be done. The solution maintains that one-boxers (the people who think you should take only box B) are misunderstanding the notion of probability in expected utility maximization. We can all agree that, in some sense, *if an action makes it more likely that you will get something you want, then that counts as a reason in favor of the action*; if it makes it less likely that you will get what you want, that counts as a reason against. Expected Utility Maximization is just a more precise and general formulation of that intuition.

Here is the mistake the one-boxers appear to be making: they read "makes it more likely" as meaning "gives you evidence". So they think that if your performing act A would give you evidence that something you want will happen, then that counts as a reason in favor of A. This point of view is called "evidential decision theory". In the Newcomb problem, if you decide to take one box instead of two, the fact that you are making that choice gives you evidence that the machine predicted that you would so choose, which means there is probably a million dollars in box B. So the one-boxers think that you are "making it more likely" that there is a million dollars in box B.

In fact, however, rational agents do not endeavor to *give themselves evidence* that their ends will be realized; rational agents endeavor to *cause* their ends to be realized (which usually has the side effect of giving themselves evidence that their ends will be realized).[3] This point of view is known as "causal decision theory".[4] In the Newcomb problem, if you decide to take one box instead of two, this has no chance at all of *causing* there to be a million dollars in box B, so you have no reason to take one box instead of two.

To elaborate: The prediction machine scanned your brain yesterday. For simplicity, suppose there is a brain configuration b_1 that tends to cause people to choose only one box in Newcomb's problem, and another brain configuration b_2 that tends to cause people to choose both boxes.[5] The prediction machine makes its prediction based upon which of those states it detects. At the time your brain was scanned, it was in either b_1 or b_2. Since it is impossible to change the past, it makes sense to treat that state as fixed. That means that you should calculate expected utilities *given* each possible brain configuration that you might have had yesterday.

---

[3] You might object: "But if I give myself evidence that a good thing will happen, then I'll come to believe the good thing will happen, and this belief will make me feel good. So I *do* have reason to give myself such evidence after all." This might be true – but only in virtue of your having an *additional* goal, beyond having the good thing happen – namely, the goal of making yourself feel good. The only thing you have reason to do *merely by virtue of having goal G* is to (try to) bring about G. If you also have the goal of believing that G will happen, then *that* gives you a reason to cause yourself to believe that G will happen (but it does not, e.g., give you any reason to give yourself evidence that you will believe that G will happen, unless you also have a goal of believing that you will believe that G will happen . . . and so on).

[4] See Skyrms 1982; Sainsbury 2009, pp. 81–2 (but note that Sainsbury defends a different version of causal decision theory from that of Skyrms and myself).

[5] To be more precise, you can think of b_1 as a set of brain configurations, namely, those that, when the brain scanner detects one of them, it causes the prediction machine to predict that you will choose one box when placed in the Newcomb choice situation. And similarly for b_2, *mutatis mutandis*.

Now, if your brain was b_1, then there is $1 million in box B, and that will (with certainty) continue to be true whether you now choose one box or two. If, on the other hand, your brain was in b_2, then there is nothing in box B, and *that* will (with certainty) continue to be true whether you choose one box or two.[6] So the probability of your getting the $1 million is just the probability that your brain was in b_1 yesterday.

The one-boxer argument turns on the claim that *you are more likely to get the $1 million if you take one box than if you take two*. For the reason just explained, that is not true. Let's say that, since you have no idea what state your brain was in yesterday, you consider it 50% likely that it was in b_1 and 50% likely that it was in b_2. Then the probability of your getting the million dollars if you take one box is 50%. And the probability of your getting the million dollars if you take both boxes is also 50%.

Now, having gone through that reasoning (if you were persuaded by that), you have just learned something about yourself: that you are the sort of person who accepts the two-box reasoning. So now you might be more confident that your brain was in fact in b_1 yesterday. Let's say you are now 90% confident that your brain was in b_1 yesterday. If you like, you can redo the expected utility calculation using this new probability. Now the probability of your getting the million dollars if you take one box is 10%, and the probability of your getting the million dollars if you take both boxes is 10%. But the probability of your getting the *thousand* dollars is zero if you take one box, and 100% if you take both. So again, you should take both. In the relevant sense, taking both boxes makes you more likely (in fact, 100% likely) to get the thousand dollars and does *not* make you any less likely to get the million dollars.

Why is this the correct sense of "making more likely"? Because this is the sense that matters to one who is trying to bring about good things, and not merely to produce evidence of good things. Since you know that

---

[6]To state the point mathematically: $P(M|T_1\&B_1) = P(M|T_2\&B_1) = 1$, and $P(M|T_1\&B_2) = P(M|T_2\&B_2) = 0$, where M = [Box B contains a million dollars], T_1 = [You take one box], T_2 = [You take both boxes], B_1 = [Your brain was in b_1], and B_2 = [Your brain was in b_2]. As we say, the past brain state "screens off" your decision from the question about whether the box contains a million dollars.

your past brain state, whether it was b_1 or b_2, cannot now be changed, the relevant question is whether, *given* that brain state (and more generally, given all the things that you cannot affect), taking one box will make you more likely to get what you want.

5.3.2 Two-Boxing Maximizes Expected Utility: Doing the Math

Taking the above points into account, we can reformulate the principle of expected utility maximization. Earlier, we said that the rational choice is the one with the highest expected utility, where the expected utility of a choice is calculated by multiplying, for each possible outcome, the probability that the outcome will occur if you make that choice by the benefit you will receive if that outcome occurs, and then summing these products for all outcomes. In other words,

$$\mathrm{EU}(A) = \mathrm{P}(O_1 \mid A) \cdot \mathrm{V}(O_1) + \mathrm{P}(O_2 \mid A) \cdot \mathrm{V}(O_2) + \ldots$$
$$= \sum_i \mathrm{P}(O_i \mid A) \cdot \mathrm{V}(O_i)$$

where EU(*A*) is the expected utility of choice *A*; the possible outcomes of the choice are O_1, O_2, O_3, and so on; P($O_i|A$) is the probability of O_i occurring given that you do *A*; and V(O_i) is the value to you of outcome O_i.[7]

How should we modify this to take account of the reasoning of section 5.3.1 above? Here is a way: we should understand "P($O_i|A$)" as denoting the probability-weighted average value of P($O_i|A$) *given* each of the alternative hypotheses about how the fixed facts about the world might be.

In other words: let's refer to all the things that you cannot affect as "the fixed world". There are many ways that the fixed world could be; call them W_1, W_2, W_3, and so on.[8] Then the proper value of P($O_i|A$) to use in an expected utility calculation is

---

[7] Here we assume that the O_i form a partition and that they include everything that matters to value.

[8] Assume that the W_i form a partition.

$$P\left(O_i \mid A, W_1\right)P\left(W_1\right) + P\left(O_i \mid A, W_2\right)P\left(W_2\right) + P\left(O_i \mid A, W_3\right)P\left(W_3\right) + \cdots$$
$$= \sum_j P\left(O_i \mid A, W_j\right)P\left(W_j\right).$$

Plugging this into the formula for expected utility[9]:

$$EU(A) = \sum_i V(O_i) \cdot P(O_i \mid A)$$
$$= \sum_i \left(V(O_i) \cdot \sum_j P(O_i \mid A, W_j)P\left(W_j\right) \right).$$

On this understanding of Expected Utility Maximization, here is how we should assess the expected utilities in Newcomb's problem. The possible outcomes of the scenario are that you get $0, that you get $1000, that you get $1,000,000, and that you get $1,001,000. We assume for simplicity that the value you get from each outcome is just equal to the amount of money you get. Then:

Expected utility from taking one box
  = (0)(Probability of getting $0 if you take one box)
  + (1000)(Probability of getting $1000 if you take one box)
  + (1,000,000)(Probability of getting $1,000,000 if you take one box)
  + (1,001,000)(Probability of getting $1,001,000 if you take one box)

The first term cancels since it is something multiplied by zero. The second and fourth terms are both zero, since there is no chance of winding up with either 1,000 or 1,001,000 if you take one box. So the above reduces to

---

[9] My formula here is mathematically equivalent to Skyrms' (1982, p. 697) formula for expected utility in causal decision theory.

(1,000,000)(Probability of getting $1,000,000 if you take one box)

= (1,000,000)[P(B_1)(Probability of getting $1,000,000 if you take one box, given B_1) + P(B_2)(Probability of getting $1,000,000 if you take one box, given B_2)]

= (1,000,000)[P(B_1)(1) + P(B_2)(0)]

= 1,000,000 · P(B_1)

where B_1 is the proposition that your brain was in state b_1 yesterday, and B_2 is the proposition that it was in state b_2. Next, we find the expected utility from taking two boxes:

Expected utility from taking two boxes

= (0)(Probability of getting $0 if you take two boxes)

+ (1000)(Probability of getting $1000 if you take two boxes)

+ (1,000,000)(Probability of getting $1,000,000 if you take two boxes)

+ (1,001,000)(Probability of getting $1,001,000 if you take two boxes)

The first term is zero. The third term is also zero since there is no way of getting exactly $1,000,000 if you take both boxes. So the above reduces to

(1,000)(Probability of getting $1,000 if you take two boxes)

+ (1,001,000)(Probability of getting $1,001,000 if you take two boxes)

= (1,000)[P(B_1)(Probability of getting $1,000 if you take two boxes, given B_1) + P(B_2)(Probability of getting $1,000 if you take two boxes, given B_2)]

+ (1,001,000)[P(B_1)(Probability of getting $1,001,000 if you take two boxes, given B_1) + P(B_2)(Probability of getting $1,001,000 if you take two boxes, given B_2)]

$$= (1,000)[P(B_1)(0) + P(B_2)(1)]$$
$$+ (1,001,000)[P(B_1)(1) + P(B_2)(0)]$$
$$= 1,000 \cdot P(B_2) + 1,001,000 \cdot P(B_1)$$

Since B_1 and B_2 are the only alternatives in this scenario, $P(B_2) = 1 - P(B_1)$. So the above reduces to

$$= 1,000(1 - P(B_1)) + 1,001,000 \cdot P(B_1)$$
$$= 1000 + 1,000,000 \cdot P(B_1)$$

These formulas give the expected utilities in terms of $P(B_1)$, the probability that your brain was in b_1 when it was scanned yesterday. But it does not matter what this probability is, because whatever it is, 1000 + 1,000,000 · $P(B_1)$ is greater than 1,000,000 · $P(B_1)$. So taking two boxes gives more expected utility than taking one box.

For illustration: suppose that at the start of your deliberations, you have no opinion about whether your brain was in b_1 or b_2, so you assign probability ½ to each alternative. Then the calculated expected utilities would be 500,000 for taking one box, and 501,000 for taking both boxes. So you should take both boxes.

But after doing these calculations, you become pretty sure that you are going to choose both boxes, and you also become pretty sure that there is going to be nothing in box B. So you lower $P(B_1)$ to, say, 10%, and raise $P(B_2)$ to 90%. If you like, you can then redo the calculations using these new probabilities: now the expected utilities are 100,000 for taking one box and 101,000 for taking both boxes. This is disappointing, but you should still take both boxes.

5.3.3   Why This Is the Best Solution

Intuitively, expected utility maximization and dominance reasoning are both rational. This is a reason for thinking that they are not truly in conflict. In fact, the Dominance Principle seems as if it ought to be a *special case* of Expected Utility Maximization – namely, the case where you know for certain which act will give you greater *actual utility* (not merely expected utility). In that special case, surely Expected Utility Maximization ought to recommend that one take the act that in fact maximizes utility – surely that is in accord with our intuitive understanding of what the principle is getting at.

All this is to say that, if there is an interpretation of the two rational choice principles that reconciles them, then, other things being equal, we should prefer that interpretation over one that makes them incompatible. The account given above reconciles the two principles. Evidential decision theory does not – it requires us to simply reject the Dominance Principle. So we should prefer causal decision theory over evidential decision theory.

5.4   The Case of Perfect Reliability

Now consider a variation on the Newcomb case. Imagine that the scenario is as described before, except that the machine is not merely 90% but *100%* reliable. It never makes an error. Many, even among those who prefer two boxes in the original case, think that surely in *this* case you should take one box.

But, it appears, the above reasoning says otherwise: even in the case of 100% reliability, you should still take two boxes. The dominance argument still applies: either box B contains $1 million, or it contains nothing. If it contains $1 million, then you should take both boxes, since you will then get $1,001,000 instead of $1,000,000. If it contains nothing, then you should take both boxes, since you will then get $1,000 instead of nothing. So you should take both boxes. As you go through this reasoning, you realize with a sinking feeling that box B is in fact empty. This doesn't dissuade you from taking both boxes, though, since you now know that the best you can do is to get the thousand dollars.

This is also the way to maximize your expected utility. The expected utilities are, again, as follows:

Expected utility from taking one box: $1,000,000 \cdot P(B_1)$
Expected utility from taking two boxes: $1000 + 1,000,000 \cdot P(B_1)$

The latter is still larger than the former. Nothing has changed, because the reliability of the device did not appear anywhere in the calculations.

And the argument about causal versus evidential probabilities still applies. Choosing one box now gives you *conclusive* evidence that you will get $1 million. But it still cannot *cause* this result, since the million dollars was already placed in the box yesterday. Choosing two boxes gives you conclusive evidence that box B is empty, but, again, it cannot cause this to be the case. So by the reasoning of section 5.3.1, you still have no reason to choose one box instead of two.

You might think this is a problem. Surely in the 100% reliability case, you should take one box. Since the standard two-boxer arguments apply in the 100% reliability case just as much as they apply in the 90% reliability case, that just shows that the standard two-boxer arguments must be wrong. Or so one might claim.

I don't think that's correct. My diagnosis: normal methods of prediction could plausibly be highly reliable, but not 100% reliable. There are only two ways in which a prediction device could be 100% accurate. The first is if all our actions are entirely pre-determined. The machine knows what we are going to do because, given the antecedent causes, that is the only thing we *can* do. However, if this is the case, then there is no free will, and if there is no free will, then deliberation doesn't make sense (we cannot rationally deliberate on the assumption that we have no choice about anything), and it makes no sense to speak of what choice one "should" make.[10]

---

[10] I here assume that determinism is incompatible with free will, which is controversial. For defense of this assumption, see my 2000.

The second way a prediction device could be 100% accurate would be if there is backwards causation, that is, a person's decision at a given time somehow reaches into the past and causes the machine to predict that very decision.

This, I suppose, is how crystal balls and other forms of precognition are supposed to work (they would work this way if they worked). When you see an ordinary object, this works by the object's causing you to have a sensory experience of it. Analogously, when you "see" the future (if you could do so), this would work by the future events' causing you to have an experience representing them. This ability of course would not *have* to be 100% reliable. But *in order* to be 100% reliable, in a world where the future isn't predetermined, you would have to have some such ability to be affected by the future.

But in this case, the reasoning for taking two boxes no longer applies, since it is no longer true that you cannot affect the past prediction. If you take one box, that could cause there to be a million dollars in that box – not by causing the money to suddenly appear there now, but by causing the money to have been put there yesterday.

So, if the machine is 100% reliable due to backwards causation, then you should take one box. If the machine is 100% reliable because every-thing is predetermined, then you have no free will, in which case it does not make sense to discuss what you should or should not do. If the machine could somehow be 100% reliable *without* either backwards cau-sation or determinism, then you should still take both boxes. However, this last alternative is not really possible.

The case of the merely 90% reliable predictor does not face this prob-lem, because a machine *might* be 90% reliable without backwards causa-tion or determinism. Assuming that that is the case, our earlier reasoning in favor of two boxes applies.

5.5 Rationality and Long-Run Benefit

5.5.1 One-Boxers as a Group Do Better

Here is another argument for one-boxing. Our conception of rationality should have some connection with being better off or having one's goals better satisfied. (Let's assume that our only goal is to be better off, so that these two notions of rationality, as promoting one's interests and as promoting one's goals, will coincide. This isn't true in general, but it could be true of some agents.) Of course, it need not be that rational people *always* wind up better off, since even the most rational people are sometimes fooled, and even the best laid plans sometimes go awry. But there ought to be a general tendency for the rational to be better off.

Newcomb gives us a scenario in which one-boxers typically wind up better off than two-boxers. This isn't just an occasional accident, like someone who foolishly spends his life savings on the lottery and then luckily wins. It is systematic and predictable. If you watch a large group of one-boxers and a large group of two-boxers go into a Newcomb choice situation, you know that the one-boxers, on average, are going to come out well ahead. This might tempt us to think that it is the one-boxers, after all, who are the rational ones. We might even be tempted to *define* rationality in terms of whatever ways of thinking and choosing systematically tend, in the long run, to get agents what they want.

I think this line of thinking does not really make any progress over the original one-box argument. The scenario in which you track a large group of one-boxers and a large group of two-boxers, and the one-boxers wind up better off, fails to support one-boxing, because rationality is not about trying to satisfy the goals of *your group*. It is about trying to satisfy your own goals.

There are other well-known cases in which a group of rational individuals systematically does worse than a group of non-rational individuals. Consider the Prisoner's Dilemma, in which each of two people has a choice between two actions, "cooperating" and "defecting".[11] If one

---

[11] For a stronger parallel between Newcomb's Problem and the Prisoners' Dilemma, see Lewis 1979. Lewis argues that the other player in the Prisoner's Dilemma acts like a sort of "predictor" of one's

player cooperates while the other defects, then the defector gets the best available outcome while the cooperator gets the worst. If both cooperate, then both get the second-best outcome. If both defect, then both get the second-worst outcome. The payoffs are shown in the following table ("1,4" means player 1 gets 1 unit of good while player 2 gets 4, etc., where larger numbers are better):

		Player #2	
		Cooperate	Defect
Player #1	Cooperate	3, 3	1, 4
	Defect	4, 1	2, 2

By stipulation, both players want to get higher numbers for themselves, and that is all they care about. In this case, the rational choice for each is to defect; this is generally accepted in decision theory. To figure out what Player 1 should do, first suppose Player 2 will cooperate. Then Player 1 should defect, since doing so will give him 4 units of benefit instead of 3. Now suppose Player 2 will defect. Then again, Player 1 should defect, since doing so will give him 2 units instead of 1. So either way, Player 1 is better off defecting, and this is all he cares about. Parallel reasoning shows that Player 2 is better off defecting. Thus, both players, if rational, wind up defecting and getting the 2-unit payout.

If both players instead cooperate, then they are irrational. However, groups of people who are irrational in that particular way will reliably tend to end up better off (getting 3-unit payouts instead of 2) when playing Prisoner's Dilemma with each other, than groups who are rational. This does not show that cooperating is really rational, because, again, rationality (in the sense we're concerned with here) is not about making

---

own behavior, since there is likely to be a nonzero statistical correlation between the choices of the two players; therefore, by cooperating, one gives oneself evidence that the other player will cooperate, though one does not cause the other player to cooperate. Thus, says Lewis, the Prisoners' Dilemma is a kind of Newcomb problem.

the group of like-minded people better off. It is about making *yourself* better off.

5.5.2 One-Boxers Tend to Do Better in any Given Case

In reply, one might say the issue is not really about what happens in a large collection of cases. The point is simply that in each case, one-boxers are more likely to walk away with a million dollars than two-boxers are; the fact that one-boxers as a group do better in the long run is just a symptom of the fact that they are *more likely* to do better in *any given* case.

This, however, is nothing but a repeat of the original argument for one-boxing: the claim that taking one box makes you more likely to get the million dollars. We have already explained above why this is false. In the relevant sense, taking one box instead of two has no effect on your chances of getting the million.

5.5.3 One-Boxers Do Better in Repeated Games

One might propose a case in which a single individual is going to participate in many Newcomb choices. If you repeat the Newcomb choice a thousand times, then you will come out, overall, with about $900 million if you are a consistent one-boxer, and only $101 million if you are a consistent two-boxer. Doesn't this show that one-boxers are more rational?

But two-boxers can reasonably argue that this is a different choice situation. Because the game is repeated, it is possible for your choice in any given iteration (except the last) to *affect* what happens in a future iteration. It is plausible that if you choose one box the first time, this might cause you to get $1 million the *next* time. Perhaps choosing the one box will put your brain into the state of a one-boxer's brain, so the next time it is scanned, the machine will predict a one-box choice.

To avoid this argument, we might suppose that your brain is scanned only once at the beginning, and this one scan is the basis for the machine's predictions in all subsequent cases where you play the game. In that case, according to causal decision theory, you should always pick both boxes, since you cannot affect the machine's predictions. But people who do so wind up repeatedly getting only $1,000 instead of $1 million. Does this, finally, show that there is something wrong with my conception of rationality?

I don't think it does. Here is the more fundamental reply to all the arguments of this sort. It is possible to cook up an unusual scenario that rewards irrationality. Here is a simple one: a machine scans your brain to find out whether you have any intransitive preferences or not. If you do, then the scientists operating the machine reward you with $1 million. If you have only transitive preferences, then they beat you up. In this scenario, people with intransitive preferences wind up, systematically and predictably, much better off than people with only transitive preferences. But that hardly shows that intransitive preferences are rational.

In case you think intransitive preferences actually *are* rational,[12] you can change the example to use any other common criterion of irrationality – the sunk cost fallacy, hyperbolic discounting, even self-contradiction.[13] The criteria for rationality could be as uncontroversial as any ever are. A machine scans your brain to see whether you are guilty of these errors, and then someone rewards you if you are. Predictably and systematically. Surely this does not show that the sunk cost fallacy, hyperbolic discounting, and inconsistency are rational.

5.5.4   Being a One-Boxer Is Predictably Advantageous

Here is another try at the one-box argument: *Being the sort of person* who would choose one box in Newcomb's problem is clearly advantageous, as such people tend to walk away rich. Furthermore, being this sort of per-

---

[12] Some philosophers think this; see Rachels 1998; Quinn 1990.

[13] The sunk cost fallacy consists of thinking that because you previously expended some resources on option A, you now have a reason for favoring A – for instance, that you should sit through a movie you aren't enjoying, simply because you paid for it. Hyperbolic discounting consists of ascribing drastically more weight to near-term benefits than to longer-term benefits – for instance, spending all night drinking and partying when you have an important exam the next day. You might think the example of self-contradiction does not fit with the others because it is an instance of epistemic irrationality, not practical rationality. If you prefer, assume the example is one of *using* contradictory assumptions to *make choices*.

son clearly does *cause* you to receive the money. It is because you are this sort of person in general (which means you are, in general, in brain state b_1) that the machine predicts that you will choose one box, and that gets you the $1 million. So if you can decide what sort of person to be, you clearly should decide to be a one-boxer. Having done so, you will choose one box in the Newcomb situation.

The standard analysis of this, which I endorse, is as follows: there are two distinct decision theoretic questions: (i) If given the choice between one box and two boxes in the Newcomb scenario, which should I choose? (ii) If given the choice, before my brain is scanned, between being a one-boxer and being a two-boxer, which should I choose? The answer to (i) is "two boxes". The answer to (ii) is "one-boxer". These are two different scenarios, so it is perfectly consistent to give this pair of answers. That is, if I know in advance that I am going to be in a Newcomb situation some time in the future, and if I can control my own dispositions and attitudes, then I should work on turning myself into the sort of person who would take one box. That is consistent with the fact that, if I am now in a Newcomb situation, and my brain has already been scanned (so it is too late to develop the brain state that would have caused the machine to predict one box), then I should now choose two boxes.

One-boxers might nevertheless argue that there is a tension between these views about the two choice problems. For one might argue:

1. It is rational to be a one-boxer (that is, to be the sort of person who would choose one box in Newcomb's scenario).
2. If *x* is rational, and *x* entails *y*, then *y* is rational.
3. Being a one-boxer entails choosing one box if one is in the Newcomb scenario.
4. Therefore, it is rational to choose one box if one is in the Newcomb scenario.

What is wrong with that argument? One objection is that the premises fail to specify the *times* at which traits or choices are rational. Let's say that you are told in advance about the Newcomb situation that you are going to face. At t_1, your brain is being scanned. Later, at t_2, you are asked to pick either one box or two. Then it is rational *at* t_1 to be a one-boxer (if you can). But being a one-boxer at t_1 does not entail choosing one box at

t_2, since by t_2, you might have lost the disposition. So we can coherently maintain that it is rational to be a one-boxer at t_1 but then to choose two boxes at t_2.

One might be tempted to posit a disposition so robust that it cannot later be changed. Assume that you can control whether you have such a disposition at t_1, and the machine will detect whether you have it. Then it would be rational to adopt that disposition. By stipulation, this is incompatible with your later changing in such a way that you would take two boxes at t_2. This gets around the preceding objection. However, it opens up the objection that, if the disposition is truly unalterable, then the agent has no control over his action at t_2, in which case principles of rational choice fail to apply – there is no meaningful question about what an agent should do in a situation in which the agent cannot control his behavior.

Here is a more general objection to the one-boxing argument. The preceding argument for the rationality of one-boxing could be applied to any paradigm form of irrational behavior. Suppose a machine scans your brain to detect whether you are prone to the sunk cost fallacy. If you are, you get a great reward. It would be rational (if possible, and if you are not already like this) to make yourself the sort of person who falls prey to the sunk cost fallacy. Suppose you could cultivate a disposition so firm that it could not later be changed, and that only such a disposition will get you the reward. Then we could argue:

1'.   It is rational in this scenario to make oneself prone to the sunk cost fallacy.
2'.   If x is rational, and x entails y, then y is rational.
3'.   Being prone to the sunk cost fallacy entails making decisions based on that fallacy when given the opportunity.
4'.   Therefore, making decisions based on the sunk cost fallacy when given the opportunity is rational.

(The conclusion here can be understood as conditional on the supposition that you initially face the scenario in which you are to be rewarded for having the unalterable disposition to commit the sunk cost fallacy – just as the conclusion in the one-boxer's argument above must be understood as conditional on the supposition that you are given advance notice that you will face a Newcomb choice.) Again, the argument could be adjusted to conclude that *any* paradigm form of irrationality is actually rational (in the scenario imagined) – hyperbolic discounting, acting on intransitive preferences, acting on contradictory beliefs, and so on. I take that to be a *reductio ad absurdum* of the argument.

Where did the reasoning go wrong? The false step is premise 2, "If x is rational, and x entails y, then y is rational." It could be rational to cause yourself to later behave irrationally, say, because, as in the above scenarios, someone will reward you for the later irrationality. That is not a contradictory supposition.

What would make the later action irrational? Wouldn't the mere fact that the later action flowed from an earlier rational choice render the later act rational too? No. The later action might be irrational because, say, it violates the Dominance Principle, or it fails to maximize the agent's expected utility at the later time, or it commits the sunk cost fallacy, etc.

5.6   Uncertainty About Decision Theory

Let's take a final variant on the Newcomb situation. In this variant, box B still contains either $1 million or nothing, but box A only contains a dollar. Everything else is as before. Does this alter what we should choose?

Now it seems much more tempting to go for one box. Who cares if you miss out on one measly dollar? To be clear, a dollar has *some* value – if you saw one on the street, you'd pick it up. But its value is very low.

But the arguments for two-boxing still apply. As long as a dollar is worth *something*, two boxes dominates one box: if there is nothing in box B, then you're choosing between $0 and $1; if there is $1 million in box B, then you're choosing between $1,000,000 and $1,000,001. $1 is better than $0, and $1,000,001 is better than $1,000,000. So either way, you should take both boxes. Similarly, according to section 5.3.2, the expected utility of taking one box is $1,000,000 \cdot P(B_1)$, and the expected utility of taking two boxes is $1 + 1,000,000 \cdot P(B_1)$. The latter is greater.

So in terms of the theoretical arguments, this scenario is no different from the original version of the Newcomb choice situation. But it seems different; it seems rational to take one box in this new scenario.

Here is my account of this. I believe the account of rational choice that I gave earlier. Nevertheless, I am not *100% certain* of it. I think the one-boxers are very probably wrong, but I am not dogmatic about this – I concede that there is a chance they might be right.

On my preferred account of rational choice, taking two boxes in the *new* Newcomb situation (the one with $1 in box A) is very slightly better than taking one box – namely, by a margin of one expected dollar. But on the alternative account (the one-boxers' view), taking one box is *much* better than taking two – namely, by a margin of 799,999 expected dollars. Since I am to *some* degree uncertain about the right theory of rational choice, I should give some weight to both theories, proportional to my confidence in each. But then, even a very small uncertainty about my account of rational choice enables the possible advantage of one-boxing to outweigh that of two-boxing, when the apparent advantage of two-boxing is so small.

Consider the following situation: suppose there is a lottery with a prize of $1 million. There are ten tickets, exactly one will win, and the tickets cost $1. Should I buy one? I will probably lose money if I do. But I should still buy a ticket if I care about *money*, because buying a ticket gives me a very large *expected monetary profit*.

Similarly, even though taking two boxes probably has greater expected utility than taking one box, I should still take one box if I care about *expected utility*, since the *expected expected utility* of taking one box is higher. Expected expected utility is a mathematical construct used for decision-making in cases where you are uncertain of the correct account of expected utility. Expected expected utility is found by adding up, for each possible theory of rational choice, the expected utility of an action according to the theory, weighted by the epistemic probability of the theory itself being correct.

Admittedly, something about this reasoning is weird. It looks like there are now three theories of rational choice in play:

R_1 *Causal decision theory:* The rational choice is the one that maximizes expected utility, calculated as described in section 5.3.2.

R_2 *Evidential decision theory:* The rational choice is the one that maximizes expected utility, calculated using evidential probabilities, as in section 5.1.

R_3 *Maximize EEU:* The rational choice is the one that maximizes expected expected utility (EEU), calculated by taking a weighted average of the expected utilities of an action according to each viable theory of rational choice, weighted by the probabilities of the theories.

These seem to be three incompatible theories: they all name different criteria for rational choice, which could diverge in some cases. So if R_3 is correct, then R_1 and R_2 are both false. And if, hypothetically, I were completely convinced that R_3 was correct, then I'd have to assign probability zero to R_1 and R_2. Then, when I tried to apply R_3, I'd have to assign zero weight to R_1 and R_2, which of course leaves the EEU undefined. Surely this is not right.

This puzzle can be resolved by introducing a distinction between ideal rationality and bounded rationality. Ideal rationality is what an ideal rational agent – one with unlimited intelligence, reasoning abilities, and understanding of all relevant reasons – would practice. Bounded rationality is what a being like us should practice, *given* our various imperfections.[14]

To illustrate, suppose I am playing chess. Suppose that on move 63, the move *pawn to e6* on my part would *in fact* put me in a position to ultimately win the game, even with perfect play by my opponent. However, I am not aware of this fact at the time; it will only be revealed

---

[14] The term "bounded rationality" was introduced by Simon (1955) to describe the sort of approximately-rational decision-making appropriate under conditions of limited knowledge and calculating abilities. I extend the notion to include conditions of ignorance about rational choice theory itself.

This distinction between ideal and bounded rationality is (even) less clean cut than it sounds. Rather than a simple qualitative distinction between idealized and bounded senses of rationality, what we really have is a spectrum of different degrees of idealization in different respects. Almost any rational criticism of an action presupposes *some* degree of idealization. For instance, we criticize agents for committing the sunk cost fallacy, which is widely taken to be irrational. But one could argue that in *some* sense, it is rational to commit this fallacy, *given* the actual limitations of most who commit it, including the fact that they can't see at the time that it is a fallacy.

after the game when we analyze the position using computers. Furthermore, suppose that, as of move 63, I am short on time and in danger of losing to my opponent on time. I consider moving pawn to e6, but I realize that it would take me several minutes to think through the consequences of that move. So I reject it and focus on moves that are easier to think through but which (later analysis will reveal) do not enable me to force a win.

Now, in some sense, pawn to e6 was the correct move, the move I "should have" made in my position. At the same time, there is another sense in which I was rational to reject that move. Roughly speaking, an ideal player would have moved pawn to e6, but I would not have been wise to do this, given my known limitations.

R_1 and R_2, I take it, are theories of ideal rationality. The ideal rational agent would follow one of them – almost certainly R_1, in my opinion. R_3 is a theory of bounded rationality for beings like us. It tells us to weight the theories of *ideal* rationality by the probabilities we assign to them. My arguments leading up to this section have all been addressed to ideal rationality. Only this section addresses bounded rationality. So it is consistent to hold that R_1 and R_3 are both correct in their own domains.[15]

Can the principle of EEU Maximization (R_3) be used to justify choosing one box in the *original* Newcomb scenario, with the $1,000 in box A? The answer depends on how convincing you find the arguments for causal decision theory, and how much more you value a million dollars than a thousand dollars. In principle, you could well be boundedly rational in choosing one box for this reason, even with a high confidence in causal decision theory. But the ideal rational agent would (very probably) take two.

References

Huemer, Michael. 2000. "Van Inwagen's Consequence Argument," *Philosophical Review* 109: 524–43.

---

[15] Of course, you might now wonder what you should do if you are uncertain even about the correct theory of *bounded* rationality, for instance, if you are uncertain as to whether R_3 is correct. But that question is too difficult and confusing to address here.

Lewis, David. 1979. "Prisoners' Dilemma Is a Newcomb Problem", *Philosophy & Public Affairs* 8: 235–40.

Nozick, Robert. 1969. "Newcomb's Problem and Two Principles of Choice", pp. 114–46 in Nicholas Rescher, ed., *Essays in Honor of Carl G. Hempel.* Dordrecht: D. Reidel.

Quinn, Warren S. 1990. "The Puzzle of the Self-Torturer", *Philosophical Studies: An International Journal for Philosophy in the Analytic Tradition* 59: 79–90.

Rachels, Stuart. 1998. "Counterexamples to the Transitivity of Better Than", *Australasian Journal of Philosophy* 76: 71–83.

Sainsbury, Richard M. 2009. *Paradoxes*, 3rd ed. Cambridge: Cambridge University Press.

Simon, Herbert A. 1955. "A Behavioral Model of Rational Choice", *Quarterly Journal of Economics* 69: 99–118.

Skyrms, Brian. 1982. "Causal Decision Theory", *Journal of Philosophy* 79: 695–711.

6

The Surprise Quiz

6.1 The Paradox

A professor announces to his class that there will be a surprise quiz next week.[1] And by a surprise quiz, he explains, he means one such that the students can't predict, prior to the time he actually gives it, that the quiz is coming on that day. "Thus," he urges, "you'd best study the material this weekend!" The class meets five days a week, Monday through Friday.

The students go home and try to deduce when the quiz will occur. "Suppose it comes on Friday," one student reasons. "Then we'd know by the end of Thursday's class that it was coming on Friday, since that would be the only day of the week left. So then it wouldn't be a surprise. So the quiz can't be on Friday."

"What about Thursday?" says another. "Since we've just eliminated Friday, that means that if it hasn't come by Wednesday evening, we'd

---

[1] This chapter's paradox goes back at least to O'Connor 1948. According to Rescher (2001, p. 112n19), the paradox was discussed by Quine in a paper circulated in the early 1940s and later published as Quine 1953, though the paradox's inventor is unknown (Quine does not claim the credit). Quine's version concerns a scheduled hanging, but I find the quiz version much nicer.

To forestall overly cute responses to the coming paradox, assume that the professor's announcement includes the information that there will be one *and only one* quiz that week.

© The Author(s) 2018
M. Huemer, *Paradox Lost*, https://doi.org/10.1007/978-3-319-90490-0_6

know it was coming on Thursday, and it wouldn't be a surprise. So it can't be on Thursday either."

By similar reasoning, they eliminate Wednesday, then Tuesday, then Monday. (After eliminating Tuesday, you might think they'd conclude that it must be on Monday. But if Monday is the only possible day, then it wouldn't be a surprise if it comes on Monday. So it can't be given on Monday either, for the same reason that eliminated every other day.) The students breathe a sigh of relief, knowing that the surprise quiz cannot be given at all. They spend the weekend partying and getting drunk instead of studying.

The next week, the professor gives a quiz on Wednesday. Everyone is surprised.

Now there are two problems here. First, the initial conclusion that a surprise quiz cannot be given (if pre-announced as above) is extremely implausible. Note that the reasoning could be extended to any number of days, so if a professor had said, at the beginning of the students' college careers, that they'd be given a surprise test at some time during the next *four years*, there would still, allegedly, be no day on which it could be given.

Second, we can derive contradictory conclusions, for if we accept the initial reasoning, the students should expect there to be no surprise quiz – which means that they will be surprised if it is given on any day. If the surprise quiz cannot be given on any day, then it can be given on any day.[2]

6.2 Rejecting the Assumptions

The reasoning of the paradox rests on the following assumptions about the students:

Credulity: The students believe without question everything the professor asserts (up until the end, when they conclude that the quiz can't be

---

[2] Scriven (1951, p. 403) makes this point.

given). Thus, when he says there will be exactly one test and it will be a surprise, they don't doubt this.

Perfect reasoning: The students believe all the logical consequences of their beliefs. Thus, they can be counted on to follow through the reasoning ascribed to them above, for any number of days.

Self-awareness: The students are fully aware of their own mental states and abilities. Thus, they *know* that they would follow through this reasoning, and thus that they would not be surprised, e.g., if the quiz were on Friday.

I'm sorry to report that these are not realistic assumptions for actual students. Many actual students, alas, fail to believe (or hear, or remember) many things I tell them, many fail to draw the logical consequences of their beliefs, and many are mistaken about their own abilities. Could this be the problem? Perhaps it *would* be impossible to surprise ideal (perfectly-reasoning, perfectly self-aware, credulous) students.[3] It remains the case that *actual* students can be, and often are, given surprise quizzes of just the sort described in the example, since they lack these cognitive perfections.

This is not a satisfactory response, for two reasons. First, it is highly implausible that one cannot give a surprise quiz to an ideal student no matter how many days one has to choose from. Imagine the class has 1,000 days, and the professor announces on the first day that a surprise quiz will occur on some day. He has his computer pick a random number. It picks 773, and he gives the quiz on that day. Could we really say it won't be a surprise?

Second, again, we can derive a contradiction. If the ideal student reasons to the conclusion that the surprise quiz cannot be given on any day, then the student will, after all, be surprised if it is given on any day. The reasoning defeats itself.

Perhaps the problem is that the assumptions of the paradox are not merely unrealistic but *contradictory*: a perfect reasoner cannot be perfectly credulous. Suppose the teacher announced: "Two and two are five."

---

[3] O'Connor (1948) takes this view; Cohen (1950) apparently concurs.

A credulous student would believe the announcement, but any perfect reasoner would reject it as necessarily false.[4]

This is true. But a relaxed version of the paradox could be constructed with weaker assumptions. Suppose the students are not *perfect* reasoners, but merely pretty good ones – good enough to follow the reasoning described in the paradox. They are not perfectly credulous either, so they are not unconditionally disposed to believe *everything* the professor says; they would not, for example, believe that two and two were five if the professor said so. They are, however, reasonably credulous: they are *prima facie* disposed to accept the professor's statements about the conduct of the class, unless and until they have good reasons for doubting those statements. This looks like enough to get the paradox going.

6.3 What Is Surprise?

Confusion often results from our thinking in terms of vague, qualitative categories instead of quantitative concepts. The paradoxical reasoning is conducted in terms of what the students believe or don't believe, and whether they are surprised or not surprised. But rather than simply believing or not believing a proposition, individuals may have varying *degrees of confidence* – otherwise known as "credences" or "subjective probabilities" – in a proposition. Bearing this in mind, what does it mean for a person to be "surprised" by an event? Here are three interpretations:

i)   You are surprised by an event when you previously had *zero* credence that it would occur. On this interpretation, no rational person should ever be surprised by anything, and certainly the students should not be surprised by a quiz, no matter when it occurs. For on every night, they should recognize at least some chance that there will be a quiz the next day.

ii) You are surprised by an event when you previously assigned it *less than 100%* credence. On this interpretation, every rational person

---

[4] Or perhaps they would both accept and reject it . . . and thereafter accept every proposition.

should be surprised by every contingent event. Certainly the students should be surprised by any quiz, whenever it might occur, for at no point could anyone be 100% certain that there will be a quiz. (The professor may have forgotten the quiz, changed his mind about it, gotten hit by a car on the way to campus, and so on.)

iii) You are surprised by an event when you previously considered it sufficiently unlikely, that is, your credence that it would occur fell below some threshold, t.

Interpretations (*i*) and (*ii*) are surely not what was intended by the original setup of the paradox. Let us therefore assume (*iii*).[5]

What is the "surprise threshold" (the credence level above which an event counts as non-surprising)? This is both vague and context-dependent. It is vague because no one has settled the precise meaning of "surprise" in English; thus, there are some probability levels such that, if an event with that subjective probability occurs, you will be *sort of* surprised and sort of not surprised.

It is context-dependent, because whether an event with subjective probability p is surprising may depend upon what sort of event it is, what the alternatives were, and even how much we care about it. If it is ten degrees warmer outside than the weather report predicted, I am surprised. But when I hear that some person unknown to me has won the lottery, I am not surprised, even though that win was much less likely than the unusually warm weather. (It was highly probable that *someone* would win, but not that *that specific* person would win.) But this context sensitivity does not matter for our purposes, because we can assume a constant context. We are only considering the surprisingness or unsurprisingness of a quiz occurring on a given day in the specified scenario – this should not give rise to changing thresholds.

For our purposes, it won't matter *where* the threshold is, only that there is some vague threshold in the present context, which is neither zero nor

---

[5] Some authors interpret surprise in terms of lack of *knowledge* or *justified belief* (O'Connor 1948; Levy 2009, pp. 136–7), rather than merely insufficient credence. *Pace* Levy, the assumption that the students are self-aware, good reasoners renders mention of justification superfluous – the students will have a high credence in p if and only if they are justified in having a high credence in p. Mention of knowledge is similarly unnecessary for understanding the paradox.

one. We shall also later consider the consequences of stipulating a perfectly precise threshold.

Now, on my view of vagueness defended in chapter 3, the vagueness of "surprise" means that predictions of "surprise" fail to express propositions; hence, the teacher's initial announcement, strictly speaking, lacks propositional content. This, however, is no obstacle to entertaining the rest of the paradox, nor is this vagueness the source of the paradox. The teacher's announcement has sufficient meaning to be aptly made, just as most statements of ordinary language do, and it can and should modify the students' mental states in a manner *similar* to how their mental states would be modified by a sentence with a determinate propositional content. We can aptly continue to use vague language in (approximately) describing these changes in the same manner that (as I contended in chapter 3) we aptly use vague language all the time in ordinary life.

6.4   Quiz Comes if and Only if Surprising

Let us revisit the possibility of a Friday quiz. If the quiz has not come by the end of class on Thursday, what should the students think? This depends on what they assume about the professor's intentions, which is not made clear by the initial scenario. They might assume.

i) The professor is committed to giving a quiz, whether or not it will be a surprise. (Assume they believe this with near-total certainty.)

ii) The professor is committed to giving a quiz if and only if it will be a surprise. If he can't make it a surprise, then he has no interest in giving it.[6]

Case (*i*) is easy: in this case, the students expect a quiz on Friday, which consequently will fail to surprise. Case (*ii*), however, generates a (sub-) paradox, which is the subject of the present section; for the rest of section 6.4, we shall assume (*ii*).

---

[6] Janaway (1989, p. 394), for example, reads the scenario according to (i). Wright and Sudbury (1977, pp. 53–5) in effect consider both ways of taking the scenario.

6.4.1 Self-Undermining Beliefs with a Vague Surprise Threshold

Come Thursday night, one student says, "Well, it looks like the quiz is coming tomorrow."

Another says, "But wait. Since you just predicted that, that means it won't be a surprise. Since he has no interest in giving a non-surprise quiz, the prof won't give a quiz at all."

A third replies, "But wait. Since you just predicted *no* quiz, that means that it *would* be a surprise if he gave one. Since he wants to give a surprise quiz, he probably will give it tomorrow."

A fourth replies, "But wait . . ."

This is a case of a self-undermining belief system. If the students think there will be a quiz, they can infer that there won't. But if they think there won't, they can infer that there will.[7] What can the students rationally do?

Answer: assign an intermediate degree of belief. Since "surprise" has a vague threshold, assign a degree of belief such that, if a quiz is given, it will be a borderline case of a surprise.

The idea is illustrated by figure 6.1. The vague surprise threshold is indicated by the fuzzy vertical region above "*t*" on the graph. The solid gray line represents possible credences that a student could assign, on Thursday night, to there being a quiz on Friday. If the student initially assigns a low credence, then they can infer that it should really be a high credence – hence, low values of *x* ("initial credence") map to high values of *y* ("inferred credence"). But if the student initially assigns a high credence, they can infer that it should be a low credence – hence, high *x*-values map to low *y*-values. This is just the puzzle described above, put in terms of credences rather than simple belief and non-belief.

The student reaches a stable credence only when "initial credence" equals "inferred credence" – meaning that the student must find a credence such that, if he assumes that credence initially, he can infer only that he should have that very credence, not one either higher or lower. (In mathematical terms, we are seeking a "fixed point", a point where $x = y$.) This happens in the region of the vague surprise threshold, because if he

---

[7] This aspect of the puzzle is discussed by Cave (2004) and Levy (2009, p. 147).

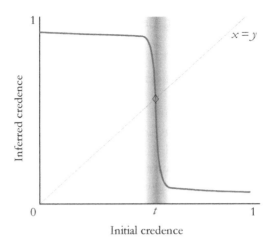

Fig. 6.1 Optimal credence with a vague surprise threshold

assigns a credence in that region, he will be uncertain whether the professor would consider the Friday quiz to be a surprise or not; hence, he will be unsure whether he can infer that the quiz would not be given. The stable credence is indicated by the small diamond in the middle of the graph.

6.4.2   Self-Undermining Beliefs with a Precise Threshold

Suppose we stipulate a perfectly precise surprise threshold. Say the professor specified that in his sense of the word, if your credence in some event is *exactly* 60% or below, then the event will count as "surprising" if it happens; if your credence is above 60%, the event will be unsurprising.

Now it appears that the proposal of section 6.4.1 fails. If the students assign a credence *at* the threshold (60%), then they know that the quiz, if it happens, will count as a surprise. Since the professor wants that, he will very probably give the quiz – with much more than 60% probability. So if your credence is 60%, it should be much more than 60%. There is no stable credence. In mathematical terminology, we've constructed a function with no fixed point (it does not cross the "$x = y$" line in figure 6.2).

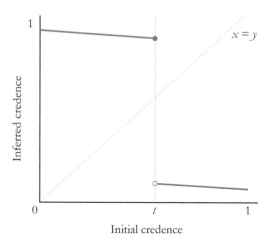

Fig. 6.2   Credences with a precise surprise threshold

Not so. In chapter 4 on the self-torturer paradox, we saw that it is not possible to discern the *precise* degree of intensity of a pain. That point generalizes to any continuously variable property of a mental state, since for any such property, a series of pairwise-indistinguishable but non-identical mental states can be constructed analogous to the pairwise-indistinguishable pains in the self-torturer example. In fact, I hold that it is impossible to know the precise value of *any* continuous variable whose value is metaphysically contingent. But for present purposes, let us just focus on mental states.

For example, imagine a series of one thousand cups of water, cup 1 through cup 1,000, each having a very slightly higher physical temperature than the last. You try feeling the water in each cup, in sequence. For any two adjacent cups, you can't tell which one feels warmer to you. But by the end, you can tell that cup 1,000 feels much warmer than cup 1. This shows that there can be temperature sensations so similar that one cannot introspectively distinguish them, even though one is in fact warmer-feeling than the other. And that means that one cannot introspectively identify the precise degree to which something feels warm or cold.

Or take a series of paintings, painting 1 through painting 1,000. For any two adjacent paintings, you cannot tell which gives you more aesthetic pleasure. But painting 1,000 is definitely much more aesthetically pleasing than painting 1. This shows that there can be differences in aesthetic pleasure too small to introspectively identify. Thus, you cannot identify the precise degree of aesthetic pleasure of an experience.

The same point holds for any continuously variable property of a mental state.

Thus, even if one had a credence of precisely 0.6 in some proposition, one could not know that this was the case. A credence of 0.6 would be introspectively indistinguishable from a credence of 0.600001 or 0.599999. Therefore, the students need only adopt a credence very close to 0.6 that a quiz will come on Friday, and they will be uncertain whether the quiz, if it comes, will count as a surprise or not. If rational, that is what they would do. The graph of figure 6.1 applies again, but this time, the fuzzy vertical region down the middle of the graph represents the region in which the students are unsure whether they have crossed the threshold, rather than the region in which it is vague whether they have crossed the threshold.

All of that is counterfactual reasoning about what would happen on Thursday night if a quiz hadn't been given so far. On Sunday night, the students conduct that reasoning and thus conclude that *if* the quiz were on Friday, it would be a borderline case of a surprise (if "surprise" is vague), or they would be uncertain whether it was a surprise (if "surprise" is precise). They are therefore uncertain, on Sunday, whether the quiz can be given on Friday.

6.4.3   The Rest of the Week

Consider next what happens if the quiz is left till Thursday. Suppose it is Wednesday night, and no quiz has so far occurred. What would the students think? They would think: "The quiz will occur on Thursday, or Friday, or there will be no quiz." Suppose they assign a very high credence to Thursday, clearly higher than the surprise threshold t. Then they realize that this means that it won't be a surprise on Thursday. Assuming again that the professor has no interest in a non-surprise quiz, they should lower their credence that it will come on Thursday. So the credence cannot be clearly above t.

What if they assign a low credence to Thursday, one clearly below the surprise threshold? Then they realize that this means that the quiz *would* be a surprise on Thursday. As discussed earlier, it is merely *unclear* whether it would be a surprise on Friday. So this is *some* reason for thinking that the professor would prefer Thursday over Friday, but it is not a *decisive* reason, since they are not sure the quiz couldn't be on Friday. It follows that at this point they should assign a higher credence to Thursday than to Friday. But nothing else follows – it does not, e.g., follow that they should assign a credence higher than *t*. So, unlike the case with a Friday quiz, we do not have a problem of self-undermining beliefs here. They can simply assign a probability to a Thursday quiz that is greater than the probability of a Friday quiz, but less than the surprise threshold. For instance, there would be nothing paradoxical if, on Wednesday night, they assign 50% credence to a quiz coming on Thursday, 45% to its coming on Friday, and 5% to there being no quiz. Then, if the quiz comes on Thursday, it will be surprising.

Things only get easier from there. On Tuesday night, if there has been no quiz, what do the students think? They again assign a lower probability to Friday than to Wednesday or Thursday, since they aren't sure a Friday quiz would count as a surprise. But they know a Thursday quiz would count as a surprise, so there is no need to assign a lower probability to Thursday than Wednesday. So they assign the same probability to Wednesday as to Thursday. If the quiz comes on Wednesday, then they are surprised (even more so than they would be by a Thursday quiz – that is, their credence will have been even farther below the threshold).

Similarly, there is no problem with a surprise quiz on Tuesday or Monday.

6.5   Quiz Comes, with or without Surprise

At the beginning of the last section, we said that the students' reasoning could be conducted on either of two assumptions:

i)   The professor is committed to giving a quiz, whether or not it will be a surprise.

ii)   The professor is committed to giving a quiz if and only if it will be a surprise.

For simplicity, we assume that one of these is held with near-total certainty. In section 6.4, we adopted assumption (*ii*). In this section, we shall adopt (*i*). Assume that the professor would *prefer* the quiz to be a surprise, though he would give it even if it weren't going to be a surprise, and the students know this.

6.5.1   No Friday Surprise

In this case, if Thursday night arrives and no quiz has been given, the students should adopt a very high credence that a quiz will come on Friday. Not 100%, because there is always a chance that the professor will have forgotten, changed his mind, gotten hit by a car, etc. But very high. They will also know that this quiz won't be a surprise.

They reason that through easily on Sunday night, so they know that if the quiz occurs on Friday, it won't be a surprise. Since they think the professor would prefer the quiz to be a surprise (though he does not care about this as much as he cares simply that there be a quiz), they infer that the quiz very probably will not be on Friday.

6.5.2   Borderline Thursday Surprise

Now suppose that no quiz has come by Wednesday night. What would the students think? A pair of students might have this dialogue:

Student A: He's giving the quiz Thursday or Friday. He prefers it to be a surprise, and it wouldn't be a surprise on Friday. So he'll probably give it Thursday.

Student B: Since you just made that prediction, it wouldn't be a surprise on Thursday either. So actually, it is no more likely to come Thursday than Friday.

A: Since you just made *that* prediction, it *would* be a surprise tomorrow. [Assume that the surprise threshold is more than 50%.] So he'll probably give it tomorrow.

B: Since you just made that prediction . . .

Again, we have a self-undermining belief system. If one initially assigns a high credence to a Thursday quiz, one can infer that it should really be a little below 50% (since Thursday and Friday are equally likely, and there is also a small chance of no quiz). But if one initially assigns a low credence (such that the quiz would be surprising), one can infer that it should really be a high credence. That is, if the credence is clearly above the threshold, it needs to be lowered, and if it is clearly below the threshold, it needs to be raised.

The solution is to assign a credence at about the threshold. As per sections 6.4.1–6.4.2 above, the result is that if the quiz occurred on Thursday, it would be a borderline case of a surprise, or the students would be uncertain whether it was a surprise.

6.5.3   The Rest of the Week

The reasoning for the rest of the week is parallel to that of section 6.4.3 above. If the quiz has not occurred by Tuesday night, the students would think: "If it occurs on Friday, it won't be a surprise. If it occurs on Thursday, it will be a borderline case, or we're not sure whether it will be a surprise." That is some reason, but not a conclusive reason, for thinking the professor would prefer Wednesday over Thursday. So the students assign a higher probability to Wednesday than Thursday, and a higher probability to Thursday than Friday.

But there is no need for the probability they assign to a Wednesday quiz to be near the surprise threshold. If P(Quiz on Wednesday) is less than t but greater than P(Quiz on Thursday), it doesn't follow that it should really be much higher, e.g., that it should be clearly above t. The consideration that if it comes on Wednesday then it will be a surprise does not, e.g., mean that it must be on Wednesday; there is still a chance it will be on Thursday, since the professor might consider that to be surprising enough. Thus, the quiz can be given on Wednesday and still be a surprise.

There is then no problem with a Tuesday or Monday quiz either.

6.6   Surprising as Not-Most-Expected

There is a version of the story where it would be impossible to give a surprise quiz. Suppose we define an "expected" event as one that was antecedently considered the most likely of the alternatives (for some natural classification of the relevant alternatives). Thus, the quiz will count as expected provided that, the night before it actually happens, the students consider the following day the most likely day for the quiz to occur. And suppose we define a "surprise" quiz as one that is not expected. That is, a quiz coming on day n will count as surprising if and only if, on the night of day $n - 1$, the students did *not* consider day n the most likely day for the quiz.

On this definition of "surprise quiz", the professor cannot follow through on his promise to give a surprise quiz. He cannot do it on Friday, since on Thursday night, trivially, the students would consider Friday the most likely day for the quiz, it being the only day left.

Since he clearly cannot do it on Friday, on Wednesday night, the students would consider it more likely that the quiz would come on Thursday than on Friday. True, this means the Thursday quiz would not be a surprise. But there is a nonzero chance that the professor would not have figured this out. It is easier to figure out that a Friday quiz wouldn't be a surprise than to figure out that a Thursday quiz would not be a surprise. So it is more likely that the professor would have failed to figure out that the Thursday quiz wouldn't be a surprise. So, as of Wednesday night, it would be more likely the quiz would occur on Thursday than on Friday.

Similarly, on Tuesday night, a Wednesday quiz is the most likely; on Monday night, a Tuesday quiz is most likely; and on Sunday night, a Monday quiz is most likely. That is, the students should always consider the next day to be the most likely. If it doesn't come on day n, they should update their beliefs to consider day $n+1$ to be the most likely.

So the professor can't give a surprise quiz. But this is not paradoxical. This is just a result of the peculiar definition of "surprise", under which an event can fail to be a surprise even though one assigned it a low absolute credence. It is still possible to give surprise quizzes in other, more ordinary senses.

References

Cave, Peter. 2004. "Reeling and A-Reasoning: Surprise Examinations and Newcomb's Tale", *Philosophy* 79: 609–16.

Cohen, Laurence Jonathan. 1950. "Mr. O'Connor's 'Pragmatic Paradoxes'", *Mind* 59: 85–7.

Janaway, Christopher. 1989. "Knowing About Surprises: A Supposed Antinomy Revisited", *Mind* 98: 391–409.

Levy, Ken. 2009. "The Solution to the Surprise Exam Paradox", *Southern Journal of Philosophy* 47: 131–58.

O'Connor, Daniel J. 1948. "Pragmatic Paradoxes", *Mind* 57: 358–9.

Quine, Willard van Orman. 1953. "On a So-Called Paradox", *Mind* 62: 65–7.

Rescher, Nicholas. 2001. *Paradoxes: Their Roots, Range, and Resolution.* Chicago, Ill.: Open Court.

Scriven, Michael. 1951. "Paradoxical Announcements", *Mind* 60: 403–7.

Wright, Crispin and Aidan Sudbury. 1977. "The Paradox of the Unexpected Examination", *Australasian Journal of Philosophy* 55: 41–58.

7

The Two Envelopes

7.1 The Paradox

A friendly experimenter has approached you and shown you two identical-looking envelopes, envelope A and envelope B.[1] All you know is that both contain money, and one of them contains twice as much as the other. (Let's say they contain checks, so you can't tell anything from the thickness.) The experimenter offers to give you one of them, whichever one you choose.

Let's say you choose envelope A. She hands it over. But just before you open it to see how much money you got, she says, "Before you open that, would you like to trade it for envelope B?"

Assume that the friendly experimenter has no particular agenda (she is not, for example, trying to get envelope A for herself because she knows what's in it). Her job is to go around offering these envelopes to people,

---

[1] This chapter's paradox derives from Kraitchik 1942, pp. 133–4. The original version concerned a pair of neckties: persons A and B each own a necktie; each knows the value of his own tie but not that of the other person. They have a chance to make a deal whereby a third party will judge the quality of the ties, and the person with the superior tie will have to give his tie to the other. Each reasons that he will either lose his tie, or gain a better tie (with equal probability?); since the potential gain is greater than the potential loss, the deal is to his advantage. Kraitchick then discusses a version involving sums of pennies.

and every time, no matter which envelope the person chooses, she is supposed to ask if they want to trade it for the other. (Why? I don't know;
maybe it's an experiment on the endowment effect.[2])

Should you trade your envelope for the other one? There are three possible answers: (*i*) "Yes, you should switch", (*ii*) "No, you should keep your
envelope", and (*iii*) "It doesn't matter; you should be indifferent between
switching and keeping."

Most people think the third answer is obviously correct. But here is an
argument for the first. The envelope in your hand contains some amount
of money. Call this amount a. The other envelope contains either $2a$ or
$a/2$. Each of those possibilities is equally likely, given your (lack of) information. So if you switch, there is a 50% probability that you will gain a
dollars, and a 50% probability that you will lose $a/2$ dollars. The amount
you stand to gain is twice as great as the amount you stand to lose. So it's
a good bet. Your expected profits from switching and from not switching
are as follows:

Switch envelopes: $(.5)(2a) + (.5)(a/2) = 1.25a$
Keep envelope A: a

$1.25a$ is greater than a, so you should switch.

After you do so, but before you open your new envelope, the experimenter offers you the chance to switch *back* to the original one. We can
construct a similar argument to show that you should switch back. Let b
be the amount of money you *now* have, the amount in envelope B. The
other envelope, which you originally chose, contains either $2b$ or $b/2$,
with equal probability. So your expected profits are as follows:

Switch back to A: $(.5)(2b) + (.5)(b/2) = 1.25b$
Keep envelope B: b

So switch back.

---

[2] This is the phenomenon where people value something more merely because they presently have
it (Thaler 1980, pp. 43–7).

Finally, we can construct an argument that it doesn't matter whether you switch. Let c be the total amount of money in the two envelopes. One of them contains $(1/3)c$ and the other contains $(2/3)c$. Given your (lack of) information, each envelope is equally likely to be the one containing $(1/3)c$. So, whichever envelope you presently have, your expected profits of switching and not switching are as follows:

Switch envelopes: $(.5)(2/3c) + (.5)(1/3c) = c/2$
Keep envelope: $(.5)(1/3c) + (.5)(2/3c) = c/2$

If you switch, you are equally likely to go from $1/3c$ to $2/3c$, or from $2/3c$ to $1/3c$. So it doesn't matter.

This last argument, intuitively, has the correct conclusion. But all three arguments seem parallel. How is it that the first two are wrong and the third correct?

7.2   The Use of Probability in the Paradox

7.2.1   An Objection

Some who hear the paradox think that the paradoxical reasoning misuses the notion of probability. In calculating the expected utility of switching envelopes, you are supposed to assign 50% probabilities each to the alternatives (*i*) that you would gain a dollars and (*ii*) that you would lose $a/2$ dollars. But one of these alternatives is, in an objective sense, not possible, because the amounts in the two envelopes have already been determined. If envelope B in fact has the greater amount, then there is no real chance of your losing money by switching; if envelope B in fact has the lesser amount, then there is no chance of your gaining money by switching. One of these alternatives is already determinately the case, and you have no chance of altering it. So there is something suspect about the 50% probabilities assigned to the two alternatives.

7.2.2 Three Interpretations of Probability

The above objection is not correct; the paradoxical reasoning does not misuse the concept of probability. To see this, let us first consider how probability can be understood. Several interpretations of probability appear in the literature; here are three prominent ones:

i. *Epistemic Probability:* The epistemic probability of a proposition for a particular person is the degree to which that person's evidence supports the proposition, or the degree of justification the person has for the proposition. A proposition with probability 1 is a proposition that one has conclusive justification for accepting; a proposition with probability 0 is a proposition that one has conclusive justification for rejecting. Note that epistemic probability is relative to an individual and depends on that individual's current information.
ii. *Subjective Probability (a.k.a. credence):* The subjective probability of a proposition for a particular person is the degree of confidence the person actually has in that proposition (whether or not this confidence is justified). A proposition with probability 1 is one of which the person is absolutely convinced. Subjective probability, like epistemic probability, is relative to an individual.
iii. *Propensity:* The propensity of an event is the degree to which the causally relevant factors have a tendency to produce that event. An event with probability 1 is one that must happen; it could not be avoided. Also, if an event has already occurred, its propensity is 1, since it cannot be altered. Note that propensities are objective and not relative to individuals. An event has a particular propensity independent of what we believe or know and independent of whether there are any people around at all.

These are commonly accepted as three distinct, legitimate senses of "probability". (It does not matter which of these, if any, best matches the meaning of "probability" in English. We are not here to debate semantic questions.)

7.2.3   Rational Choice Uses Epistemic Probabilities

In rational choice theory, it is commonly held that the rational choice is the one that maximizes the agent's expected utility, where the expected utility of an action is calculated by adding up, for every possible result of the action, the *probability* that the result would occur if one performed the action times the value to the agent of that result.

What is the correct interpretation of probability here? By that, I mean: what is the interpretation that makes Expected Utility Maximization a correct principle of rational choice?

The answer is either epistemic or subjective probability (but only, I think, if your subjective probabilities are rational, in which case they are hard to distinguish from epistemic probabilities). The answer is not propensity.

Why not propensity? Consider what I shall call the Simple Envelope Case. In this case, you are presented with two indistinguishable envelopes, with only the information that one contains $2 and the other $4. (Assume that you care only about money, and you value $4 twice as much as $2.) This time, there is no question about switching. The question is simply: which envelope should you take? There are three answers: (*i*) you should take the one on the left, (*ii*) you should take the one on the right, (*iii*) it doesn't matter; you should be indifferent between the two envelopes.

The correct answer is of course (*iii*). How could that answer come out of an expected utility calculation? Here is how: since we have no evidence favoring either envelope to be the one containing the $4, each envelope has a 50% epistemic probability of containing $2, and a 50% probability of containing $4. So the expected value of the envelope on the left is (.5)($2) + (.5)($4) = $3; similarly, the expected value of the envelope on the right is $3.

But in this case, just as in the original two-envelope case in section 7.1, the amounts in the envelopes have already been determined. So one of the envelopes has a 100% *propensity* to contain the $2, and the other has a 100% propensity to contain the $4. Neither has any 50% propensity. So, if decision theory used propensities rather than epistemic probabilities, then the above argument would be an error, and the two envelopes would *not* have the same expected value.

7.2.4   Probabilities in Causal Decision Theory

In our discussion of Newcomb's Paradox in chapter 5, we learned that the correct interpretation of the probabilities in expected utility calculations is the interpretation offered by causal decision theory, rather than evidential decision theory. This is because rational agents seek to cause good outcomes, not merely to have evidence of good outcomes.

You might think this conflicts with the conclusion of section 7.2.3. Doesn't causal decision theory hold that we must use causal probabilities rather than evidential probabilities? And doesn't that mean that we should *not* use epistemic probabilities as I just claimed?

No, it doesn't. Despite the name, the probabilities used in causal decision theory are still epistemic or subjective. They are not propensities, frequencies, or any other sort of physical probabilities. What is "causal" about causal decision theory is not the type of probabilities that are used, but what the probabilities are applied *to*. In one version of causal decision theory (which we have not discussed), the probabilities are applied to subjunctive conditionals. In my version of causal decision theory, from section 5.3.2, the expected utility of an action is defined as follows:

$$\mathrm{EU}(A) = \sum_i \mathrm{V}(O_i) \cdot \mathrm{P}(O_i | A)$$

where the O_i are the possible outcomes of your action, $\mathrm{V}(O_i)$ is the value you receive if outcome O_i occurs, and $\mathrm{P}(O_i|A)$ is the probability of O_i occurring if you do A. That conditional probability, in turn, is calculated as follows:

$$\mathrm{P}(O_i | A) = \sum_j \mathrm{P}(O_i | A, W_j) \cdot \mathrm{P}(W_j)$$

where the W_j are the possible ways the unalterable world might be (the sets of circumstances that you cannot affect). The notion of causation comes in in identifying those circumstances. It does not enter into the interpretation of probability. All of the probabilities in the above two equations are epistemic probabilities.

The reason for this is that an agent cannot rationally be criticized for what the *actual effects* of their actions are or would have been per se; they can only be rationally criticized for what they *had reason to believe* about what those effects would be. Hence, in decision theory, causation should only enter into the contents of the propositions to which one assigns epistemic probabilities.

7.3   The Use of Variables in the Paradox

The expected utility calculation for switching envelopes,

$$EU(\text{switch}) = (.5)(2a) + (.5)(a/2) = 1.25a$$

appears confused. The expected utility of a particular action is a specific quantity. "*a*" is a *variable*, not the name of a specific quantity; hence, "$1.25a$" does not name a possible value for the expected utility of anything.

The actual expected utility of switching (more precisely, the expected monetary payout, which we're using as a proxy for utility) would be calculated by adding up, for each possible dollar value that one might get, the probability of getting that amount multiplied by the amount. In this calculation, one must plug in the specific dollar amounts, $1, $2, and so on.

You might object: "But *a is* a specific quantity. By stipulation, it is the amount of money in envelope A, whatever that is. This amount is *unknown*, but that does not prevent it from being a specific amount."

Okay. But the argument claims that the expected dollar payout of keeping your own envelope is *a*, and that of the other envelope, $1.25a$. So now the claim is that the *expected* dollar amount in your envelope is equal to the amount that is *actually* in the envelope, *whatever that is*. For example, if (unbeknownst to you) there is actually $1 in your envelope, then the expected payout of your envelope is $1; if there is actually (unbeknownst to you) $100 in it, then the expected payout is $100.

This is false. The expected value of a variable, by definition, is determined by the information you have available to you (more specifically, by your epistemic probabilities); it is not determined by whatever is the *actual* value of the variable.

Assume for simplicity that the envelopes must contain integer dollar values. Then the expected amount of money in envelope A is:

$$\$1{\cdot}P(A_1) + \$2{\cdot}P(A_2) + \$3{\cdot}P(A_3) + \ldots$$

where $P(A_1)$ is the probability that envelope A contains $1, $P(A_2)$ is the probability that it contains $2, and so on. The value of this sum depends on your probability distribution, but it is very unlikely to equal the actual amount that is in the envelope; indeed, it is unlikely even to be one of the possible amounts.

Consider this analogy: the average number of children for an American family is 1.87. So if you pick a random American family, 1.87 is the *expected value* of the variable "number of children in the family". But that is never the *actual* value – no family has 1.87 children. Similarly, the expected monetary value of envelope A is (almost certainly) not its actual value.

On this diagnosis, the argument for switching given in section 7.1 is badly confused. So is the argument for keeping your envelope, and *so is the argument that it doesn't matter*. The argument that it doesn't matter gets the correct conclusion, but it does so by means of the same conceptual confusion as the other two arguments.

So what is the correct analysis?

7.4   The Correct Analysis

Again, assume for simplicity that the envelopes must contain integer dollar amounts. The expected utility calculation for an action starts by listing the possible ways that the unalterable world might be, that is, the circumstances that are beyond your control. One assigns a probability to each of these circumstances. Then, for each of these circumstances, one assesses how much benefit one would gain if that circumstance obtains and one performs the action in question. In the case of switching or keeping one's original envelope, then, one could make the following table[3]:

---

[3] Cf. Clark's (2002, p. 204) parallel table and analysis.

Possible Circumstance	Probability	Payout if you keep	Payout if you switch
A contains $1, B contains $2	p_1	$1	$2
B contains $1, A contains $2	p_2	$2	$1
A: $2, B: $4	p_3	$2	$4
B: $2, A: $4	p_4	$4	$2
A: $3, B: $6	p_5	$3	$6
B: $3, A: $6	p_6	$6	$3
⋮	⋮	⋮	⋮

I have left the probabilities as "p_1", "p_2", and so on, because I don't know what these probabilities should be. They have to be some series of numbers for which the (infinite) sum is 1. Fortunately, we won't need the exact numbers. Here is the important point: The first circumstance in the table ("A contains $1, B contains $2") is identical to the second ("B contains $1, A contains $2"), except that A and B have been switched. But the two envelopes are indistinguishable, and you have no different information about the one than about the other. It seems that you should assign the same probabilities to any two circumstances that differ only in that "A" and "B" have been interchanged. So you should assign probabilities such that $p_1=p_2$, $p_3=p_4$, $p_5=p_6$, and so on. Note: you should *not* assign $p_1=p_3$, $p_3=p_5$, and so on. Circumstances involving different total amounts of money do not have the same probabilities; larger amounts are generally less likely to be in the envelopes than smaller amounts (for example, it is highly unlikely that someone is going to give you a check for $1 billion).

The expected utilities of switching and of keeping your envelope are calculated as follows, based on the above table:

EU(keep)   = $(p_1)($1) + (p_2)($2) + (p_3)($2) + (p_4)($4) + \ldots$
EU(switch) = $(p_1)($2) + (p_2)($1) + (p_3)($4) + (p_4)($2) + \ldots$

Since $p_1=p_2$, and $p_3=p_4$, and so on, this reduces to:

EU(keep)   = $(p_1)($1) + (p_1)($2) + (p_3)($2) + (p_3)($4) + \ldots$
EU(switch) = $(p_1)($2) + (p_1)($1) + (p_3)($4) + (p_3)($2) + \ldots$

The expressions on the right hand sides of those two equations are identical, only with the terms slightly rearranged.[4] So the expected value of switching and of keeping your envelope are the same. So it doesn't matter if you switch.

Now you might ask: don't the above equations commit the putative error mentioned at the start of section 7.3, that of using variables in place of numbers? "p_1", "p_3", and so on, are variables, not names of specific quantities. Therefore, the right hand sides of the above equations are not possible expected values.

In reply: Yes, these are variables rather than specific values, but no, that isn't a problem. Granted, the above equations don't tell us what the expected values are, unless and until we figure out what p_1, p_3, and so on are, plug those in, and then do the calculations. But this is okay. We didn't need to know what the expected values are of switching and of keeping your envelope. All we wanted to know was: which has more expected value? No matter what values you plug in for p_1, p_3, and so on, the above two sums will be equal to each other. Different people can reasonably use different probabilities, depending on how generous they think the experimenter might be. All will still agree that it doesn't matter whether you switch envelopes.

References

Clark, Michael. 2002. *Paradoxes from A to Z*. London: Routledge.
Kraitchik, Maurice. 1942. *Mathematical Recreations*. New York: W.W. Norton.
Thaler, Richard. 1980. "Toward a Positive Theory of Consumer Choice", *Journal of Economic Behavior and Organization* 1: 39–60.

---

[4] Rearrangement can sometimes make a difference in infinite sums. However, in this case, assuming that the probabilities sum to 1, the two infinite sums on the right hand sides will come to the same amount.

Part III

Paradoxes of Probability

8

The Principle of Indifference

8.1 The Principle of Indifference

The Principle of Indifference is a principle about how to assign probabilities to propositions in the absence of evidence:

Principle of Indifference: If there is no reason to favor one alternative over another, then the two are equally likely.

Thus, if we have n alternatives, with no reason to prefer any alternative over any other, each alternative has probability $1/n$. This is meant to apply to *epistemic* probability, which is a measure of the degree of justification or evidential support a proposition has. (Of course it does not apply to other kinds of probability.)

What if we have a variable with a continuum of possible values, and no information except that its value falls within certain boundaries? A natural extension of the above formulation is to say that in this case, equal-sized ranges (within the given boundaries) are equally likely to contain the variable's true value; in technical terms, the probability density should be uniform. For instance, if you know that X takes some real-number value between 1 and 4, then the probability of its falling between 1 and 2

© The Author(s) 2018
M. Huemer, *Paradox Lost*, https://doi.org/10.1007/978-3-319-90490-0_8

is ⅓ (2 minus 1, divided by 4 minus 1). I shall take this also to be part of the Principle of Indifference.[1]

There are some cases that can't be covered by the Principle of Indifference, such as those where there are infinitely many possible discrete values, or a continuous variable with no limits on its value. In these cases, assigning equal probabilities to all alternatives, or to equal-sized ranges, results in the total probability being either 0 (if all the assigned probabilities are zero) or infinity (if the probabilities are nonzero). We won't talk about such cases, as I don't have a solution for how to assign probabilities in such cases. But we will have plenty of paradox to worry about even without these cases.

8.2   The Paradoxes of the Principle of Indifference

8.2.1   The Colored Book

A new book by your favorite author has just been published. So far, all you know about the cover design is that the cover is either red or green or blue. Given just this information, what is the probability that the book is blue?[2]

Here are two attempts to solve the problem using the Principle of Indifference.

Solution 1:   The book is red, green, or blue. With no information to favor any of these alternatives over any other, each has probability ⅓ .

---

[1] This might be entailed by the original formulation, because for any pair of equal-sized intervals, we would have no reason to think the true value more likely to fall into one interval than the other. (For *different*-sized intervals, we *have* a reason to think one is more likely to contain the true value – namely, that it's larger.) So equal-sized intervals must in general contain equal probability, so the probability density must be uniform.

[2] This example is from Keynes 1921, p. 43. Keynes' intention, however, is not to refute the Principle of Indifference but to refine it (pp. 55–64).

Solution 2:   The book is either red or not red. With no reason to favor either of these alternatives over the other, each has probability ½. Similarly, it is either green or not green, each with probability ½; and blue or not blue, each with probability ½. But then the probability of its being red, green, or blue is ½ + ½ + ½ = 1½, which is impossible.

8.2.2   France and England

Suppose you know nothing about France, England, and the U.K., other than that all three are places, and England is a proper part of the U.K. (So you are even more geographically challenged than the average American high school student.) On this information, what is the probability that England is larger than France?[3] You have no information suggesting which region is more likely to be the larger, so the probability is ½ that England is larger, and ½ that France is larger. (We assume that no two territories are exactly the same size.)

Now, what is the probability, on the same information, that the U.K. is larger than France? Again, with no reason to favor "the U.K. is larger than France" over "France is larger than the U.K." or vice versa, both of these alternatives have probability ½.

But this cannot be. Since you know the U.K. contains England as a proper part, the U.K. has to be bigger than England. Since you know for sure that the U.K. is larger than England, the U.K. has to be more likely than England is to be larger than France.

8.2.3   The Car Ride

Sue has taken a car ride of 100 miles. It took her between one and two hours; equivalently, her (average) velocity was between 50 and 100 miles per hour. This is all you know. Based on this information, what is the probability that her trip lasted between an hour and an hour and a half?[4]

---

[3] From Keynes 1921, p. 44.
[4] From Fumerton 1995, p. 215.

Solution 1:   The range of possible times is from 1 to 2 hours. So the probability of the actual time falling between 1 and 1½ hours is (1½ − 1)/(2 − 1) = ½.

Solution 2:   If Sue's trip took 1 hour, then her (average) velocity was 100 miles per hour. If her trip took 1½ hours, then her velocity was 100/1½ = 66 ⅔ miles per hour. So the trip was between 1 hour and 1½ hours if and only if her speed was between 66 ⅔ mph and 100 mph. The total range of possible speeds was 50 mph to 100 mph. So the probability that her speed was between 66 ⅔ and 100 is (100 − 66 ⅔)/(100 − 50) = ⅔.

And the only problem here is that one half does not equal two thirds.

The above calculations are both mathematically correct. If you phrase the problem in terms of possible times, you get a different answer than if you phrase it in terms of possible velocities. Given a velocity, you can calculate the corresponding time, and vice versa, but the relationship between the two is nonlinear. Thus, a given range of possible times correlates to a different-sized range of possible velocities, as illustrated in figure 8.1. This kind of problem recurs in the next two examples.

Range of Possibilities

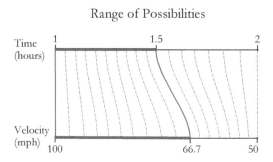

Fig. 8.1 Mapping between time and velocity

8.2.4   The Cube Factory

There is a factory in Princeton that produces cubes, for some unknown reason. All you know about their size is that they are at most 2 inches wide. Equivalently, they are at most 8 cubic inches in volume. Given just this information, what is the probability that the cubes are between 0 and 1 inch wide (equivalently, between 0 and 1 cubic inch in volume)?[5]

Solution 1:   We are given that the width is between 0 and 2. Thus, the probability of its falling between 0 and 1 is $(1 - 0)/(2 - 0)$ = ½.

Solution 2:   The width is between 0 and 1 if and only if the volume is between 0 and 1. We are given that the volume is between 0 and 8. The probability of its falling between 0 and 1 is thus $(1 - 0)/(8 - 0)$ = ⅛.

Again, we get different answers depending on what variable we describe the problem in terms of – in this case, width or volume.

8.2.5   The Circle and Chord

There is a circle with an equilateral triangle inscribed in it (figure 8.2). Someone has chosen a chord of the circle at random. What is the probability that this chord is longer than a side of the triangle?

Solution 1:   Rotate the inscribed triangle so that one of its sides is parallel to the chosen chord. Now imagine a radius of the circle drawn perpendicular to the chosen chord, as in figure 8.2a. The chord intersects the radius at some distance from the center of the circle. If that distance is less than half the radius, then the chord is longer than the side of the triangle. If it is more than half the radius, then the chord is shorter than the side of the triangle. (This can be proven

---

[5] From van Fraassen 1989, p. 303.

(a)

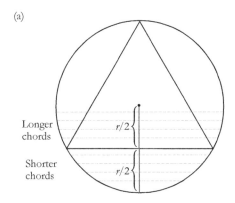

(b)

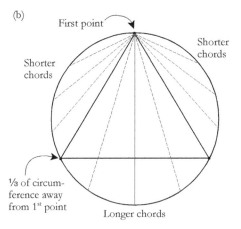

(c)

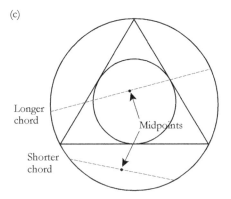

Fig. 8.2 Bertrand's Paradox: (a) solution 1, (b) solution 2, (c) solution 3

geometrically and is apparent from the diagram.) With no reason to favor either of these alternatives over the other, we give equal probability to each. So the probability of the chord being longer than a side of the triangle is ½.

Solution 2:   The chord has two endpoints. Take either endpoint, and rotate the triangle so that the endpoint coincides with a vertex of the triangle, as in figure 8.2b. The other endpoint is some distance away along the circumference of the circle. If that distance is *less* than a third of the circumference, in either direction, then the chord is shorter than a side of the triangle. This is true of two thirds of the points on the circumference. If the distance is *more* than a third of the circumference away, then the chord is longer. This is true of one third of the points on the circumference. So the probability of the chord being longer than a side of the triangle is ⅓.

Solution 3:   Imagine a circle inscribed within the equilateral triangle, as in figure 8.2c. The midpoint of the chosen chord is either inside this smaller circle or outside it. If the midpoint is inside the smaller circle, then the chord is longer than a side of the triangle. If the midpoint is outside the smaller circle, then the chord is shorter than a side of the triangle. The smaller circle has one quarter of the area of the larger circle; therefore, the chord's midpoint has probability ¼ of falling within the smaller circle. So the probability of the chord being longer than a side of the triangle is ¼.

This last problem is known as Bertrand's Paradox, after Joseph Bertrand, who introduced it in 1889.[6] I have left it till last since it is more complicated than the others, but it is the same sort of problem.

All of these problems, from the colored book through the circle and chord, follow a common pattern. They all derive contradictory results by applying the Principle of Indifference to different ways of describing the same problem. In the case of discrete alternatives, there are different ways

---

[6] Bertrand 1889, pp. 4–5.

of dividing up the space of possibilities. In the case of continuous alternatives, there are different variables in terms of which the possibilities can be described.

8.3   Wherefore Indifference?

8.3.1   Theories Rejecting the PI

Probably the dominant response to the paradoxes of the Principle of Indifference is to declare the Principle false. It is said that the above examples show the Principle to be inconsistent.[7]

How, then, should we answer the questions about the colored book, France and England, and so on? It is usually said that these questions, as posed, have no determinate answers. For instance, with no information other than that a book is red, blue, or green, one simply cannot calculate a probability that the book is blue. Some would say that we always need empirical information to assign probabilities – for instance, statistics on how often publishers produce blue books, or at least some experience with book covers and their appearances. This I call the Empiricist view.[8]

Others say that, in the absence of evidence, it is permissible to assign *any* probability to the book's being blue, as long as all of one's probabilities cohere with each other. This is the Subjectivist view.[9] Both Empiricism and Subjectivism about probability are popular views, and both reject the Principle of Indifference.

We should distinguish *qualification* from wholesale *rejection* of a principle. If we wish to qualify the Principle of Indifference, we might hold that the principle applies only in a certain range of cases, or that it requires additional principles, for example, governing how one should partition the space of possibilities.

---

[7] van Fraassen 1989, ch. 12; Howson and Urbach 1993, pp. 59–62; Shackel 2007.

[8] See Reichenbach 1938, pp. 340, 348–57 (defending the "straight rule", according to which the probability of A occurring in circumstances C = the number of observed occurrences of A divided by the number of observed occurrences of C); van Fraassen 1989, ch. 12.

[9] de Finetti [1937] 1964; Howson and Urbach 1993.

To reject the principle wholesale, on the other hand, would be to say that there is nothing at all to it – that in no case is it correct that two alternatives must be assigned equal probability due to a lack of information favoring either over the other. Empiricists and Subjectivists reject the Principle of Indifference in opposite ways: Empiricists think that in the absence of relevant evidence, one cannot assign any probabilities; Subjectivists think that in the absence of relevant evidence, one may assign any coherent probabilities one likes. The Principle of Indifference, by contrast, counsels adopting a specific probability distribution for such cases.

Following are some reasons why a wholesale rejection of the PI is unsatisfactory.

8.3.2 The PI Is Intuitive

First, there is something extremely intuitive about the Principle of Indifference. So much so that in probability problems, it is generally not necessary even to state the Principle; one can simply presuppose it, and most audiences see nothing controversial. Take the Simple Envelope problem from chapter 7: you are to choose between two indistinguishable envelopes, one of which contains $2 and the other of which contains $4. You have no information about which is which. Which one should you choose?

The standard answer: it doesn't matter, since each is equally likely to contain the larger amount. This turns on the Principle of Indifference. Those who reject the Principle must therefore say that this answer is not correct. Empiricists must hold that we cannot say whether the two envelopes are equally likely to contain the larger amount until we have some experience with envelopes like these. This doesn't mean that one should be indifferent between the two – it means that we can't assign expected utilities to the two options, so we can't say anything at all about whether one envelope should be preferred over the other, and if so, which one.

Subjectivists must say that one can rationally assign any probability to either envelope containing the larger amount, provided one is consistent. So a person could decide, for no reason, that the envelope on the left was 99% certain to contain the $4 – and there would be nothing unreasonable about this.

Neither of these views seem correct. It seems that the correct probabilities in the scenario are 50/50. There are many similar cases in which all people uncorrupted by philosophy share the intuition that a set of alternatives are equally likely, where the best explanation for this is something like the Principle of Indifference.

8.3.3   The PI Is an Analytic Truth

The Principle of Indifference also has a straightforward rationale based on the meaning of "epistemic probability". The epistemic probability of a proposition for a person, by definition, is a matter of how strongly their evidence supports or undermines that proposition.[10] If one's evidence does not favor either of two alternatives over the other, then it supports the two alternatives to the same degree; hence, they have the same epistemic probability. Note that "supporting to the same degree" is compatible with "not supporting at all". Compare: if I donated to neither Oxfam nor UNICEF last year, then I "gave the same amount" to both charities, namely, zero.

This last analogy might seem to suggest that if one has no evidence for A, then the epistemic probability of A must be zero. This is mistaken, simply because the probability scale, by convention, includes degrees of counter-support as well as positive support; hence, "P(A) = 0" means that one's evidence conclusively refutes A, not that it merely fails to support A.[11] What probability, then, indicates that A is neither supported nor undermined by one's evidence? The answer can only be: $1/n$, where n is the number of alternative possibilities.

How could one avoid this argument?

(i) One might try a different definition of epistemic probability. One might say: "The epistemic probability of A is the degree of justification you have for A" or "The epistemic probability of A is the credence that an ideally rational agent would have in A." But the

---

[10] Taking evidence broadly, to include everything that might serve as a source of epistemic justification for or against a proposition.

[11] Exception: if A has probability zero simply because A is one of a continuous infinity of possibilities, this does not mean that one's evidence refutes A.

argument for the PI succeeds on these formulations too, and on any formulation in the vicinity: if there is no reason at all for preferring one alternative over another, it is hard to see how one could have a higher degree of justification than the other, nor yet how an ideally rational agent would have more credence in one than in another. So how could one have higher probability than the other?

(ii) Perhaps the critics of the Principle of Indifference would reject the notion of epistemic probability altogether. This is highly undesirable theoretically, as there are many contexts in which epistemic probability appears to be in play. How can we understand expected utility in decision theory, without epistemic probability? How could we understand such statements as "The theory of evolution is *almost certainly* true" without epistemic probability?

(iii) Perhaps we could accept the general notion of epistemic probability, but claim that epistemic probabilities are indeterminate when one lacks relevant evidence; a proposition can only have a determinate epistemic probability in the light of some evidence that supports or undermines it. This does not accommodate intuitions about cases such as the Simple Envelope problem, where we lack evidence about the alternatives; it is, however, meant to accommodate such judgments as "The theory of evolution is almost certainly true."

I maintain, however, that it does not accommodate even those cases. I have discussed this elsewhere, so I will be very brief here.[12] Our best account of how evidence renders a conclusion probable or improbable relies on the conclusion's having an initial probability. According to Bayes' Theorem, the probability of a hypothesis, *h*, in the light of some evidence, *e*, is given by:

$$P(h|e) = \frac{P(h) \cdot P(e|h)}{P(e)}$$

where P(*h*) is the *initial* probability of *h*, P(*e*) the initial probability of *e*, and P(*e*|*h*) the likelihood that *e* would hold if *h* were true. So if P(*h*) is

---

[12] See Huemer 2017; 2009, pp. 27–9.

indeterminate, then P($h|e$) is also indeterminate. Thus, if nothing has a probability prior to empirical evidence, then nothing has a probability in the light of empirical evidence either.

8.3.4   The PI Underlies the Least Controversial Probability Assessments

Here is a common mistaken thought: There are more and less controversial ways of assigning probabilities. Applying the Principle of Indifference is one of the most controversial and least reliable ways. More reliable ways rely on randomization techniques or inductive evidence.[13]

This is mistaken because the least controversial, most reliable ways of assigning probabilities are themselves based on the Principle of Indifference. We simply tend to overlook this fact because we instinctively presuppose the PI in probabilistic reasoning.

If you draw a card from a normal deck, what is the probability that the card will be an ace? Answer: There are 52 cards, including 4 aces; therefore, the probability is 4/52. This is not an arcane philosophical hypothesis; this is as banal and uncontroversial a probability assessment as one can find. But this answer rests on the assumption that each of the 52 cards is equally likely to be the one drawn. This, in turn, rests on the absence of evidence favoring any card over any of the others.

Reply: "No, no, it rests on the assumption that the deck is *shuffled* before the drawing, which randomizes the cards' order. If you don't shuffle the deck, then you can't say anything about the probability of drawing an ace."

Counter-reply: That reasoning also presupposes the Principle of Indifference. There are many possible precise sequences of movements that would count as shuffling a deck of cards. If you reproduce *precisely* the same deck-shuffling movements a million times, starting from a deck in precisely the same initial state, you will get the same sequence of cards

---

[13] See, for example, Rawls 1999, pp. 145–50, explaining why the parties in his original position thought experiment allegedly cannot rationally rely on the Principle of Indifference (which Rawls refers to as "the principle of insufficient reason") when making decisions.

in the shuffled deck every time. (There is no intervention of quantum mechanical randomness at the level of playing cards!) The reason we consider shuffling to "randomize" the order of cards is that human beings never in fact reproduce precisely the same movements when they shuffle decks, and we never in fact know enough about a particular deck-shuffling to be able to predict the order of the cards. Nevertheless, given the precise way that you shuffled the deck, and the precise initial state that it was in, the resulting sequence of cards is uniquely determined.

So in what sense is it true that, say, the ace of spaces has a 1/52 probability of winding up on top? The answer is that, of all the possible ways of shuffling the deck, about 1.92% of them (1/52) result in the ace of spades being on top, and the same goes for each other card . . . and we *have no reason to think* that the actual deck-shuffling you did was any more or less likely to fall into *that* class of possible ways of shuffling than into any of the other classes that also contain 1.92% of the possible ways of shuffling a deck. In other words, given ignorance of the precise details of the deck-shuffling, we apply a uniform probability distribution over possible ways of shuffling the deck.

A similar point applies to all other uncontroversial probability assignments. Suppose I want to know what proportion of philosophers are Platonists. I take a random sample of 400 philosophers and ask them how they feel about the Forms. 20% of the sample think Platonism is true. Though the sample was only a small fraction of the total population of philosophers, I infer that about 20% of philosophers are Platonists. Why?

Let's say there are a total of 10,000 philosophers in the world. There are many possible ways of choosing a sample of 400 philosophers out of 10,000. (How many? There is a formula for that; the answer is 10,000!/(400!)(9,600!).) Of these ways, the overwhelming majority constitute representative samples, in the sense that the proportion of Platonists in the sample would be close to the proportion in the general population – this fact is provable within combinatorics, and it holds regardless of the proportion of Platonists in the population. If we *assign equal probability* to each of the possible ways of choosing the sample, then we can infer that it is highly probable that our sample is representative.[14] That equal-probability assignment rests on the Principle of Indifference.

If you are tempted to say that the equal probability assignment instead rests on the fact that our sampling technique randomizes the selection of survey respondents, recall the above point about shuffling cards. Given the *full, precise details* of how survey respondents were selected, and the initial conditions of the world, the actual selection was fully determined. The sampling technique only "randomizes" in the sense that it makes the results fully *unpredictable* to us – that is, it prevents us from having any reason to think Platonist philosophers more likely than any other, equal-sized group of philosophers to get the survey.

That is what all "randomization" techniques do (unless you have access to some quantum mechanical device). So all probability assessments that rely on an assumption of randomization – which includes all those that are considered the most reliable and least controversial – rest on the Principle of Indifference.

8.4   Interpreting the Principle of Indifference: The Explanatory Priority Proviso

Not everything in the world is equally fundamental; some things are explained by other things. The things that do the explaining are more fundamental than, or *explanatorily prior* to, the things that get explained. Some examples:

(i) The properties and relations of an object's parts generally explain the features of the whole. The table is solid *because* its molecules have a stable configuration with relatively fixed distances from each other,

---

[14] This is not quite correct: since we know who the members of our sample are, we needn't assign probabilities to different hypotheses about who they are. The correct statement is too complicated for the main text: let *n* be some particular possible number of Platonists that the population might have. Consider each possible way of distributing *n* instances of "being a Platonist" across the 10,000 members of the population. Assign equal probability to each of those. It will turn out that most of those ways would result in our sample of 400 being roughly representative. This will turn out to be true for each *n* between 0 and 10,000. Thus, the prior probability of our sample being roughly representative is high, no matter what probability distribution we give to *n*. This is essentially the basis for David Stove's (1986, pp. 55–75) probabilistic defense of induction, though Stove does not bring out the dependence on the Principle of Indifference explicitly.

not vice versa. (Note: explanatory priority is a necessary but not a sufficient condition for explanation. Microscopic features in general, including those that are not relevant to explaining solidity, are prior to such macroscopic features as solidity.)

(ii) Earlier events explain later events, and causes explain their effects. The Treaty of Versailles helps to explain World War II, whereas World War II could play no role in explaining Versailles, since World War II hadn't yet happened at the time the Versailles Treaty was signed.

(iii) General facts are explained by the more specific facts that make them true. An apple is colorful in virtue of being red, not vice versa. Michael Jordan is tall in virtue of being six feet six inches, not vice versa.

This relation of explanatory priority must be taken account of in assigning probabilities: if one set of possible facts is explanatorily prior to another, then the *initial* probabilities we assign to the more fundamental possibilities must constrain the probabilities of the less fundamental possibilities, not vice versa. Given two variables, X and Y, if X explains Y, then the initial probability distribution for Y must be derived from that for X (or something even more fundamental). Here, by "initial probabilities", I mean probabilities prior to relevant evidence. Thus, if we are applying the Principle of Indifference, we should apply it at the more fundamental level. I call this the Explanatory Priority Proviso to the Principle of Indifference.[15] This will prove key to resolving the paradoxes of section 8.2.

8.5   Solutions

8.5.1   The Colored Book

The paradoxical reasoning claims that the book has an equal chance of being red or non-red, an equal chance of being green or non-green, and an equal chance of being blue or non-blue, so that the total probability of its being red, green, or blue is 1½ (see section 8.2.1).

---

[15] This is explained and defended further in Huemer 2009.

The color categories we use in ordinary language – such as "red", "green", and "blue" – are not fundamental. When an object is red, it is always red in virtue of its having some other, precise color shade, including a precise hue, saturation, and intensity. These perfectly precise shades lack names in English, but they are the more fundamental properties.

Therefore, given the Explanatory Priority Proviso of section 8.4, the correct application of the Principle of Indifference would not be to assign equal probabilities to "red" and "non-red", nor would it be to assign equal probabilities to "red", "green", and "blue". It would be to assign a uniform probability distribution over *the color solid*, that is, the space of possible precise color shades. This is a three-dimensional space with hue, saturation, and brightness as dimensions. (Since each of these dimensions has a limited range of possible values, it is possible to have a uniform, nonzero probability distribution over the space.) Each perfectly precise color is a point in the color solid. Given no information other than the ordinary understanding of colors based on our visual experiences of color, it would be rational to assign a uniform probability distribution over the region of the color solid that counts as red, green, or blue. The probability of the book's being blue is then equal to the proportion of that region that counts as blue.

If you view color samples arranged by visual appearance to human observers (for example, Munsell color chips), you will see that there are more visually discriminable shades of blue than there are of either green or red. Blue is a larger color, so to speak; it occupies more of the color solid. Thus, the book is more likely to be blue than to be either of the other given colors. Taking this into account, a reasonable estimate of the probability of the book's being blue is about 40%.

All this is assuming, again, that you have nothing to go on but the ordinary notion of color based on our visual experience thereof; thus, that you have no knowledge of the physical properties underlying the phenomenon of color, no knowledge of the processes by which book cover designs get selected, and so on.

If you have background information about the physical properties that underlie the phenomenon of color, then you must assign a uniform probability distribution over the possible ways that these underlying physical properties might be, rather than the possible visually discriminable color shades. This is because the physical properties would be explanatorily prior to the colors that we see.

If you have background information about how book covers are chosen, then you must instead assign a uniform probability distribution over the possible mental states of the people choosing the book cover (their beliefs, preferences, and other states relevant to their choice of book covers). This would be explanatorily prior (because causally prior) to the physical properties of the book cover. Of course, figuring out the results of such a probability distribution would be very difficult, as it involves us in trying to enumerate possible states of an editor's mind. Fortunately, our goal here is not to figure out what the actual probability would be in that situation. Our goal is merely to explain why the paradoxical reasoning is mistaken. It is mistaken because it applies the Principle of Indifference to the wrong sets of possibilities.

Here is another way of describing the error. It is said that since we have no reason to think the book more likely to be red than not, we should assign probability ½ to its being red and ½ to its not being red. But in fact, we have a reason to think the book more likely *not* to be red than to be red. This reason is that there are more color-shades that count as non-red than shades that count as red. So the Principle of Indifference does not apply to the set of alternatives {red, non-red}.

Similarly, it is said that of the alternatives "red", "green", and "blue", we have no reason to favor any of the three over any other. This is false, because we have a reason to favor blue over red: there are more shades of blue than there are shades of red. Likewise, we have a reason to favor blue over green: there are more shades of blue than there are of green. So the Principle of Indifference does not apply to the set of alternatives {red, green, blue}.[16]

8.5.2   France and England

The paradoxical reasoning claims that "England is larger than France" has the same probability as "France is larger than England", and also that "The U.K. is larger than France" has the same probability as "France is

---

[16] Cf. Keynes' (1921, p. 59) treatment of the case.

larger than the U.K." But these can't both be true, given the knowledge that England is a proper part of the U.K. (see section 8.2.2).

This reasoning misapplies the Principle of Indifference twice. "England is larger than France" does not have the same probability as "France is larger than England", because in the example, we are given that England is smaller than the U.K., whereas we are *not* given that France is smaller than the U.K. France *might* be smaller than the U.K. for all we know, but England is *definitely* smaller. So our information speaks to the smallness of England (slightly) in a way that it does not speak to the smallness of France. If you had to bet, you should bet on England to be the smaller region.

Similarly, if you had to bet on which was larger, the U.K. or France, you should bet on the U.K. to be the larger, since you have information that (slightly) speaks to the largeness of the U.K. (namely, that at least it is larger than England), with no parallel information speaking to the largeness of France.

A correct application of the Principle of Indifference would be something like this. Given that the U.K. is larger than England, and assuming no two territories are of exactly equal size, there are the following possible sets of relationships:

1. U.K. > England > France
2. U.K. > France > England
3. France > U.K. > England

(where ">" denotes the larger-than relation). We assign equal probability to each of these alternatives. The probability of England being larger than France is then ⅓, and the probability of the U.K. being larger than France is ⅔.

8.5.3   The Car Ride

The paradoxical reasoning claims that the probability of Sue's trip having lasted between 1 and 1½ hours is ½, and the probability of her velocity being between 66 ⅔ and 100 mph is ⅔. This can't be, since we know that the time was between 1 and 1½ if and only if the velocity was between 66 ⅔ and 100 (see section 8.2.3).

The correct solution is the one based on velocity; the solution based on time is in error. This is explained by the Explanatory Priority Proviso: Given a fixed distance, the speed at which Sue drove causally explains the amount of time that her trip took, not vice versa. If someone asks, "How come it took so long?", you could answer, "Because she was driving very slowly." But if someone asks, "Why was she driving so slowly?", you could not sensibly answer, "Because it took her a long time."

The priority relation in question is metaphysical, not psychological or conceptual. Thus, it does not matter that velocity is commonly defined in terms of a ratio of distance to time; how we define things does not matter to what we should consider likely to happen. Actual dependence relations in the objective world (that we know about) do matter. So what matters is the causal relation, not the conceptual relation.

So the correct probability is ⅔.

8.5.4   The Cube Factory

The paradoxical reasoning claims that the probability of the cube's side being less than 1 inch is ½, and the probability of its volume being less than 1 cubic inch is ⅛; yet the side is less than 1 if and only if the volume is less than 1 (see section 8.2.4).

In this case, both solutions are conceptually in error, but the solution given in terms of volume gives the correct probability.

The size of an object is determined by the amount of material present and its arrangement. Assuming a fixed arrangement, the size is determined by the quantity of material. For instance, if the object is a cube of iron, its size is determined by the number of iron atoms. The cube may take up a lot of space because there are so many atoms in it; it is not the case that there are many atoms in it because it takes up a lot of space. Therefore, given the Explanatory Priority Proviso, the correct application of the Principle of Indifference is to assign a uniform probability distribution over the possible amounts of material that might be present. This has the same result, mathematically, as a probability distribution based on volume, since volume for an object of a given material is proportional to the quantity of material (at least approximately, for ordinary objects – of course, if you have an object with the mass of a star, matters may be different).

So the correct probability in this case is ⅛.

8.5.5   The Circle and the Chord

The paradoxical reasoning claims that the probability of the chord being longer than the side of the triangle is ½, and ⅓, and ¼ (see section 8.2.5).

It is stipulated that the chord was chosen at random. However, there are many ways of choosing a chord that would qualify as "choosing a chord randomly". One way is to randomly select a point on the circumference, then randomly select a second point on the circumference, then connect the two. Another method is to randomly select a direction, then randomly select a distance (between zero and the length of the radius), then draw a chord whose midpoint is the chosen distance from the center of the circle, in the chosen direction. A third method is to randomly select a point inside the circle, then construct a chord with that point as its midpoint. These methods correspond to the three solutions discussed in section 8.2.5.

The method of selection is explanatorily prior to the result obtained. Therefore, the correct application of the Principle of Indifference would be to assign a uniform probability distribution over the possible methods of random selection. Each possible method of random selection generates its own probability distribution, including, in particular, a probability for the chosen chord to be longer than the side of the triangle. We need to take an average of these probabilities. Thus, suppose we have exactly three possible random selection methods, M1, M2, and M3. Then the overall probability of the chord being longer than the side of the triangle is given by:

$$P\left(\text{chord is longer than side}\right) = \frac{1}{3} P \begin{pmatrix} \text{chord is longer than} \\ \text{side if M1 is used} \end{pmatrix}$$

$$+ \frac{1}{3} P \begin{pmatrix} \text{chord is longer than} \\ \text{side if M2 is used} \end{pmatrix}$$

$$+ \frac{1}{3} P \begin{pmatrix} \text{chord is longer than} \\ \text{side if M3 is used} \end{pmatrix}$$

⅓ is the probability of each of the three possible methods having been the method of selection. Applying this to Bertrand's three methods of selecting a chord, this yields

$$P\left(\text{chord is longer than side}\right) = \left(\frac{1}{3}\right)\left(\frac{1}{2}\right) + \left(\frac{1}{3}\right)\left(\frac{1}{3}\right) + \left(\frac{1}{3}\right)\left(\frac{1}{4}\right) = \frac{13}{36}.$$

In other words, with no information suggesting that any of Bertrand's methods is more likely to have been the chosen method of selecting a chord, we consider each method equally likely, and thus take the average of Bertrand's three solutions.

But this is assuming that Bertrand's three methods are the only random selection methods. Some think that there are actually infinitely many random selection methods, perhaps because every probability distribution over the set of possible chords corresponds to a possible "random selection method".[17]

This is not correct. Not every possible probability distribution can be produced by something that we would recognize as random selection. Only probability distributions that are *uniform* over some *natural variables* (for example, the distance of the chord from the circle's center, or the distance between the points where the chord intersects the circumference) count as random selection methods. Bertrand's three methods qualify. There may also be other methods one can think of that qualify.[18]

---

[17] Aerts and de Bianchi 2014; Shackel 2007, pp. 173–4.

[18] Here is one more: select a random position in the circle, then select a random angle, then construct a chord that passes through the chosen point, with the chosen angle to the vertical. See Marinoff 1994 for more methods.

How can we ensure that we have enumerated every random selection method? I know of no way of ensuring this. However, the correct application of the Principle of Indifference would be to assign equal weight to every such method that one is aware of. This avoids paradox. If one becomes aware of an additional method not previously considered, this does not threaten a paradox; one should simply incorporate that method, and recalculate the probability accordingly.

"But," one might ask, "which was the correct probability? Was the probability one originally calculated correct? If so, how could the new probability, calculated after discovering a new selection method, also be correct?"

In reply, there are two ways of thinking about epistemic probability. One way is that the probability of a proposition is the degree of belief one should rationally have in that proposition, given one's present information and taking into account one's cognitive limitations. On this account, the probability of the chord being longer than the side of the triangle changes when you acquire new information, namely, the information that there is an additional possible random selection method you had not previously considered.

Another way of thinking about probability is more idealized: perhaps the probability of a proposition is the degree of belief that an ideal reasoner would have in it, where this ideal reasoner sees all logical possibilities and all the logical consequences of his beliefs. On this account, ordinary people may often be unable to determine the probability of a proposition. We could only *estimate* the probability of the chord being longer than the side of the triangle, by enumerating as many random selection methods as we can. When we discover additional methods, we can then revise our estimate, seeking to make it more accurate.

In either case, there is no paradox, that is, there is no valid way of deriving incompatible probabilities. In the idealized conception of probability, there is a single correct answer to Bertrand's problem, though we may not know it. In the less idealized conception, there are probabilities that change as our logical and mathematical knowledge increases, but there are never two different probabilities for the same person at the same time.

8.6   A Philosophical Application: The Problem of Induction

8.6.1   The Traditional Problem

Inductive reasoning is (roughly) reasoning that extrapolates from particular cases, applying what is known to be true of observed cases to the unobserved.[19] For instance, suppose that I observe a large number of honey badgers, and all of them turn out to be mean. I might then inductively infer (a) that the *next* honey badger I meet will be mean, or even (b) that all honey badgers are mean.[20]

This type of reasoning appears to presuppose some such principle as the following:

The Uniformity Principle: Unobserved objects of a given kind tend to be similar to observed objects of that kind.

If we *don't* assume anything like the Uniformity Principle, then it is unclear why, after observing some mean honey badgers, we would expect the hitherto *unobserved* ones to be mean, rather than nice.

Therefore, it seems that we need some reason for believing the Uniformity Principle; otherwise, all our inductive conclusions will be unjustified. What reason can we give for believing the Uniformity Principle?

Notice, first, that we cannot verify the Uniformity Principle by observation, since the Uniformity Principle makes a claim about unobserved objects. By definition, we cannot know by observation that *unobserved* things are similar to observed things. Second, the Uniformity Principle

---

[19] More precisely, inductive reasoning is reasoning that non-demonstratively infers, from the fact that certain things of kind A have feature B, that other things of kind A also have B. The fact that certain A's have B need not be observed; it might be, say, intuited or discovered by inference. For instance, from the fact (*i*) that each of the first billion even numbers can be written as the sum of two prime numbers, one might inductively infer (*ii*) that all even numbers can be written as the sum of two prime numbers. Nevertheless, I shall continue to speak of observed and unobserved objects, since the most common and widely discussed examples of induction involve inference from the unobserved to the observed.

[20] For more on the character of the honey badger, see Randall 2011.

does not seem to be a self-evident truth, or derivable from self-evident truths, like the fact that 2+2=4 or the fact that there is no largest prime number. One reason for saying this is that it seems perfectly possible that unobserved things should be completely different from observed things, whereas things that are self-evident are things that could not possibly have been false. Third, the Uniformity Principle could not be known by induction, since any inductive argument for the Uniformity Principle would have to be circular, given that induction presupposes the Uniformity Principle.

But these three alternatives – observation, (inference from) self-evident truths, and induction – seem to exhaust the possible ways in which we might try to justify the Uniformity Principle. Since none of them work, it looks as though the Uniformity Principle cannot be justified. Since the Uniformity Principle is the basis for all inductive reasoning, it looks as though inductive reasoning cannot be justified.

This conclusion is known as inductive skepticism. Note that inductive skepticism is *not* the view that inductive conclusions are not *conclusively justified*, or that they are merely probable and never certain. Inductive skepticism is the view that there is *no justification whatsoever* for *any* inductive conclusion.[21]

This view is crazy. Nearly all our beliefs about the world around us depend on induction, including, for example, my belief that the sun will rise tomorrow, my belief that other people exist and have mental states, even my belief that the world outside this room exists. It is absurd to say that all of these beliefs are completely unjustified, just like, say, the belief that purple unicorns built the Taj Mahal.

The problem of induction is the problem of explaining how induction is justified. What went wrong in the argument for inductive skepticism?

8.6.2   A Probabilistic Formulation of the Problem

The problem of induction, it turns out, is closely connected to the paradoxes of the Principle of Indifference. Consider a simplified version of

---

[21] This view is defended by Hume (1975, pp. 25–39) and Popper (1961, pp. 27–30), among others.

the honey badger inference: assume that there are two personalities an animal can have: nice and mean. Assume that you can tell by observing an animal for a short time whether it is nice or mean. You are about to observe a honey badger. Given no further information than the preceding, what is the probability that it will be mean? Using the Principle of Indifference, we can assign equal probabilities to the two alternatives; thus, the answer is "½".

Now consider a slightly modified problem. Suppose that things are as described above, except that this time, you know that 98 honey badgers have previously been observed, and all of them proved to be mean. Given this information, what is the probability that the next one you observe will be mean?

Here is one way to calculate that. Consider the sequence of 99 honey badger observations (the previous 98 plus the one you are about to do). There are 2^{99} possible outcomes for this sequence of observations. Each outcome can be described by listing, for each observed badger, whether it was nice or mean. (The first possible outcome is 99 nice badgers. The second possibility is 98 nice badgers followed by one mean one. The third is 97 nice badgers, one mean, then one nice. And so on.) Applying the Principle of Indifference, we can consider each of these possibilities to have an equal initial probability, namely, $1/2^{99}$. Now, to calculate the probability of the 99th badger being mean *given* that the first 98 badgers were mean, we simply take the following ratio:

$$\frac{\text{The number of sequences in which the first 98 badgers are mean and the } 99^{th} \text{ is also mean}}{\text{The number of sequences in which the first 98 badgers are mean}}$$

This ratio is ½. (There is one possible sequence in which the first 98 badgers are mean and the 99th is mean, and one sequence in which the first 98 badgers are mean and the 99th is nice.)

Notice that this is the same as the initial probability that the next observed badger would be mean, *before* you knew that 98 previous badgers were observed to be mean. In symbols:

$$P\left(M_{99} \middle| M_1, ..., M_{98}\right) = P\left(M_{99}\right)$$

The probability of badger #99 being mean *given* that badgers 1 through 98 were mean is the same as the initial probability of badger #99 being mean. In other words, the information about the niceness or meanness of the first 98 observed badgers is completely irrelevant. It tells us nothing about what the next badger will be like. This is the inductive skeptic's conclusion.

Thus, inductive skepticism is actually supported by (a certain way of applying) the Principle of Indifference.

8.6.3   A Solution

Above, we applied the Principle of Indifference to the possible sequences of observation results. But, just as in the case of the earlier problems involving the Principle of Indifference, there are other ways of describing the possibilities in the honey badger problem, and hence there are other ways of applying the Principle of Indifference to the problem, which result in different answers.

Here is one of them. Assume that there is in general a fixed *objective chance* for a randomly chosen honey badger to be mean. This objective chance (unlike epistemic probabilities) is a matter of objective, physical facts about honey badgers, their environment, and the laws of nature; it is not dependent on our knowledge or evidence concerning honey badgers, or anything else about our minds. This objective chance is initially unknown to us, but we may be able to make inferences about the value of the objective chance. Assume also, as is widely accepted, that *if* you knew that the objective chance of a honey badger being mean was c, then the epistemic probability for you of a given badger being mean, given only that information, would be equal to c.

Now suppose we apply the Principle of Indifference to the possible values of this objective chance. This requires that we assign a uniform probability density to the possible values of the objective chance. Thus, for example, the epistemic probability that the objective chance is between 0 and 0.1 is 1/10; the epistemic probability that the objective chance is between .3 and .7 is 4/10; and so on.

This approach gives us a non-skeptical solution. Informally, what happens is that our observations of badgers give us information about the value of the objective chance of honey badger meanness. As we collect more and more instances of mean badgers, this tends to confirm that this objective chance is high, since otherwise it would be very unlikely that we would observe so many mean badgers. That, in turn, enables us to predict that the next observed badger will probably be mean. Working this out mathematically requires a little knowledge of calculus and probability theory. Because some readers are averse to reading mathematical derivations, I will relegate the derivation to the following subsection. For now, I will just tell you the result: in general, we can show that if the first n badgers are all mean, then the probability of the next one being mean given just that information is $(n+1)/(n+2)$.[22] So, given that the first 98 badgers were mean, the probability of the next one being mean is 99%. This is a strong rebuttal to inductive skepticism.

Why should we apply the Principle of Indifference in this way, rather than the manner described in the previous section that leads to inductive skepticism? Because of the Explanatory Priority Proviso: the objective chance of honey badger meanness is a pre-existing, physical fact about how the honey badger system works. This sort of fact could be used to (partly) explain our observations, whereas the reverse is not true (the sequence of observation results does not explain the objective chance). So the objective chance is explanatorily prior to the particular sequence of observation results. Therefore, the Principle of Indifference should be applied to the possible values of the objective chance, not to the possible sequences of observation results.

Now, the preceding reasoning all assumes that there are such things as stable, objective chances. So you might wonder: how do we *know* that there are such things? Isn't this something that we would have to learn by induction – and wouldn't that involve us in the sort of circular reasoning that the inductive skeptic initially warned us against (section 8.6.1)?

The answer is that we can construct a probabilistic argument for the existence of stable objective chances, and this argument does not require

---

[22] This is the famous Rule of Succession, first employed by Bayes (1763, scholium to Proposition 9) and later Laplace (1995, pp. 10–11) and Carnap (1962, pp. 567–8).

any circular reasoning. We may start by assigning, say, a 50% probability to the hypothesis that there are stable objective chances, and a 50% probability to the hypothesis that there are no such things. From this point, the degree of uniformity in our experiences gives us information about whether stable objective chances exist or not. As we notice more and more stable patterns in our experience, it becomes more and more (epistemically) probable that stable objective chances exist, since otherwise such stable patterns would be unlikely. Notice that this does not involve any sort of circular reasoning: the starting position does not amount to assuming that there are stable objective chances, since it does not require assigning a high prior probability to this hypothesis.[23]

8.6.4   The Mathematics of the Inductivist Solution

Let A_n be the proposition that all of the first n observed badgers are mean (where n can be any positive integer). What is the initial epistemic probability of A_n? In general, the probability of A_n *given* that the objective chance of a mean badger is c, is c^n. (For instance, if badgers have a .7 objective chance of being mean, then, given just this information, the probability of finding 99 mean badgers in a row is $(.7)^{99}$.) If there were finitely many possible values of the objective chance, then we would simply add up, for each possible value of the objective chance, the (epistemic) probability that the objective chance has that value times the (epistemic) probability of A_n *given* that the objective chance has that value (which, again, would be c^n). But because we are "summing" for infinitely many alternatives, we need to use an integral and a probability density. The appropriate formula is the following:

$$P(A_n) = \int_{c=0}^{1} c^n \rho(c) dc$$

where $\rho(c)$ is the (epistemic) probability density for the objective chance. In accordance with the Principle of Indifference, we take this probability

---

[23] This is shown in my 2009, pp. 24–6.

density to be uniform, which requires that $\rho(c) = 1$ for all c between 0 and 1. Plugging this into the above equation yields

$$P(A_n) = \int_{c=0}^{1} c^n dc = \frac{c^{n+1}}{n+1}\Bigg|_0^1 = \frac{1^{n+1}}{n+1} - \frac{0^{n+1}}{n+1} = \frac{1}{n+1}.$$

Now, we would like to know the probability of the $(n+1)^{th}$ badger being mean given that the first n are mean. This is equivalent to $P(A_{n+1}|A_n)$, which, from the definition of conditional probability, is $P(A_{n+1} \& A_n)/P(A_n)$. Applying the above expression for $P(A_n)$ we obtain:

$$P(A_{n+1}|A_n) = \frac{P(A_{n+1} \& A_n)}{P(A_n)} = \frac{P(A_{n+1})}{P(A_n)} = \frac{\frac{1}{(n+1)+1}}{\frac{1}{n+1}} = \frac{n+1}{n+2}.$$

Thus, when we observe 98 mean badgers in a row, the probability of the next one being mean is 99/100.

8.7 Another Application: The Mystery of Entropy

8.7.1 Why Entropy Increases

The Second Law of Thermodynamics – the Entropy Law – states that the entropy of a closed system always increases until the system reaches maximum entropy, at which point entropy will remain constant. Roughly, this means that the world becomes less ordered, or more random, over time. This explains the fact that when a warm object comes in contact with a cold object, heat flows from the warm to the cold; we never see heat spontaneously flowing from the cold to the warm. Similarly, when you put a spoonful of cream in your coffee, the cream disperses throughout the coffee; you never see the cream gather back into a single spot.

This is sometimes said to be the key to understanding "the arrow of time", or how the future direction in time differs from the past direction. Most of the laws of physics are time symmetric, that is, they treat the forward and backward directions of time the same, so that for any process that satisfies the laws, a similar process happening in reverse would also satisfy the laws. The entropy law is one of very few exceptions – it treats the future and past differently.[24] This makes it a very philosophically interesting law.

Why is the entropy law true? Imagine an insulated box filled with air. At time t, the left half of the box, for whatever reason, is ten degrees warmer than the right half. The entropy law predicts that, say, a minute in the future, the two sides of the box will be more uniform: heat will have moved from the warmer side to the cooler, bringing their temperatures closer together. Heat will not move from the colder side to the warmer side. Why is this?

The molecules in any macroscopic object are in rapid, random motion. In a gas, these molecules are free to move throughout their container. The temperature of a given material is just the average kinetic energy that the molecules have in virtue of this random motion. To say the left half of the box is warmer than the right half is to say that the average kinetic energy of the molecules in the left half is greater than that of the molecules in the right half.

Let "M_t" stand for the given macroscopic state of the box at time t, that is, the state in which the left half is ten degrees warmer than the right half. There are many possible *microscopic* states of the box that would realize M_t – that is, different sets of precise locations and momenta for the molecules that would make it true that the left half of the box was ten degrees warmer than the right half. Of these many micro-states, the *overwhelming majority* would lead to a future in which the halves of the box are more uniform in temperature. Therefore, if (in accordance with the Principle of Indifference) we assign a uniform probability distribution to the possible states that realize M_t, we should expect the halves of the box to have a more uniform temperature a minute later, which counts as an increase in entropy.

---

[24] If the wave function collapse in quantum mechanics is real, the law governing it is also temporally asymmetric. Also, some elementary particle interactions violate temporal symmetry.

How do I know that most realizations of M_t result in the box being more uniform in temperature after t? Since the air molecules in the box are moving randomly, periodically one of them crosses from the left side to the right side of the box, and periodically one crosses from the right to the left. Consider the first molecule to cross from the left to the right after t. We know nothing about this molecule except that, at t, it is on the left. By stipulation, the molecules on the left at t have a higher average kinetic energy than those on the right at t. So, on average, we would expect this molecule to be more energetic than the average molecule on the right side of the box. Therefore, probably, when it crosses over it will result in raising the temperature of the right side of the box.

Parallel reasoning shows that the first molecule to cross from the right to the left will probably *lower* the temperature of the left side. If we repeat this for trillions of trillions of molecules, the probability becomes *extremely* high that, on net, the left half of the box gets cooler and the right half warmer. So high that we should never expect to see an exception in real life. This continues to be true until the two halves of the box are the same temperature.

That seems to explain the entropy law. Notice how the explanation turns on the Principle of Indifference.

Now, you might think: "Wait, the Principle of Indifference is a *normative epistemological* thesis, a thesis about what we are justified in believing. But the Second Law of Thermodynamics is an empirical, physical law. How can a normative epistemological principle explain the truth of an empirical law of physics?" Well, the above explanation for the entropy law does not make it *physically impossible* for heat to move from the cold side to the warm side; it is just that, given the appropriate initial probability distribution, we should have an *incredibly tiny credence* that we would ever observe that happening.

8.7.2   The Reverse Entropy Law

Now here is a puzzle to think about. The entropy law, as standardly understood, is time-asymmetric. It predicts entropy increasing in only one direction in time. We just gave a probabilistic explanation for why entropy should increase in the future. But why is there a temporal asymmetry? Why can't we construct a parallel piece of reasoning that treats the backward direction in time in the same way that the above reasoning treats the forward direction? This reasoning would lead to what we might call the Reverse Entropy Law, which states that the entropy of a closed system always increases *into the past* until it reaches maximum entropy; more colloquially, that entropy has spontaneously decreased over time, from a maximum-entropy state.

Let's try to construct that reasoning. Again, assume that at *t*, the left half of the box is warmer than the right. As noted earlier, the molecules are in random motion, and periodically one crosses from one side of the box to the other. Consider the *last* molecule that crossed over from the right to the left, before *t*. We know nothing about this molecule except that, at *t*, it is on the left side of the box. By stipulation, the molecules that are on the left side of the box at *t* have higher average kinetic energy than those on the right. Applying the Principle of Indifference, any of these molecules is equally likely to have been the last one that crossed over. So, on average, we would expect this molecule to have higher kinetic energy than the average molecule that is on the right side at *t*. Therefore, probably, when it crossed over it resulted in *lowering* the temperature of the right side; the right side was warmer just before it crossed over.

Similarly, consider the last molecule that crossed from the left to the right before *t*. All we know is that, at *t*, it is on the right. The molecules on the right at *t* are, on average, less energetic than those on the left at *t*. So probably, this molecule is less energetic than the average molecule that is on the left at *t*. So when it departed the left side, it raised the average energy level of the left side.

Thus, probably, just before *t*, the left side was cooler and the right side warmer than it is at *t*. If we repeat the reasoning for trillions of trillions of molecules, the probability becomes overwhelming that the left side was cooler and the right side warmer in the past. That is, there is an overwhelming probability that entropy was higher in the past.

Notice that this reasoning is all perfectly parallel to the reasoning from section 8.7.1 above, except with the temporal directions switched. There is no mathematical or logical error here. If there's an error, it's a philosophical one having to do with the nature of time.

According to the reasoning of section 8.7.1, if you see a system in a state of less-than-maximal entropy, you should expect that, a minute later, it will be in a higher entropy state. This was taken to imply that, *in any spontaneous process, entropy increases.*

Similarly, the reasoning of *this* section tells us that, if you see a system in a state of less-than-maximal entropy, you should infer that, a minute *ago*, it *was* in a higher entropy state.[25] Why, then, can we not infer that, *in any spontaneous process, entropy decreases?*

8.7.3   Reverse Entropy Is Crazy

Perhaps we could accept the Entropy Law *and* the Reverse Entropy Law. Or more precisely, we could accept this generalization: *given* that a closed system has some nontrivial degree of order at *t*, it tends to have higher entropy both before and after *t*. Entropy increases as you move farther in time from the low-entropy state, *in either direction.* Call this the Two-Way Entropy Law (figure 8.3).[26]

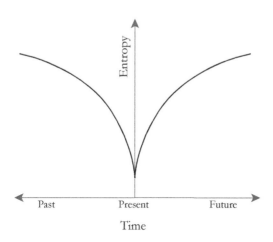

Fig. 8.3   Two-Way Entropy Law

---

[25] For further explanation, see Hurley 1986.

[26] Why is Fig. 8.3 drawn as it is? The farther we are from thermal equilibrium, the higher the proportion of possible transitions that lead toward equilibrium rather than further away. Thus, the lower entropy is, the higher the *rate* at which entropy increases. So as we move forward from the low-entropy time, entropy increases at a decreasing rate, i.e., the curve is concave down. The curve in the past direction is just the mirror image of the future-oriented curve.

The Two-Way Entropy Law is a coherent theory. It is, however, completely crazy. Suppose you come upon a cup of coffee with a bit of cream in the middle of it. You didn't see how it got that way; all you know is what it is like now. You should expect that, a minute later, that cream will be uniformly dispersed throughout the coffee. This much is common sense.

According to the Two-Way Entropy Law, you should also think that, a minute in the past, that cream *was* widely dispersed throughout the coffee. From that dispersed state, the cream spontaneously gathered together in the middle, in a time-reversed version of the sort of dispersion we usually see. You should assign *the same probability* to this hypothesis about the past as you do to the hypothesis that the cream is going to disperse in the future.

Or suppose that you see a rock in the air, unsupported. You just got a glance for an instant, so you don't get to see what happens to the rock after that moment, nor what happened to it before.

You should assume that the rock will fall to the ground. As it hits the ground, its energy will be transmitted to the molecules in the ground, which wind up moving a little faster, that is, the rock's kinetic energy is converted into thermal energy and sound waves in the ground. You expect that thermal and sound energy to disperse outward from the site of impact. The rock will then probably continue to sit on the ground for a long time.

According to the Two-Way Entropy Law, the future that you predict for this system is perfectly analogous to the past that you should retrodict. So probably the rock was sitting on the ground for a long time to begin with. A very large number of molecules in the ground, starting from very far away in all different directions, started, by chance, moving toward the rock. Not all of the molecules in the ground, of course; rather, of the trillions of trillions of molecules in the ground surrounding the rock, it just happened that a slightly larger percentage of them were headed towards the rock than away from it. These molecules bumped into other molecules closer to the rock, which bumped into other molecules still closer, and so on. And these molecules happened to be on trajectories such that a large number of them all wound up colliding with the rock at about the same time and knocking it into the air. That's probably how it got in the air.

"But," you say, "that sequence of events is astronomically improbable. How could there be a coherent view on which one *expects* that to be true?"

Indeed, that sequence of events is astronomically unlikely, considered in itself. The Two-Way Entropy theory does not deny this. It only says that *given* the state of the rock at the moment you saw it, the foregoing story is the most likely explanation. Of course, it's incredibly unlikely that a rock would be in the air like that at any given time. *Something* incredibly unlikely has to have happened. The alternative – that the rock was in an *even lower* entropy state before you saw it – is (allegedly) even more unlikely.

You might point out that we don't actually observe such decreasing-entropy events. We see many low-entropy states, but whenever we observe a low-entropy state coming into being, what we seem to recall is that it evolved from an *even lower* entropy state, not from a high-entropy state. For instance, of all the times I recall seeing some cream in the middle of some coffee, it always started out with the cream completely separate from the coffee and then being poured into it.

But that is assuming that we can trust our memory. If we don't assume any temporal asymmetry in the physics, then our memories are exactly as likely to be reliable indicators of the past as they are to be reliable indicators of the future. Or so one might argue.

You have certain expectations about your own future and that of the world around you. Not very precise expectations, but broad, qualitative expectations about how things will go. Based on the Two-Way Entropy Law, you should also think that a time-reversed version of that is most likely how the present state of yourself and the world around you *came about* – including your current brain state, including your current collection of memories, and so on. It is highly unlikely that the current state of the world (including your current collection of seeming-memories) is going to lead to a time-reversed version of the events that you seem to recall happening over the past year. Your memories don't predict the future. Similarly, then, the current state of the world (including your current collection of seeming-memories) is highly unlikely to *have arisen* from the events that you seem to recall happening over the past year. That is, your memories probably don't reflect the real past.

All this is assuming that we start with knowledge only of the present, macroscopic state of the world, and we reason from there to hypotheses about the past in the same way that we reason to hypotheses about the future.

Of course, if we could not trust our memories, then we would have no way of coming to know the basic physical theory that the above reasoning takes for granted. So the Two-Way Entropy theory cannot be justified. But that observation does not address the problem. The intellectual problem is to explain why our physical theory does not support Reverse Entropy, as it does the regular Entropy Law. If our current physical theory predicts that it is incredibly unlikely that our memories are reliable, then that would be strong evidence against that physical theory.

8.7.4   The Reverse Argument Misuses the Principle of Indifference

I assume I don't have to argue against the Two-Way Entropy theory. It's probably too crazy even for a philosopher to embrace.[27] What is needed is a *diagnosis* of the error. The argument for the Reverse Entropy Law seems parallel to the account of why the real Entropy Law holds. Is there something wrong with the account of the real Entropy Law? Or is the parallel reasoning somehow relevantly different?

Here is a possible diagnosis. The reasoning for the real Entropy Law respects the Explanatory Priority Proviso to the Principle of Indifference given in section 8.4. It begins with a uniform distribution over states of the world at a time, and uses this to constrain judgments about the probabilities of states at a *later* time.

The reasoning for the reverse law does the opposite: it begins with a uniform probability distribution over states at a given time, and uses this to constrain the probabilities for states at an *earlier* time. Because earlier states of the world are explanatorily prior to later states, it is an error to

---

[27] Though perhaps I should reserve judgment until Peter Unger has weighed in.

reason in this way. Given the Explanatory Priority Proviso, the correct application of the Principle of Indifference is to assign uniform probabilities to possibilities at an earlier point in time, and infer probabilities at a later point, not vice versa.

Now to explain that more clearly: recall the box in macroscopic state M_t at time t, where the left half is warmer than the right. Our above reasoning (section 8.7.2) considers the most recent molecule that crossed from the right side to the left before t. Since this molecule is on the left at t, we are supposed to take its expected energy level to be the average of the molecules that are *on the left at t*, and therefore take its expected energy level as higher than the average of the molecules on the right. Therefore, this molecule, in crossing over, probably cooled down the right side. So the two sides were probably closer in temperature in the past. Call this "the Reverse Argument" (because it supports the Reverse Entropy Law).

Here is an alternative argument. Consider the last molecule that crossed from right to left. Since this molecule *was* on the right side shortly before t, its expected energy level is the average of the molecules that were on the right side at that time. Since only one molecule has crossed from right to left since that time, that average must be almost identical to the average at time t. The molecules on the right at t are relatively low-energy molecules. So we should expect the last molecule that crossed over from the right to be a low-energy molecule. More precisely, we should take the expected energy level of that molecule to be the average energy level of the molecules on the right just before t. Which means that when it crossed over, it cooled the left side. Call this "the Forward Argument" (because it suggests entropy increasing forwards in time).

Parallel reasoning shows that the last molecule that crossed from the left to the right probably heated up the right side. Hence, before t, the two sides of the box were probably *even more* disparate in temperature, with the right side hotter and the left side cooler.

The difference between the Reverse Argument and the Forward Argument comes down to two different ways of applying the Principle of Indifference. For simplicity, let's assume that there are just two kinds of molecules, fast and slow. The box contains equal numbers of each kind, but at t, the left side contains 60% of the fast molecules and only 40% of the slow molecules, while the right side contains 60% of the slow molecules and 40% of the fast ones. If *x* is the last molecule that crossed from right to left just before *t*, what are the odds of *x* being a fast molecule?

The Reverse Argument: *x* is on the left at *t*, where 60% of the molecules are fast. *x* is equally likely to be any of the molecules that are on the left at *t*. So it has a 60% chance of being fast, and a 40% chance of being slow.

The Forward Argument: just before *t*, before *x* crossed over, there were a certain number of molecules on the right side, of which 60% were slow. Consider each possible way of choosing one of those molecules to be the one that crosses over. 60% of these ways result in a slow molecule crossing over, so the odds are 60–40 that a slow molecule was the last one to cross over.

Here is an analogy (see figure 8.4).[28] The average height of people in the Netherlands is 6.0 feet, while the average height in Indonesia is 5.2 feet. Issi recently moved from Indonesia to the Netherlands. Assume that people's height does not change when they move from one country to another. What is the expected value of Issi's height given the preceding information?

Answer 1:   Issi's expected height is 6 feet, since she is now in the Netherlands, and that is the average for people in the Netherlands.

Answer 2:   Issi's expected height is 5.2 feet, since she was just in Indonesia, where that was the average height.

Answer 2 is better, because it takes account of explanatory priority: Issi was originally in Indonesia, and her original height explains her present height, not vice versa.

You might want to say: "Actually, we should look at the collection of all people who first live in Indonesia and then move to the Netherlands. If we know the average height of *that* group, that will be Issi's expected height." But assume you do not have that information, or the group is too small to have reliable statistics. Then Answer 2 above is best.

_____

[28] Thanks to Iskra Fileva for this analogy.

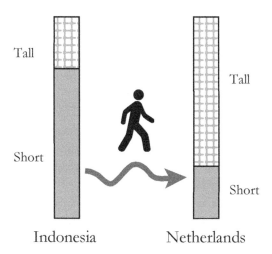

Indonesia   Netherlands

Fig. 8.4   Migrant from Indonesia to the Netherlands

8.7.5   The Isolated Box

I think there is something right about the preceding line of thought. But there seems to be something wrong with it as well.[29] Take this scenario: assume that you know at the start that the box of gas molecules has been isolated for a long time (long enough to have reached thermal equilibrium long ago, whatever its initial state). Stipulate that there has been nothing to interfere with the random motion of the particles in it during this time. Now, at time t, you measure the temperature with thermometers on opposite sides of the box, finding the left side, to your great surprise, 10 degrees warmer than the right. What is the best account of what happened?

You should think that the box was in thermal equilibrium for a while, then it reached its current low-entropy state by a random fluctuation away from thermal equilibrium, and it will soon return to thermal equilibrium again. Such a fluctuation is *incredibly* improbable, but it's the only explanation that makes sense given the rest of the scenario.

---

[29] I thank Randall McCutcheon (p.c.) for pointing this out.

But the reasoning of the preceding subsection (section 8.7.4), if correct, would seem to apply to this scenario just as well as to the case where the box's history is merely unknown. According to the argument of section 8.7.4, we should think that a few seconds before t, the box was probably in an *even lower* entropy state than it is at t, with the two sides even more divergent in temperature. This goes back to the time the box was created, when it was in an incredibly low-entropy state; by chance, it must have failed to ever reach thermal equilibrium since then. But this is very unreasonable; this requires an even greater improbability than the hypothesis of the preceding paragraph.

In this example, we are supposed to assume (i) that the box has been undisturbed for a long time, with nothing to interfere with the random motions of the particles therein, and (ii) that your temperature measurements at t are completely trustworthy. In any realistic case, these assumptions could not be justified (once you seemingly observe the ten-degree temperature difference, you should infer that your temperature measurements are not accurate, that the box was not really isolated, or something similar). Nevertheless, *if* we take assumptions (i) and (ii) as fixed, then the hypothesis of an incredibly coincidental thermodynamic fluctuation is the correct inference.

So there are two kinds of cases:

(a) Cases like the Indonesia/Netherlands case, in which we should accept the Forward Argument.

(b) Cases like that of the isolated box considered here, in which we should accept the Reverse Argument.

What is the key difference between (a) and (b)?

I think the difference is that in type (b) cases, we are given that a system has been isolated long enough, with nothing to interfere with the random behavior of its particles, to reach thermal equilibrium. In reality, the world never gives us such guarantees. In reality, if you see a significant difference between two large groups, the rational inference is never that it came about by some astronomical coincidence; the rational inference is that some mechanism produced it systematically, even if the mechanism is wholly unknown to you.

Thus, if we observe that people in the Netherlands are on average 0.8 feet taller than those in Indonesia, we should not take this to be the result of purely random distribution of human heights. We should assume that some mechanism systematically produces taller people in the one region than in the other. This mechanism might, for example, have to do with differing evolutionary pressures in different climates – but one need not know anything about the mechanism to be justified in concluding that there is *some* systematic mechanism or other. The idea that such large groups of people have such a large average height difference by pure chance is just so improbable that we are justified in inferring that there is some more fundamental cause, even if we can't guess what it might be. From there, it is reasonable to expect that the person who recently migrated from Indonesia was a relatively short person.

Similarly, the idea that the universe has its present low-entropy state by pure chance is so incredibly improbable that we should assume that there is *some* (presently unknown) more fundamental cause that preferentially brought about an extremely low-entropy universe fourteen billion years ago, or whenever our physical universe came into being. We should assume this, even if we don't know what could make the universe have such low entropy. Of this, we will have more to say in our discussion of the Fine Tuning Argument in section 11.2.

References

Aerts, Diederik and Massimiliano Sassoli de Bianchi. 2014. "Solving the Hard Problem of Bertrand's Paradox", *Journal of Mathematical Physics* 55: 083583.
Bayes, Thomas. 1763. "An Essay Towards Solving a Problem in the Doctrine of Chances", *Philosophical Transactions of the Royal Society* 53: 370–418.
Bertrand, Joseph. 1889. *Calcul des Probabilités*. Paris: Gauthier-Villars.
Carnap, Rudolf. 1962. *Logical Foundations of Probability*, 2nd ed. Chicago: University of Chicago Press.
de Finetti, Bruno. [1937] 1964. "Foresight: Its Logical Laws, Its Subjective Sources", tr. Henry Kyburg, pp. 99–158 in Henry Kyburg and Howard Smokler, eds., *Studies in Subjective Probability*. New York: Wiley.
Fumerton, Richard. 1995. *Metaepistemology and Skepticism*. Lanham: Rowman & Littlefield.

Howson, Colin and Peter Urbach. 1993. *Scientific Reasoning: The Bayesian Approach*, 2nd ed. Chicago: Open Court.

Huemer, Michael. 2009. "Explanationist Aid for the Theory of Inductive Logic", *British Journal for the Philosophy of Science* 60 (2009): 1–31.

Huemer, Michael. 2017. "There Is No Pure Empirical Reasoning," *Philosophy and Phenomenological Research* 95: 592–613.

Hume, David. 1975. *Enquiry Concerning Human Understanding* in L. A. Selby-Bigge and P. H. Nidditch, eds., *Enquiries Concerning Human Understanding and Concerning the Principles of Morals*, 3rd edn. Oxford: Clarendon.

Hurley, James. 1986. "The Time-asymmetry Paradox", *American Journal of Physics* 54: 25–8.

Keynes, John Maynard. 1921. *A Treatise on Probability*. London: Macmillan.

Laplace, Pierre Simon. 1995. *Philosophical Essay on Probabilities*, tr. Andrew Dale, New York: Springer.

Marinoff, Louis. 1994. "A Resolution of Bertrand's Paradox", *Philosophy of Science* 61: 1–24.

Popper, Karl. 1961. *The Logic of Scientific Discovery*. New York: Science Editions.

Randall. 2011. "The Crazy Nastyass Honey Badger" (video), YouTube, January 18, https://www.youtube.com/watch?v=4r7wHMg5Yjg, accessed December 10, 2017.

Rawls, John. 1999. *A Theory of Justice*, revised ed. Cambridge, MA: Harvard University Press.

Reichenbach, Hans. 1938. *Experience and Prediction: An Analysis of the Foundations and the Structure of Knowledge*. Chicago: University of Chicago Press.

Shackel, Nicholas. 2007. "Bertrand's Paradox and the Principle of Indifference", *Philosophy of Science* 74: 150–75.

Stove, David C. 1986. *The Rationality of Induction*. Oxford: Clarendon.

van Fraassen, Bas. 1989. *Laws and Symmetry*. Oxford: Clarendon.

9

The Ravens

9.1 A Paradox of Confirmation

Inductive reasoning is a kind of reasoning in which we draw generalizations from particular cases (see discussion, section 8.6 above). For instance, if you see many black ravens, with no exceptions, you might infer that all ravens are black, even though you have not seen all the ravens in the world.

Philosophers have tried to describe the rules governing this type of reasoning. Under what conditions does some observation count as inductive evidence for a generalization? The following principles seem especially intuitive[1]:

I. Observation of an A that is B supports the generalization [All A's are B].
II. Observation of an A that is not B refutes the generalization [All A's are B].
III. Observation of a non-A is irrelevant to the generalization [All A's are B], that is, provides evidence neither for nor against it.
IV. If two propositions are logically equivalent, then they are supported or refuted by precisely the same observations.

---

[1] Conditions I-III are advanced by Nicod (1930, p. 219). Hempel adds the fourth. The paradox is first discussed in Hempel 1945, pp. 13–21.

© The Author(s) 2018
M. Huemer, *Paradox Lost*, https://doi.org/10.1007/978-3-319-90490-0_9

Note that we are not asking under what conditions an observation *conclusively* supports a generalization. Nor are we asking when an observation supports a generalization *enough* that one could be justified in believing the generalization based solely on that observation. We are only asking under what conditions an observation provides *at least some* support, however small, for a given generalization. With that understood, the above four principles seem like a reasonable start on an answer. Thus, for example, if I observe a black raven, I thereby have (at least a little) evidence for thinking that all ravens are black; if I observe a white raven, I have (conclusive) evidence *against* the idea that all ravens are black; and if I observe a non-raven, I do not thereby have any evidence either for or against the claim that all ravens are black.

The above four principles, however, are jointly incompatible. For suppose I observe a purple shoe. This object is not a raven, so, by principle III above, this observation is irrelevant to [All ravens are black].

The object is, however, a non-black non-raven. Therefore, by principle I, this observation supports [All non-black things are non-ravens]. But [All non-black things are non-ravens] is logically equivalent to [All ravens are black] (both generalizations simply deny that there are any non-black ravens). So, by principle IV, the observation of the purple shoe must support [All ravens are black].

Which is it, then: does the shoe observation support [All ravens are black], or is it irrelevant?

9.2   Solution

The answer depends on how the observation was gathered. We can imagine at least three ways in which a purple shoe observation might come about:

Method 1: An object is randomly selected from the class of non-ravens (figure 9.1). Imagine that there is a giant bag labeled "non-ravens", where you know at the start that everything in the bag is something other than a raven. You pick an object out of the bag, and it turns out to be a purple shoe. In this case, the observation is irrelevant: you have acquired no evidence either for or against the hypothesis that all ravens are black. This

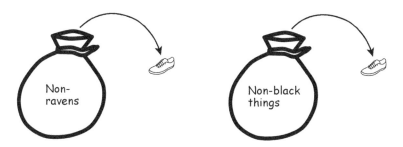

Fig. 9.1 Ways of collecting an observation of a non-black non-raven

is because, even if there were some non-black ravens in the world, you could not have discovered any of them by this method.[2]

Method 2: There is a giant bag labeled "non-black things". You pick one object randomly from the bag, and it turns out to be a purple shoe. In this case, you gain *some* evidence that all ravens are black. This is because, if there were some non-black ravens, you *could* have discovered one by this method. Your failure to discover one is evidence that there aren't any. It is only a very small amount of evidence, because the class of non-black things is extremely large; thus, even if there are some white ravens out there (or whatever other non-black color they might be), there is only a very small chance that you would find one by this method. You would have to sample a great many non-black things before becoming confident that none of them are ravens.[3]

It may seem that the above two suggested methods are contrived – when does one ever come across a bag full of non-ravens? It is, however, possible to make observations in ways that are relevantly like that. For instance, suppose I am trying to find out whether all ravens are black, and I decide to gather evidence by checking the shelves in a local shoe store. Ravens tend not to frequent shoe stores, so this is relevantly like looking in the bag of non-ravens. This is a poor method, since it is extremely improbable that I would find a non-black raven, even if non-black ravens exist. (The probability is not *zero* – there *might* be a raven in the store – so in fact I could gather some very tiny amount of evidence in the shoe

---

[2] Cf. Hempel 1945, pp. 19–20.
[3] Cf. Rescher 2001, p. 226.

store.) To gather stronger evidence, I should look in a place that non-black ravens would be more likely to visit, if such creatures existed. More generally, for any given hypothesis, I should test the hypothesis under the conditions that would be most likely to refute the hypothesis if the hypothesis were in fact false.

Method 3: I select a random observable object from the universe, and it turns out to be a purple shoe. Or, to be more realistic: I go looking around my environment, with no particular effort to find either ravens or non-ravens, black things or non-black things, just examining whatever I run into. Among other things, I see a purple shoe. In this case, I acquire, again, a very small amount of evidence that all ravens are black. This is because this method has a (very small) chance of yielding an observation of a non-black raven, if such things exist.

Which of the four principles of confirmation are mistaken, then? The important mistake is principle III, "Observation of a non-A is irrelevant to the generalization [All A's are B]." This is not always true, because it is possible for an observation of a non-A to be made in conditions such that, antecedently, there was some chance that the observation would have turned out to be of an A that is non-B, if such objects existed. The reason why principle III *sounds* true is that, when we hear about observations of non-A's, we tend to imagine conditions such that it is antecedently known, before making the observation, that the object will be a non-A. We then ask, *given* that an object is a non-A, does it matter whether it is a B? The answer to that is of course no. In other words, when we hear "observation of an A …", we tend to think of something like the scenario of drawing an object from the bag of A's; when we hear "observation of a non-A …", we think of drawing an object from the bag of non-A's. But there are other ways of making an observation.

Principle I, "Observation of an A that is B supports the generalization [All A's are B]", is similarly mistaken. If the observation is collected in such a way that it could not have turned up a counterexample to the generalization – as in the case of an object randomly selected from the class of B things which turns out to be an A – then the observation is irrelevant to the generalization [All A's are B].

References

Hempel, Carl G. 1945. "Studies in the Logic of Confirmation (I)", *Mind* 54: 1–26.

Nicod, Jean. 1930. *Foundations of Geometry and Induction*, tr. Philip Paul Wiener. London: Kegan Paul, Trench, Trubner & Co.

Rescher, Nicholas. 2001. *Paradoxes: Their Roots, Range, and Resolution*. Chicago, IL: Open Court.

10

The Shooting Room

10.1 The Paradox

Somewhere in the world is an awful place called "the shooting room".[1] The people who own the shooting room have decided to play an evil game. They play the game once and only once. The game works like this: first, they call one person, randomly selected from all the people in the universe, into the room. When called into the room, a person is forced to go. The sinister organizers then flip a fair coin. If it lands heads, they shoot the person, whereupon the game ends.

If the coin lands tails, they let the person go, then call 9 new people into the room, and flip the coin a second time. If it lands heads on the second toss, they shoot the 9 people, and the game ends.

If it lands tails the second time, they let the 9 people go, call 90 new people into the room, and flip the coin a third time. If it lands heads, they shoot the 90 people, and the game ends.

If it lands tails, they let the 90 people go, call 900 new people into the room ... and so on. The game continues until some shooting occurs. In general, for each round n after the first one, the organizers call $9 \times 10^{n-2}$

---

[1] This chapter's paradox (with slight modification) is based on Leslie 1996, pp. 235–6, 251–6.

© The Author(s) 2018
M. Huemer, *Paradox Lost*, https://doi.org/10.1007/978-3-319-90490-0_10

people into the room, then flip the fair coin for the *n*th time. If it lands heads on this *n*th toss, they shoot everyone in the room and the game concludes. If it lands tails, they let the people in the room go, then begin round *n*+1.

Now suppose that you learn that a particular individual, Vic, was called into the shooting room some time ago. What is the probability that Vic got shot? There are two plausible answers to this.

Answer 1: When Vic was called into the room, a fair coin was flipped. There is a 50% chance that it landed heads, in which case Vic was shot, and a 50% chance that it landed tails, in which case Vic was released unharmed. Therefore, the probability that Vic was shot is 50%.

Answer 2: Consider what percentage of all the people called into the room get shot. If the game went for only one round, then 100% (one out of one) of the people called into the room got shot. If the game went for exactly two rounds, then the one person from the first round was released unharmed, but then the 9 people in the second round were shot, so 90% of all the people called into the room were shot. If the game went for exactly three rounds, then 10 people (from rounds one and two) were called into the room but were released unharmed, while 90 (from round three) were shot. So again, 90% of all the people called into the room were shot. And so on. In general, if the game lasted for *n* rounds (for any *n* > 1), then 90% of all the people called into the room were shot. The coin must *eventually* come up heads. So we know, with probability 1, that the percentage of people called into the room who are shot is at least 90%. Therefore, given that Vic was one of these people, the probability that he was shot is at least 90%.[2]

These two methods of calculating the answer turn on two different, plausible principles about probability. I will call them the Objective Chance Principle and the Proportion Principle:

---

[2] Leslie (1996, pp. 252–5) maintains that the 50% answer is correct if the coin flip result is genuinely random, but that 90% is correct if the coin flip is deterministic (though unpredictable to you). I think this a very odd view.

Objective Chance Principle: Given that event A happens if and only if B happens, and B has an objective chance c of occurring, the probability that A happens is c.[3]

Proportion Principle: Given that x is an A, and the proportion of A's that are B is p (with no reason for regarding x as being more or less likely to be B than any of the other A's), the probability that x is B is p.

In the present case, Vic's getting shot turns on the coin's coming up heads, which has a 50% objective chance of occurring. No other information given in the scenario affects the probability of the coin's coming up heads, so, applying the Objective Chance Principle, we should assign a 50% probability to Vic's getting shot. At the same time, you know that Vic is a person called into the shooting room, and at least 90% of people called into the shooting room are shot, and there is no reason for regarding Vic as more or less likely to be shot than any other person called into the room. Hence, applying the Proportion Principle, we should assign at least a 90% probability to Vic's being shot.

So, which of these principles must we reject: the Objective Chance Principle, or the Proportion Principle?

10.2   Solution

10.2.1   Solving the Finite Case

The paradox makes crucial use of the infinite: the setup of the problem assumes that the game can simply continue until some shooting occurs, *however long this takes.* This requires that the shooting room has infinite size, that the people running the scheme have an infinite supply of bullets, that there is an infinite population of people from which they can draw their potential victims, that they have had an infinite amount of

---

[3] This is applying Lewis' (1980, p. 266) "Principal Principle". Background assumption: our evidence includes only information about what happens at and before the time at which chance c exists. We don't, for example, have access to a crystal ball that detects future events via backwards causation.

time to complete the game (or else that they can move with unlimited speed, so that they could complete any number of rounds in a finite time), and so on. These assumptions are impossible; as a result, there is no need to answer what would result from such a scenario.[4] The question is like the question of what would occur if an irresistible force encountered an immovable object – the proper response to which is, "There cannot be any such things."

What happens if we replace the impossible assumptions with assumptions that are in principle realizable? Rather than supposing that the game can continue indefinitely, let us suppose that there is a finite but large limit to the number of rounds that the game could continue. This might be, say, because there are only so many people in the world who could be called into the shooting room; thus, if the game should get to the point where it requires calling more new people into the room than the number of new people who exist, the game simply ends with no one being shot. But we may assume that the number of available victims is very large, so that the probability of running out of potential victims is very small.[5]

This version of the scenario is metaphysically possible, unlike the original version. In this case, what is the probability of Vic's getting shot, given that Vic is called into the room? Again, there are two ways of calculating this. The first way is to look at the chance of the coin coming up heads when it is flipped while Vic is in the room. This is 50%, so Vic has a 50% probability of getting shot.

The second method is to look at the percentage of all the people called into the room who are shot. But we no longer know for sure that this percentage is at least 90; if the game goes on long enough, with the coin repeatedly coming up tails, then everyone will escape unharmed. This does not mean that we cannot use this method; it just means that the calculation must be more complex. We can still use the principle that, *given* that x% of people called into the room are shot, the probability of Vic's being shot is x%. The proportion of people shot is either 100% or 90% or 0%. So we will have to calculate the probability, given that Vic is

---

[4] See Huemer 2016, pp. 143–53, 223–8.
[5] Leslie (1996, p. 252) briefly considers such a scenario and suggests that the 90% answer would still be correct.

called into the room, that 100% of the people called into the room are shot, as well the probability that 90% of the people are shot, and that 0% of the people are shot.

Now, speaking informally, the key point is going to be that the probability of Vic being called into the room increases as the game goes on; therefore, when you learn that Vic has been called into the room, this provides evidence that the game has gone on for a long time, which in turn raises the probability that the organizers would have run out of potential victims and thus had to conclude the game with no one having been shot. After taking this into account, it is going to turn out that the overall probability of Vic's having been shot is 50%.

To illustrate, let us assume that there are only one million people in the world (the results we will derive can be generalized to any finite population). If the shooting room organizers run out of people to call into the room, then the game ends. Thus, if the coin comes up tails seven times in a row (at which point the next round of the game would require 9 million new people to be called into the room), the game ends with no one having been shot. If the coin comes up tails *fewer* than seven times before coming up heads, then some people get shot. Thus, there are eight possible outcomes of the game, which I will call O_1, O_2, and so on:

	Coin toss results	People shot	Total people called into room	Proportion of people shot	Probability of outcome
O_1	H	1	1	1	1/2
O_2	TH	9	10	0.9	1/4
O_3	TTH	90	100	0.9	1/8
O_4	TTTH	900	1,000	0.9	1/16
O_5	TTTTH	9,000	10,000	0.9	1/32
O_6	TTTTTH	90,000	100,000	0.9	1/64
O_7	TTTTTTH	900,000	1,000,000	0.9	1/128
O_8	TTTTTTT	0	1,000,000	0	1/128

We want to calculate the probability that Vic is shot, given that Vic is called into the room. Call this $P(S|C)$. (S is the proposition that Vic is shot; C is the proposition that Vic is called into the room.) According to probability theory, given that O_1, ..., O_8 are the only possible outcomes,

$$P(S|C) = P(O_1|C)P(S|O_1,C) + P(O_2|C)P(S|O_2,C) + \dots$$
$$+P(O_8|C)P(S|O_8,C) \tag{10.1}$$

The second factor in each of those terms ($P(S|O_m,C)$) can be determined by applying the Proportion Principle: we simply take the *proportion* of all people called into the room who are shot, given each possible outcome, and treat this as the *probability* of Vic being shot, given that he is called into the room and given that particular outcome. This proportion is 0.9 in each outcome, except the first (where it is 1) and the last (where it is 0). Thus:

$$P(S|O_1,C) = 1$$
$$P(S|O_2,C) = \dots = P(S|O_7,C) = 0.9 \tag{10.2}$$
$$P(S|O_8,C) = 0$$

Substituting Eq. 10.2 into Eq. 10.1 yields (with a little arithmetical manipulation):

$$P(S|C) = P(O_1|C) + (0.9)\big[P(O_2|C) + \dots + P(O_7|C)\big] \tag{10.3}$$

Next, what is the value of $P(O_1|C)$? According to Bayes' Theorem (given that $O_1, \dots, O_8$ are the only possible outcomes),

$$P(O_1|C) = \frac{P(O_1) \times P(C|O_1)}{P(O_1) \times P(C|O_1) + \dots + P(O_8) \times P(C|O_8)} \tag{10.4}$$

The values of $P(O_1)$, $P(O_2)$, and so on can be read off the table above:

$$P(O_1) = 1/2$$
$$P(O_2) = 1/4$$
$$P(O_3) = 1/8$$
$$P(O_4) = 1/16$$
$$P(O_5) = 1/32 \tag{10.5}$$
$$P(O_6) = 1/64$$
$$P(O_7) = 1/128$$
$$P(O_8) = 1/128$$

What about $P(C|O_1)$, the probability of Vic being called into the room, given that the coin comes up heads on the first toss? If the coin comes up heads on the first toss, then the total number of people ever called into the room is 1. We have assumed that the world population is one million. Therefore, the probability of Vic being the person called into the room would be one in a million. With each round that the game goes on, the total number of people who have been called into the room increases by tenfold; thus, Vic's probability of being called in multiplies by ten, up until the last round, when everyone in the world has been called in. Thus, we obtain:

$$P(C|O_1) = 1/1,000,000$$
$$P(C|O_2) = 1/100,000$$
$$P(C|O_3) = 1/10,000$$
$$P(C|O_4) = 1/1,000$$
$$P(C|O_5) = 1/100 \tag{10.6}$$
$$P(C|O_6) = 1/10$$
$$P(C|O_7) = 1$$
$$P(C|O_8) = 1$$

All of this is in accordance with the Proportion Principle for assigning probabilities. Plugging Eqs. 10.5 and 10.6 into Eq. 10.4 yields:

$$P(O_1|C) = \frac{\left(\dfrac{1}{2}\right)\left(\dfrac{1}{1,000,000}\right)}{\left(\dfrac{1}{2}\right)\left(\dfrac{1}{1,000,000}\right)+\ldots+\left(\dfrac{1}{128}\right)}(1)$$

$$= \frac{1}{35,156}$$

We can find $P(O_2|C)$, $P(O_3|C)$, and so on, using the same method. Omitting the remaining tedious arithmetic, I display the results as follows:

$$P(O_1|C) = 1/35,156$$
$$P(O_2|C) = 5/35,156$$
$$P(O_3|C) = 25/35,156$$
$$P(O_4|C) = 125/35,156 \tag{10.7}$$
$$P(O_5|C) = 625/35,156$$
$$P(O_6|C) = 3,125/35,156$$
$$P(O_7|C) = 15,625/35,156$$

Finally, plugging Eq. 10.7 into Eq. 10.3:

$$P(S|C) = \frac{1}{35,156} + 0.9\left(\frac{5}{35,156} + \frac{25}{35,156} + \frac{125}{35,156} + \frac{625}{35,156} + \frac{3,125}{35,156} + \frac{15,625}{35,156}\right)$$
$$= 0.5. \tag{10.8}$$

This result, obtained by applying the Proportion Principle for assigning probabilities, is identical to the result obtained by applying the Objective Chance Principle: the probability of Vic being shot given that he is called into the room is ½. This was just a much more tedious way of obtaining the result.

That result was obtained assuming a population size of one million. But the same result emerges for any finite population size. For instance, if we instead suppose that the population of people available for the shooting room is one billion, then the final equation will be:

$$P(S|C) = P(O_1|C) + 0.9\left[P(O_2|C) + \ldots + P(O_{10}|C)\right]$$

$$= \frac{1}{4,394,531} + 0.9\left(\frac{5}{4,394,531} + \frac{25}{4,394,531} + \ldots + \frac{1,953,125}{4,394,531}\right)$$

$$= 0.5.$$

So we need not choose between the Objective Chance Principle and the Proportion Principle. The two principles yield the same result, 0.5, for all possible population sizes. They disagree only in the impossible case of an infinite population.

10.2.2   The Impossibility of the Infinite Case

Now, you might ask: What's so impossible about an infinite population? On some current cosmological theories, the physical universe is held to be infinite. Thus, for all we know, the population of intelligent beings in the universe might actually be infinite.

Fair point. The impossibility in the original statement of the Shooting Room scenario does not really lie in the fact that the scenario assumes an infinite population. There may in fact be infinitely many persons in the universe. It is just that only finitely many of them could have been called into the shooting room, as of any given time. To see this, it suffices to reflect on the temporal processes described in the scenario. In each round of the game, some people must be gathered together, a coin flipped, and then the people in the room either shot or released. This takes time. Since the game has a first round, it must have begun at some time. Whatever that time was, only a finite time has elapsed since then. Therefore, only finitely many rounds of the game can have been played up till now. In that sense, at any given time, only finitely many people can have been called into the room. If the coin has thus far always come up tails, then, so far, 0% of all the people ever called in have been shot. This is enough for the logic of our above solution.

"But," you might think, "what if the organizers play the game faster and faster with each round? They take one day to play the first round; then, if there is a second round, they take half a day for that; then a quarter of a day for the third round; and so on. In that case, they can complete an unlimited number of rounds within two days."

This, however, is really impossible. To be thus capable of playing the game faster and faster without limit, the organizers would require an infinite store of energy located within a finite region. There cannot be such infinite energy density in any region.[6] In addition, of course, the organizers would need the ability to violate various laws of physics to be able to play the game faster and faster without limit. Since the scenario is impossible, it does not matter that the Objective Chance Principle and the Proportion Principle would conflict in this case. Since the principles agree in all genuinely possible cases, we can continue to endorse both.

References

Hamade, Rufus. 1996. "Black Holes and Quantum Gravity", Cambridge Relativity and Cosmology, University of Cambridge, http://www.damtp.cam.ac.uk/research/gr/public/bh_hawk.html, accessed May 31, 2017.
Huemer, Michael. 2016. *Approaching Infinity*. New York: Palgrave Macmillan.
Leslie, John. 1996. *The End of the World*. London: Routledge.
Lewis, David. 1980. "A Subjectivist's Guide to Objective Chance", pp. 263–93 in Richard C. Jeffrey, ed., *Studies in Inductive Logic and Probability*, vol. II. Berkeley, Calif.: University of California Press.
Wald, Robert M. 1984. *General Relativity*. Chicago: University of Chicago Press.

[6] It is metaphysically impossible for anything to possess an infinite, natural, intensive magnitude; see Huemer 2016, ch. 10. Energy density counts as a natural, intensive magnitude. You might object that, according to General Relativity, the center of a black hole has infinite energy density. This, however, is generally regarded as a problem for physicists to solve – physicists are seeking theories that eliminate the infinite quantities in such cases (Wald 1984, pp. 211–12; Hamade 1996). In any case, if the organizers of the Shooting Room gather together enough energy in a small enough space to create a black hole, it is doubtful that they would still be able to carry out their game.

11

Self-Locating Beliefs

11.1   The Sleeping Beauty Paradox

A group of scientists is about to perform a simple experiment (figure 11.1).[1] At the beginning of the week, they put a person ("Sleeping Beauty", as we will call her) to sleep by chemical means. Then they flip a fair coin. If it comes up heads, the scientists wake up Sleeping Beauty on Monday, talk to her briefly, then put her back to sleep, using a drug that causes her to forget being woken up. Beauty will then continue to sleep until she wakes up naturally a few days later.

If, on the other hand, the coin comes up tails, then the scientists wake up Beauty twice: once on Monday, and again on Tuesday. Each time, the scientists talk to her briefly, then put Beauty back to sleep using the same drug, which erases her memory of having been woken. Thus, if Beauty is woken on Tuesday, she will not remember having been woken on Monday, and she will have no way of knowing what day it is. When she is woken on Monday, she also will not know whether it is Monday or Tuesday,

---

[1] An ancestor of this section's paradox, the "paradox of the absentminded driver", was devised by Piccione and Rubinstein (1997). The present version was introduced to philosophers by Elga (2000).

© The Author(s) 2018
M. Huemer, *Paradox Lost*, https://doi.org/10.1007/978-3-319-90490-0_11

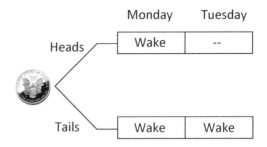

Fig. 11.1 Sleeping Beauty problem

since she won't know whether she was previously woken up and forgot it. Beauty is aware of all this at the start.

When the scientists wake Beauty, they ask her one question: "What is your credence that the coin came up heads?" (Alternately: "How likely do you consider it that the coin came up heads?")

If she is perfectly rational, what answer should Beauty give? What is the correct probability to assign to the coin's having come up heads? There are two plausible answers to this.

Answer 1: Coins have a ½ probability of coming up heads when flipped. Thus, at the start of the experiment, Beauty should have a ½ credence that the coin will come up heads. Upon being woken, she has no additional relevant evidence. She knows that she has just been woken up, but she already knew from the start that she would be woken up at least once, so this is nothing new. Therefore, she should continue to reckon the probability of the coin's having come up heads at ½.[2]

Answer 2: Suppose that the experiment were repeated with 200 subjects. Most likely, about 100 times the coin would come up heads, and the other approximately 100 times it would come up tails. There would then be a total of 300 occasions on which someone was woken up, not knowing what day it was, and asked about the probability that the coin came up heads. These 300 wakings would include:

---

[2] This is the view of Lewis (2001).

100 wakings in which the coin had come up heads, and it was now Monday
100 wakings in which the coin had come up tails, and it was now Monday
100 wakings in which the coin had come up tails, and it was now Tuesday

Suppose you participate in this experiment. At some point, you find yourself experiencing one of these 300 wakings, of which you believe roughly 1/3 are "heads wakings" (that is, occasions of someone being woken up after the coin in fact landed heads). You have no reason to think this particular waking more or less likely than any other to be a heads waking. So the probability that the coin landed heads before this waking is 1/3.

Of course, the numbers would probably not break down so evenly; perhaps the coin would come up heads 105 times, or 93 times, instead of exactly 100. But in the long run, if the experiment were performed many times, the proportion of heads results would approach ½, and the proportion of wakings on which "the coin came up heads" was true would approach 1/3.[3]

11.2   The Fine Tuning Argument

Before trying to solve the above problem, I want to tell you about another very interesting, controversial argument, which will turn out to be related to the Sleeping Beauty Problem.

According to many scientists, the conditions required for life to exist are extremely specific. I don't just mean the conditions for *human* life to exist; I mean the conditions for any sort of life that we have any understanding of. There are a number of physical parameters of the universe that must take on values in an extremely narrow range, if life is to be possible in this universe. For example, it has been calculated that if the gravitational constant differed by more than $1/10^{40}$ of its present value, stars would either be too hot or too cool to support life.[4] Similar claims are

---

[3] This argument is defended by Elga (2000).
[4] Davies 1984, p. 242. For a series of examples of fine tuning, see Leslie 1989, chs. 2–3.

made about the cosmological constant, the strength of the strong nuclear force, the strength of the electromagnetic force, and other parameters. Another interesting instance of fine tuning showed up earlier, in section 8.7: the universe apparently started out, 14 billion years ago, in an incredibly low-entropy state. The overwhelming majority of possible states for any complex system are states of thermal equilibrium (with maximal entropy). If the universe had started out in a state of thermal equilibrium, it would still be in thermal equilibrium now, which means that there would be no living things, nor would there be anything else interesting going on. So it is very lucky that the universe started with extremely low entropy.

Now, our present interest is not in evaluating the preceding scientific claims. Assume that the scientific facts are as just described. What could we infer from that? Is there an explanation for why the universe has the properties needed for life to exist? According to one line of argument, the best explanation for the universe's having such properties is that our universe was designed by an intelligent being (sometimes called "God") who wanted there to be life.[5] If the universe has *no* such designer, it is said, there is no particular reason why it should have the properties required for life to exist. Since those properties are so specific, it is overwhelmingly more likely that the universe would *not* have them than that it would. So if there were no intelligent designer, there almost certainly would not be any life. But if there were an intelligent designer, it is at least reasonably likely that there would be life. So the fact that life exists is evidence that the universe is the product of design.

The most popular non-theistic alternative is the Multiple Universes ("Multiverse") theory (figure 11.2): perhaps there are many different "universes", each with different values for the mentioned physical parameters. (Obviously, "universe" here does not refer to the totality of everything that exists. Rather, the "universes" are just very big collections of stuff that are isolated from each other, such that if you're in one of them, your own universe is all you can see.) Out of the enormous number of universes (perhaps even infinitely many), some extremely small percentage have the right parameter values for life to be possible. It is only in those universes that there is anyone to look around, measure the parameters, and find that

---

[5] Davies 1983, chs. 12–13.

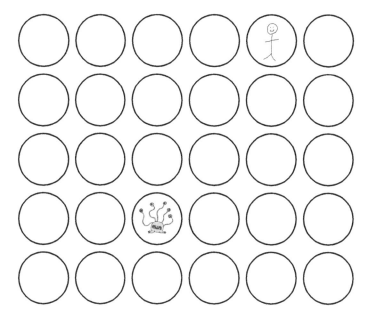

Fig. 11.2 The multiverse

they are "fine-tuned" for life. In the many other universes where life is impossible, there just is no one around to notice this fact. That is why we should not be surprised to find that the physical parameters in our universe have the values required for life to exist.[6]

Now, there may be other possible theories, but I won't consider any such here. Nor will I discuss the general plausibility of intelligent design theories, though I assume that intelligent design constitutes at least a possible rational account of the fine tuning evidence.

My main interest is in the Multiverse theory. Does the fine tuning evidence – the fact that the universe has parameters falling within very narrow ranges that are necessary for life to exist – support the existence of multiple universes? If so, does this neutralize whatever reason we would otherwise have for accepting the Design hypothesis? Some think the Multiverse theory is superior to Intelligent Design. But others think, for

---

[6] Carter 1974, pp. 295–8; Tegmark 2003; Susskind 2006.

reasons to be discussed below, that the Multiverse is not a reasonable explanation at all.

11.3   The Doomsday Argument

Now I want to tell you about one more interesting argument, which will turn out to be related to the Fine Tuning Argument and the Sleeping Beauty Problem.[7]

How much longer will the human species last? No one knows. There are many possible scenarios for our extinction: perhaps the species will be destroyed by nuclear war. Or a biological weapon will be released that kills everyone. Or a giant asteroid impact will do us in. Or we will be destroyed by superintelligent robots that we created but lost control of. And so on. Alternately, perhaps we will avoid all of these dangers and the species will go on for millions of years, perhaps even colonizing other star systems throughout the galaxy.

For simplicity, let us just consider two hypotheses:

Short-lived Species: The human species will go extinct within the next ten thousand years.
Long-lived Species: The human species will continue for more than ten thousand more years.

The Doomsday Argument is an argument designed to show that the human species is probably short-lived, rather than long-lived. The argument claims that we have evidence for this conclusion simply in virtue of the number of people who have so far existed.

Thus far, human beings have existed for at least 50,000 years (perhaps more, depending on what you count as human); however, for almost all of that time, the world population was extremely low. As a result, the total number of humans who have ever existed is surprisingly low, only

---

[7] The argument derives from Leslie 1990 (vaguely presaged by Carter 1983). For a concise, popular presentation, see Bostrom 2012.

about 108 billion, of which around 7.4 billion are alive now.[8] If you are alive now, then you are somewhere between the 100 billionth and the 108 billionth human who was ever born; that is, your "birth order" within the species is between 100 billion and 108 billion. Given the facts about population, if the human species is long-lived, then many more people will exist in the future than have existed in the past. So, if the human species is long-lived, then almost all humans who exist, throughout the species' entire lifetime, will have had a birth order much higher than 108 billion.

This means that, *if* the human species is long-lived, then your birth order is *surprisingly low*. On the other hand, if the human species is short-lived, then your birth order is not surprisingly low. In general, if some piece of evidence is more likely to exist if a given hypothesis is true than if the hypothesis is false, then that evidence, if found, raises the probability of the hypothesis. That is: if $P(E|H) > P(E|\sim H)$, then $P(H|E) > P(H)$. The probability of finding that one's birth order is less than 108 billion is greater if one belongs to a short-lived species than it is if one belongs to a long-lived species. Therefore, the fact that your birth order is less than 108 billion is evidence that you belong to a short-lived species, rather than a long-lived one.

Here is an analogy. Suppose that you are about to pick a number out of a hat. Let's say that the hat contains either ten slips of paper, with the numbers 1 through 10 written on them, or a hundred slips of paper, with the numbers 1 through 100. You know it's one of those two alternatives, but you don't know which. Now, you draw your number at random from the hat and look. It turns out to be the number 8. At this point, what should you think about the contents of the hat? Do you think it is a small hat (containing just the numbers up to 10) or a large hat (with numbers going up to 100)? You should think it is *much more likely* to be a small hat, since if it were a large hat, you would almost certainly have drawn a larger number from it. In fact, this probability can be calculated, as follows. Let

S =   [The hat contains just the numbers 1 through 10.]

---

[8] Haub 2011; U.S. Census Bureau 2017.

L =   [The hat contains the numbers 1 through 100.]
E =   [Your chosen number is 8.]

Then by Bayes' Theorem,

$$P(S|E) = \frac{P(S) \cdot P(E|S)}{P(S) \cdot P(E|S) + P(L) \cdot P(E|L)}$$

(11.1)

We assume that S and L are initially equally likely, so P(S) = P(L) = ½. If S is the case, then there were ten numbers in the hat, so there was a one in ten chance of drawing the number 8. If L is the case, then there were a hundred numbers in the hat, so there was a one in a hundred chance of drawing the number 8. Plugging this information into Eq. 11.1 yields:

$$P(S|E) = \frac{\left(\frac{1}{2}\right)\left(\frac{1}{10}\right)}{\left(\frac{1}{2}\right)\left(\frac{1}{10}\right) + \left(\frac{1}{2}\right)\left(\frac{1}{100}\right)} = \frac{10}{11} = .\overline{90}$$

So the probability that you have the small hat is just over 90%.

This is, allegedly, analogous to the reasoning in the Doomsday Argument: you are a random person chosen from the human species. It is either a long-lived species, containing many "birth order" numbers, or a short-lived species, containing relatively few "birth order" numbers. Since your birth order number is relatively small, it is more likely that you are taken from a short-lived species.

Now, there are many interesting issues surrounding this conclusion (the risk of nuclear war, the risk of environmental disaster, etc.). But I will ignore the most exciting issues. I want to focus just on the type of probabilistic reasoning involved in the argument. Assume that the factual premises of the argument are correct, especially that *if* the human species continues for much longer, then the overwhelming majority of people who ever live will turn out to be people born later than you. Do you really have evidence, just on the basis of that, that the species will die out before very long?

I have chosen to discuss the above three issues – Sleeping Beauty, the Fine-Tuning Argument, and the Doomsday Argument – in the same chapter because they all involve similar kinds of reasoning. All involve probabilistic reasoning about "self-locating beliefs" (roughly, beliefs about where you yourself are located), and all involve observational selection effects – that is, we are asked to reason about hypotheses whose truth would affect our chances of existing or otherwise being able to make observations. Most importantly, all three issues can be resolved in a similar manner.

11.4   The Multiverse: Pro and Con

Start with the Fine Tuning Argument. Again, my interest is mainly in assessing the Multiverse theory: is the theory supported by the evidence, and does it neutralize our reason for supporting the Design theory? Here, I'll first explain an objection to the Multiverse theory, then discuss a response in defense of the Multiverse, and then adjudicate between the two.

11.4.1   The "This Universe" Objection

Imagine that you are scheduled to be executed by a firing squad.[9] The firing squad contains fifty sharpshooters with loaded rifles. As the squad takes aim, you expect to die momentarily. You close your eyes. They all fire . . . And somehow, you find yourself still alive. All of the shooters have completely missed. In the moments after this happens, you reflect that this event seems so unlikely that there must be some explanation. Perhaps someone talked to all the squad members beforehand and instructed them all to miss. Or someone got into the armory last night and loaded all the rifles with blanks. Or there is some other explanation you haven't thought of. But almost certainly, it didn't happen by accident.

Now suppose it occurs to you that there might perhaps be a trillion trillion other firing squads elsewhere in the universe. You don't have any

---

[9] This example is from Leslie 1990, p. 70.

independent evidence of such other firing squads, of course. But if there *were* all these firing squads, then it would be likely that there would be at least *some* in which, by pure chance, all fifty shooters missed. It is only in such cases that the convict is able to stand there wondering about the fact that they all missed; in the cases where the squad hits their target (let us assume) the convict is instantly killed. Therefore, you conclude (?), you now have good reason to think there actually *are* all these other firing squads. And since this explains your experience, there is no need to postulate any sort of conspiracy to keep you alive. Is this good reasoning?

I take it that this pretty obviously is not good reasoning. You should not believe in the other firing squads, nor should you dispense with hypotheses about what sort of conspiracy might have kept you alive.

Why not? The problem seems to be that the Multiple Firing Squad hypothesis, even if true, simply is not an explanation for your evidence. Granted, the Multiple Firing Squad theory renders it more probable that *at least one person somewhere* would experience what you just did, that is, all shooters missing. But your evidence is not that at least one person somewhere in the universe has experienced this; your evidence is that *you* experienced this. In general, a theory should explain your *total evidence*, that is, the most informative thing that you know. So what needs to be explained is the fact that you personally survived the firing squad.

The Multiple Firing Squad theory does not explain this, because it would not, even if true, render it more probable that you would have survived. The odds of your firing squad missing are determined by such things as the number of shooters, their level of skill, their motivation, and so on. These odds are not at all affected by what goes on with other squads elsewhere. If someone starts up a firing squad on Alpha Centauri, that doesn't make your firing squad suddenly more likely to miss. If, before your scheduled execution, you are able to implicate a neighbor so that the neighbor is also sentenced to death by firing squad, you do not thereby double your chances of surviving your own scheduled execution, nor should you increase your credence that you will survive. Therefore, whatever happens with your firing squad is completely evidentially irrelevant to the existence of other firing squads.

Here is a simpler analogy.[10] You are about to flip a coin. What is the probability that it will come up heads? 50%. But wait, here is an additional piece of information: someone in the next room is flipping a coin too. Does that make it more likely that you will flip heads? No. That makes it more likely that *at least one of the coins* will come up heads, but the probability that *this* coin will do so remains 50%. So if it does come up heads, this could not be *explained* by the fact that someone flipped another coin in the next room. By the same token, if you should flip ten heads in a row, this could not be explained by there being many other people flipping coins in other rooms. Accordingly, if you flip ten heads in a row, you do not thereby acquire any reason at all to believe that many other coins have been flipped.

Champions of the Multiverse appear to be committing the very fallacy that we have just criticized. They claim that there are probably multiple universes, because this would render it probable that at least some universes would have parameters fine-tuned so as to allow life to exist.[11] This assumes that our evidence is merely that *life exists in at least one universe*. But this is not correct; our evidence is that life exists in *this universe*. This is the most informative thing that we know. And the probability of this evidence obtaining is completely unaffected by what might be happening in any other, causally isolated universes. Just as the other firing squads don't make your squad more likely to miss, and the other coins don't make your coin more likely to come up heads, the other universes do not make your universe any more likely to contain life. Thus, when we see that our universe is fine tuned to allow for life, we do not thereby acquire any reason at all to believe in other universes.[12] Nor, therefore, do we have any reason to set aside the hypothesis of Intelligent Design.

---

[10] Hacking (1987, pp. 33–4) makes the same point, using dice instead of a coin.

[11] Partisans of the multiverse have also claimed to have independent reasons for thinking there must be multiple universes (independent, that is, of the fine tuning evidence); see, e.g., Susskind 2006, ch. 11. I make no attempt to evaluate this claim; my concern is solely whether the fine tuning evidence on its own supports Multiple Universes.

[12] A similar argument is made by Hacking (1987) and White (2000).

11.4.2 In Defense of the Multiverse

Not so fast. There are other analogies that are more favorable to the Multiverse argument. Consider the fact that the Earth contains peculiar features that make it especially hospitable to life.[13] It is within a narrow range of suitable distances from the sun, it has an appropriate size, it contains a large amount of surface water, it contains a suitable quantity of heavier elements, and so on. Many would argue that this should not surprise us, because there are in fact a great many planets in the universe, of which probably the vast majority are unsuitable to life; it is only on the few planets suitable to life that any intelligent beings could have evolved to wonder about the characteristics of their planet. So of course we find ourselves on such a planet.

Now imagine someone pressing the "this planet" objection: "Oh, that only explains the fact that there is at least one habitable planet in the universe. Our evidence is not merely that at least one planet somewhere is habitable; our evidence is that *this planet* is habitable. And however many other planets there may be, they don't affect the habitability of this one. So the Multiple Planet theory does nothing at all to explain our evidence." Intuitively, this objection seems misguided. It also seems analogous to the "this universe" objection from the last subsection (section 11.4.1).

Here is another analogy.[14] Suppose we have a box containing an unknown (to us) quantity of radioactive uranium-235, which has a half-life of about 700 million years. This means that on average, about half of the atoms in any sample of U-235 will decay over a span of 700 million years; these decay events are completely random and independent of each other.

We also have a uranium-decay-detector, which can record whether or not at least one atom in the box decays in a given time period. (It has to be reset after each detected decay event.) Also, oddly enough, every individual uranium atom on Earth has a name (they were all named by scientists back in the 1960s), and the detector can also identify by name the particular atom that triggers it.

---

[13] Manson and Thrush (2003, pp. 73–4) use this analogy to rebut the "this universe" objection.
[14] Manson and Thrush 2003, p. 74. I have modified the example slightly.

You turn on the detector and leave the room for five minutes. On your return, you see that the detector has been triggered by an atom named "b0bxkd6yv2qm513aajy8qlmy4uc9z4" (that's what the atom names look like). I will just abbreviate this name to "Bob". You don't know how many additional atoms might have decayed after Bob, since only the first one is recorded.

At this point, which do you think is more likely: the box contained only one atom, or the box contained many atoms? It seems you could infer that the box contained many atoms, for if there were only one atom in the box, the probability that it would have decayed in just the last five minutes would be on the order of one in a hundred trillion. If, on the other hand, the box contained many atoms, it would be much more likely that at least one of the atoms would have decayed.

Now imagine someone pressing the "this atom" objection: "Oh, that only explains the fact that *at least one* uranium atom in the box decayed. Your evidence is not merely that at least one atom decayed. Your evidence is that *Bob* decayed. And however many other atoms may be in the box, they would have had no effect on Bob's probability of decaying. Thus, the Multiple Atom theory does *nothing at all* to explain your evidence, nor do you have any reason at all for positing multiple atoms." Again, this seems misguided, and again, it seems analogous to the reasoning of section 11.4.1 above.

11.4.3   Four Cases Resolved

We need a theory that accounts for all four of the above cases: the Firing Squad, the Coin Flip, Planet Earth, and the Uranium case. In the first two cases, there is no reason to posit multiple entities. In the last two, there is. If we can find a theory that correctly accounts for these cases, we can use it to evaluate the argument for Multiple Universes.

Here is the theory: Your evidence supports a hypothesis, H, provided that the truth of H would make it more likely that you would receive that qualitative evidence than it would be if H were false. Notice three important points about this principle:

(i) When you are evaluating a hypothesis, what needs to be explained is always *your* having a certain set of evidence, not merely *someone's* having that evidence.

(ii) The evidence itself should be understood qualitatively. By this, I mean that if two possible situations are indistinguishable to you, then they should be treated as cases in which you "have the same evidence". For instance, suppose that in case A, you observe a red bird. In case B, you observe a numerically distinct red bird which, however, is qualitatively exactly like the red bird in case A (and thus, you could not distinguish the two birds). Then I would say that you have the same evidence in case A as you have in case B.

(iii) The explanatoriness of a hypothesis is evaluated relative to the alternatives. To count as explanatory, a hypothesis needs to render the evidence *more likely than* some salient alternatives.

In the Firing Squad case, your evidence consists of an experience of surviving a firing squad. The probability of your receiving this evidence by sheer luck is very low. The probability of *your* receiving this evidence if there were multiple other firing squads elsewhere in the universe is just as low. The existence of other firing squads raises the probability that there will be some other people having that experience, but it does not affect *your* probability of having that experience. On the other hand, the probability of your surviving your firing squad if there was some kind of conspiracy to keep you alive is much higher. So your evidence supports the conspiracy theory, and it does not at all support the multiple-firing-squad theory.

In the Coin Flip case, your evidence is your experience of flipping a coin ten times and seeing it come up heads every time. The probability of your enjoying this evidence as a result of pure chance is $(1/2)^{10}$. The probability of *your* receiving this evidence if there are many other coins being flipped elsewhere by other people is also $(1/2)^{10}$. So the evidence does not support the multiple coin theory.

In the Planet Earth case, your evidence consists of your experience of living on a life-sustaining planet. If there were only one or a few planets in the universe, the probability that you would exist at all is very low. However, if there were *many* planets in the universe, it is much more likely that you would find yourself existing, and of course doing so on a life-sustaining planet. So the evidence supports the multiple-planet theory, as against the "coincidence" theory. (But see section 11.4.4 below for qualifications.) You could also consider a theory of intelligent design: perhaps an intelligent creator made the Earth and intentionally fashioned it to be life-sustaining. This, too, would render it more likely that you would find yourself existing on a life-sustaining planet. So the design hypothesis is also supported by the evidence. (I do not attempt to determine which hypothesis is better; I say only that both are possible explanations.)

Why not describe the evidence as being that *this specific* planet that you find yourself on is life-sustaining, rather than merely that you find yourself on *some* life-sustaining planet? After all, the proposition that you are on Earth and Earth is life-sustaining is more informative than the proposition that you are on some life-sustaining planet or other. The answer is that your evidence does not really identify a specific, individual planet. If you had instead found yourself on another planet, qualitatively *like* Earth but located in another galaxy, you would not have noticed the difference; thus, we should count the evidence you would have had in that case as being the same as the evidence you actually have. Therefore, your relevant evidence is that you are on *a* planet with certain characteristics, not that *this* planet has these characteristics.

Notice that a parallel argument could *not* be made to show that your evidence is not really that *you* are on a life-sustaining planet but only that *someone* is on a life-sustaining planet. For it could not be said that if someone else were having these experiences, you would not notice the difference; rather, if someone else were having experiences like your current experiences, you would not thereby receive any evidence at all, let alone evidence indistinguishable from your actual evidence. For similar reasons, in the Firing Squad case, your evidence must be that *you* survived your firing squad, and in the Coin Flip case, your evidence must be that *you* flipped ten heads in a row.

In the Planet Earth case, why not include in the evidence more information, besides just that you are on a life-sustaining planet? Why not include, say, information about the number of continents on your planet, the number of other planets in its solar system, and even the shapes of the constellations visible in the night sky from your planet? Doesn't the total evidence requirement (section 11.4.1) demand that we include all this?

In reply, that information could indeed be treated as evidence, but it is, as it turns out, irrelevant evidence. It is irrelevant because the theories under consideration do not differentially impact the probabilities of these details. The probability of your finding yourself on a planet from which a "Big Dipper" constellation is visible in the night sky is the same, regardless of whether your planet's life-sustaining properties are a mere fluke, or yours is one of many billions of planets in the universe, or your planet was created by an intelligent designer. Thus, it is permissible to ignore this sort of detail and characterize the relevant evidence as being just that you are on a life-sustaining planet. A refined version of the total evidence requirement, then, would state that we should take a more informative characterization of the evidence rather than a less informative one, whenever this makes a difference to the relative probabilities of the evidence on the alternative hypotheses under consideration.

Lastly, in the case of the uranium atoms, your evidence is that an atom named Bob decayed in the last five minutes. You know nothing about the atom that decayed except that it decayed and it was named Bob. The atom's name is irrelevant information, because the different hypotheses under consideration do not make different probabilistic predictions about the names of atoms. The relevant alternative hypotheses in this case are hypotheses regarding the quantity of uranium in the box. Hypotheses about the number of atoms in the box, whether it be many or few, do not predict anything about what an atom that decays is likely to be named. So we can disregard that information. So the relevant evidence is simply that at least one atom decayed in the last five minutes. You would be much more likely to receive this evidence if the box contained many atoms than if it contained few. So the evidence supports that the box contains many atoms.[15]

---

[15] If one wishes to count the identity of the decayed atom as part of the evidence, this results in a more complicated calculation for the posterior probability of there being many atoms in the box, but the answer will be the same. The key point: whether one or many atoms were in the box has no effect on Bob's probability of decaying; however, the probability of Bob's having been in the box when Bob decayed increases linearly with the number of atoms supposed to be in the box. Since the evidence tells you not only that Bob decayed but that Bob was in the box at the time, the evidence is rendered more probable by the Many Atoms hypothesis. So Many Atoms is confirmed.

11.4.4   Personal Identity and the Multiverse Theory

Now at last, what of the Multiverse theory? It appears that the Multiverse theory *is* supported by the evidence – namely, your experience of finding yourself in a universe that permits the existence of life. This would be more likely to happen if there were many universes than if there were only one.

This conclusion requires a caveat: the argument requires the assumption that *you could have existed in a universe other than this one.*[16] Similarly, our argument about the Planet Earth case in section 11.4.3 assumed that you could have existed on another planet.

You might well doubt this. For you might think that, whatever else you are, you are an individual, physical object. And a particular physical object can only exist in the universe it is in. If some very similar object were to exist in another universe, that object would be made of a completely separate mass of material and have been created at a different time and place, by a distinct causal chain of events. All this, plausibly, suffices to preclude that object from counting as *the same object* as the object that is here, now, in this universe. Thus, if you had not existed in this universe, you could not have existed at all, since no physical object could count as you unless it were in this universe. Or so one might argue.

An alternative view is that you would exist as long as an organism with a brain sufficiently like your actual brain had come into existence somewhere (in whatever universe).

Or perhaps your identity is tied to a particular, immaterial soul, which could have animated any body in any universe.

I cannot resolve the problem of personal identity or the nature of persons here. So I will simply note that *if* a person in another universe could count as you, then the fine tuning evidence supports multiple universes. It *also* to some degree supports Intelligent Design – that is, both theories are

---

[16] Manson and Thrush (2003, pp. 75–7) discuss this issue, inconclusively. My own sympathy for Cartesian dualism inclines me toward accepting the assumption. I don't know what causally determines whether a given immaterial mind animates a given body, but whatever it is, I think it not unreasonable that a given mind could have animated a body in a different universe. But I cannot argue for all this here.

rendered more probable by our finding ourselves existing in a fine-tuned universe. Again, I do not claim to determine which theory is better.[17]

But if a person in another universe could *not* count as you, then the fine tuning evidence gives you no reason at all to believe in other universes. By the way, in this case, your existing on a life-supporting planet is probably also not at all explained by the existence of many planets within our universe – the same reasons that would make us doubt that you could have lived in another universe should also make us doubt that you could have lived on another planet.

11.5   Against Doomsday

The Doomsday Argument makes a similar mistake to the Multiple Coin Flip and Multiple Firing Squad theories. It misunderstands our evidence by characterizing it in an overly general way. As a result, the reasoning takes hypothesized facts that could not have had any effect on our evidence as being relevant to that evidence.

Consider a related probability problem: you are informed that a person has been randomly chosen from all human beings, past, present, and future (maybe there is an alien with a time machine who can survey the species' entire lifetime and thus pick a human at random). The randomly chosen human turned out to have a birth order of about 100 billion.

In this scenario, it would be correct to say that the given evidence supports the Short-lived Species hypothesis rather than the Long-lived Species hypothesis. This is because, if the human species were long-lived, the chosen person would be more likely to have a very high birth order, than if the species were short-lived (here considering 100 billion as a rela-

---

[17] The theories are not empirically equivalent; more evidence is needed to adjudicate between them. Multiverse predicts, roughly, that we should find ourselves to be fairly typical examples of the sort of conscious beings who would exist in a multiverse filled with universes with randomly chosen parameter values. Design predicts, instead, that we should find ourselves in a universe whose parameter values are *especially* suitable or good for life, even out of those sets of parameter values that *permit* life. These predictions can differ. E.g., Multiverse might lead us to expect the initial entropy of the universe to be approximately the highest that it could be, compatible with life later being likely to evolve; Design would probably lead us to expect a lower initial entropy, perhaps the minimal physically possible initial entropy.

tively low birth order). That is, letting "E" stand for the evidence that the random person had a low birth order, "S" stand for the Short-lived Species hypothesis, and "L" stand for the Long-lived Species hypothesis, we can say that $P(S|E) > P(S)$, because $P(E|S) > P(E|L)$.

The Doomsday Argument purports to be analogous to that correct piece of reasoning. This analogy depends on the idea that, if L were true – that is, if the human species were *going to* exist for a long time to come – then you would have been less likely to find yourself existing now, and more likely instead to find yourself existing at a later time, when humanity will be in a more advanced state. Assuming that there is no backwards causation (later events cannot affect earlier events), this cannot be true. The probability of your being born at the time you were actually born is completely unaffected by anything that happens after that time. Therefore, that you were born at that time does not provide any evidence about what will happen later; in particular, it does not confirm any hypotheses about the future of the human species. Letting "Y" denote the fact that you were born at the time you were actually born, we can say that $P(Y|S) = P(Y|L)$; therefore, $P(S|Y) = P(S)$.

Now, you might think there is something fishy about the discussion of the probability of Y. You might wonder whether a proposition such as Y, which refers to the birth of a *specific individual*, has a determinate probability. Some theorists deny in general that singular events have probabilities.[18] And, even if you think some singular events have probabilities, you might think that the criteria for personal identity (the conditions for something to count as *you*) are too indeterminate or inscrutable for there to be a determinate probability that *you* would come into existence at a given time.

That, however, could not be the view of someone who advances the Doomsday Argument, since the Doomsday Argument itself turns on reasoning about the probability of your having a certain birth order; it requires us to claim that you would have been more likely to be born later if the human species were long-lived. So advocates of the Doomsday Argument would have to accept that there is such a thing as the probabil-

---

[18] The reason is that they understand probabilities in terms of frequencies with which some type of outcome occurs in a large collective. See von Mises 1957, pp. 18–20, 28–9.

ity of your being born at a given time – or at least that there is a reasonable proxy that can be used for this.

To explain what I mean by "a reasonable proxy": let Y' be a very detailed but purely qualitative description of the event of your birth. Thus, Y' will say that a baby with such-and-such characteristics was born (where these are your actual characteristics) at a certain time and place, but it will not say that the baby was *you*. Even if you doubt that Y has a determinate probability, at least Y' should have one. So perhaps we can use Y' instead of Y in our reasoning.

To repeat, the Doomsday advocate has to accept *some* description of your relevant evidence concerning your own birth – whether it be Y or Y' or something similar – in order to claim that the evidence is rendered more likely by the Short-lived Species hypothesis. But however exactly we describe the evidence, it is false that the probability of that evidence is affected by what will occur in the future.[19] The future could not have any effect on either Y or Y' obtaining, and you know that. So hypotheses about the future are neither confirmed nor disconfirmed by the occurrence of either Y or Y'.

You might think that P(Y|S) and P(Y|L) are unknowable, or indeterminate, or that there is a range of reasonable values for each of them rather than a single correct value. All of that is consistent with my argument. My argument does not require any particular value for P(Y|S) or P(Y|L) to be accepted as the correct value. My argument only requires that we *reject* the claim that P(Y|S) is determinately greater than P(Y|L). That is enough to reject the Doomsday Argument. We can be ignorant of the values of P(Y|S) and P(Y|L) and yet still be confident that P(Y|S) is not greater than P(Y|L). We can be confident of this simply because we know in general that the future does not affect the past.

Notice how this case differs from the case of picking numbers from a hat. In the hat case, when you pick a small number, you can infer that the hat probably contains few numbers rather than many numbers. This inference is legitimate because the size of the hat can in fact *affect* what number you draw. If the hat contains the numbers 1 through 1,000,000,

---

[19] More precisely, *given* a fixed history of the world prior to time t, the probability of your being born at t is independent of what occurs after t.

that fact would make it possible for you to pick a number between 11 and 1,000,000, which would be causally impossible if the hat contains only the numbers 1 through 10. Furthermore, the larger-numbered slips in the large hat are not causally isolated from the smaller ones; they can prevent the smaller ones from being chosen. The slip numbered "501", for example, can prevent the slip numbered "8" from being chosen, by getting in the way and getting itself drawn out of the hat instead. This is crucially disanalogous from the birth order case used in the Doomsday Argument, since individuals who exist later in time could not have prevented you from being born when you were.

In a sense, the Doomsday Argument is the mirror image of the Multiverse argument. The Multiverse argument asks us to infer, from the fact that we exist at all, that there are many opportunities for beings like us to exist (in the form of the many universes). The Doomsday Argument, by contrast, asks us to infer, from the fact that there haven't been very many humans so far, that there probably are *not* very many opportunities (across space and time) to exist as a human.

But the Multiverse argument does not require any problematic backward causation, since the many universes are supposed to exist simultaneously. The simultaneous existence of many universes makes it more likely that you would find yourself having evidence qualitatively like your current actual evidence (again, assuming that you could have existed in any universe that was sufficiently hospitable for beings like you).

There *could* be a version of the Multiverse theory that makes the same mistake as the Doomsday Argument: suppose we claimed that because we find ourselves existing at all, there probably *will be* many universes in the future. That argument would be fallacious, since the future universes could not have affected your odds of having the evidence you have now.

11.6   Sleeping Beauty: For a Third

We have seen the importance of correctly describing one's evidence. In the Firing Squad case, it is important that your evidence is that *you* survived your firing squad, not merely that *someone* survived a firing squad. In the Doomsday case, it is important that your evidence is that *you* were born at the time you were, not merely that *some* random person from the species' entire history was born at that time.

The Sleeping Beauty problem also turns on a fine point about the description of one's evidence. In this case, the question is which of the following is the better characterization of Sleeping Beauty's evidence:

E_1 I am woken up at least once.
E_2 I am woken up *now*.

If Beauty's evidence, upon being awoken, is E_1, then she in fact has no new evidence, since she knew from the start that she would be woken up at least once regardless of whether the coin came up heads or tails. In that case, she should stick with her initial credence that the coin would come up heads, namely, ½.

If, however, Beauty's evidence, upon being awoken, is E_2, this is new information that she did not have at the start of the experiment. She can rationally update her credences about the coin toss on the basis of this information. In the statement of E_2, "now" refers to the specific time at which Beauty has just found herself awoken. She does not know whether this time is on Monday or Tuesday. All she knows about this particular time is that it is a time at which she was woken by the scientists. But times at which a subject of this experiment is woken up are more likely to be Mondays than to be Tuesdays. Specifically, they are *twice* as likely to be Mondays, since, if the experiment were repeated many times, there would be twice as Monday wakings as Tuesday wakings. Beauty has no reason to think she is special or that this time is special, so she should take the probability of the present time being a Monday to be equal to the probability, in general, of a-time-that-a-subject-of-this-experiment-is-woken-up being a Monday. That is, she should take it to be twice as likely that now is Monday as it is that now is Tuesday. So she should assign credence 2/3 to its being Monday, and 1/3 to its being Tuesday.

Of course, on the supposition that now is Tuesday, the coin definitely came up tails, not heads. On the supposition that now is Monday, it is just 50% likely that the coin came up heads, since this was 50% likely antecedently, and the fact that Beauty is woken on Monday does not add any new information (she was definitely going to be woken on Monday, regardless of how the coin landed). Now let

Heads = [The coin came up heads]
Tails = [The coin came up tails]
Mon = [Now is Monday]
Tues = [Now is Tuesday]

From what we have just said, $P(Mon)=2/3$, $P(Tues)=1/3$, $P(Heads|Mon)=1/2$, and $P(Heads|Tues)=0$. Beauty can calculate $P(Heads)$ as follows:

$$P(\text{Heads}) = P(\text{Heads|Mon})P(\text{Mon}) + P(\text{Heads|Tues})P(\text{Tues})$$
$$= (1/2)(2/3) + (0)(1/3)$$
$$= 1/3.$$

Again, that is assuming that the correct characterization of Beauty's evidence is E_2, "I am woken up *now*", rather than E_1, "I am woken up at least once."

E_2 is in fact the correct characterization of the evidence, given the total evidence principle: we should use the most informative accurate characterization of the subject's evidence. Beauty knows both E_1 and E_2, but E_2 is more informative: that Beauty is woken up *now* logically entails that she is woken up at least once, but not vice versa. Therefore, we should use E_2 rather than merely E_1 to characterize Beauty's evidence.

You might worry that this analysis violates the earlier stated condition (section 11.4.3, condition (*ii*)) that one's evidence should be described purely qualitatively. "Now" does not appear to be a purely qualitative term, so how can the correct characterization of Beauty's evidence use the term "now"?

In reply, our analysis has in fact treated the proposition [I am woken up now] purely qualitatively, in the sense that we draw no distinction between cases that Beauty herself cannot distinguish. Thus, when Beauty is woken on Monday and then when she is woken on Tuesday (if she is), we treat her in both cases as having the same evidence, expressed by "I am woken up now". She does the same probability calculation, to arrive at the same "1/3" answer. This is required by the fact that she has qualitatively the same experiences in both cases.

Contrast this with a treatment that would really violate the "qualitative evidence" condition: suppose we said that on Monday, she learns something that she expresses by "I am woken up now", where "now" refers to Monday – and therefore her evidence is that she is woken up on Monday. In this case, she should calculate the odds that the coin came up heads as follows:

$$P(\text{Heads}) = P(\text{Heads|Mon})P(\text{Mon}) + P(\text{Heads|Tues})P(\text{Tues})$$
$$= (1/2)(1) + (0)(0)$$
$$= 1/2.$$

Then, if she is woken up on Tuesday, she learns "I am woken up now", where this "now" refers to Tuesday, and so she can update her beliefs based on the evidence that she has been woken on Tuesday:

$$P(\text{Heads}) = P(\text{Heads|Mon})P(\text{Mon}) + P(\text{Heads|Tues})P(\text{Tues})$$
$$= (1/2)(0) + (0)(1)$$
$$= 0.$$

This analysis would be violating the qualitative evidence condition by treating cases indistinguishable to the subject as cases of different evidence. By contrast, the reasoning for the 1/3 answer, in which the same numbers get plugged into the equation on Monday and Tuesday, treats qualitatively indistinguishable evidence the same.

References

Bostrom, Nick. 2012. "A Primer on the Doomsday Argument", http://www.anthropic-principle.com/?q=anthropic_principle/doomsday_argument, accessed June 3, 2017.

Carter, Brandon. 1974. "Large Number Coincidences and the Anthropic Principle in Cosmology", pp. 291–8 in M. S. Longair, ed., *Confrontation of Cosmological Theories with Observational Data*. Dordrecht: D. Reidel.

Carter, Brandon. 1983. "The Anthropic Principle and its Implications for Biological Evolution", *Philosophical Transactions of the Royal Society of London A* 310: 347–63.

Davies, Paul. 1983. *God and the New Physics*. New York: Simon and Schuster.

Davies, Paul. 1984. *Superforce: The Search for a Grand Unified Theory of Nature*. New York: Simon and Schuster.

Elga, Adam. 2000. "Self-locating Belief and the Sleeping Beauty Problem", *Analysis* 60: 143–7.

Hacking, Ian. 1987. "The Inverse Gambler's Fallacy: The Argument from Design. The Anthropic Principle Applied to Wheeler Universes", *Mind* 96: 331-40.

Haub, Carl. 2011. "How Many People Have Ever Lived on Earth?", Population Reference Bureau, http://www.prb.org/Publications/Articles/2002/HowManyPeopleHaveEverLivedonEarth.aspx, accessed June 3, 2017.

Leslie, John. 1989. *Universes*. New York: Routledge.

Leslie, John. 1990. "Is the End of the World Nigh?", *Philosophical Quarterly* 40: 65–72.

Lewis, David. 2001. "Sleeping Beauty: Reply to Elga", *Analysis* 61: 171–6.

Manson, Neil and Michael Thrush. 2003. "Fine-Tuning, Multiple Universes, and the 'This Universe' Objection", *Pacific Philosophical Quarterly* 84: 67–83.

Piccione, Michelle and Ariel Rubinstein. 1997. "On the Interpretation of Decision Problems with Imperfect Recall", *Games and Economic Behavior* 20: 3–24.

Susskind, Leonard. 2006. *The Cosmic Landscape: String Theory and the Illusion of Intelligent Design*. New York: Little, Brown & Co.

Tegmark, Max. 2003. "Parallel Universes", *Scientific American*, May: 41–51.

U.S. Census Bureau. 2017. "U.S. and World Population Clock", https://www.census.gov/popclock/, accessed June 3, 2017.

von Mises, Richard. 1957. *Probability, Statistics and Truth*, 2nd revised ed. New York: Macmillan.

White, Roger. 2000. "Fine-Tuning and Multiple Universes", *Nous* 34: 260–76.

12

Concluding Remarks

What have we learned from our examination of the ten philosophical paradoxes? In this chapter, I identify some common types of error that are involved in the paradoxes but that may also occur in other contexts. I then propose two general philosophical lessons vaguely suggested by our study of paradoxes.

12.1 Seven Varieties of Error

The human mind is prone to certain recurring types of mistake. I cannot list all of them here. Here, I will just list seven main kinds of error that contribute prominently to the paradoxes of the preceding chapters.

1. *Hidden assumptions:* Very often, our reasoning is affected by unconscious or implicit assumptions, which can be very difficult to identify. Most of the time, our ability to reason in accordance with hidden assumptions is an asset, since reasoning would be far too difficult and time-consuming if we had to explicitly identify every relevant piece of information. But occasionally, one of our assumptions is mistaken, at

© The Author(s) 2018
M. Huemer, *Paradox Lost*, https://doi.org/10.1007/978-3-319-90490-0_12

least in the particular case we are dealing with, and we are unable to diagnose the error because we have not even noticed that we made the problematic assumption.

That, I take it, is the problem in the case of the semantic paradoxes, namely, the Liar and Sorites Paradoxes. We tacitly assume, roughly speaking, that a sentence that obeys the rules of our language expresses a proposition. We rely on this assumption when we make inferences about the truth-value of the liar sentence, and when we deploy vague sentences in sorites arguments. The assumption is usually close enough to correct for practical purposes; it is only in special cases, such as liar sentences or sorites arguments, that the assumption is importantly wrong.

In the Ravens Paradox, we have another sort of assumption in play: assumptions that are *suggested* by a particular statement but that are not entailed by its literal meaning. Thus, when we hear about "an observation of a black raven", we tacitly imagine a selection process that first locates ravens, then checks their color. We then find it plausible that such an observation must give evidence that all ravens are black. But this assumption about how the observation was gathered is not in fact entailed by the description, "an observation of a black raven", and this fact matters for evaluating the principle that such observations provide evidence for the conclusion [All ravens are black].

2. *Neglect of the small:* We have a tendency to neglect very small quantities or very small differences – to treat the very small as though it were nothing. This is especially true of quantities or differences that are too small to detect. Thus, we tend to confuse *indistinguishability* with *qualitative identity*. This last mistake is aided by a tendency to confuse what is true with what can be verified. These confusions are particularly tempting in the case of mental states, where the distinction between what is and what can be known is more subtle than usual.

These mistakes are at play in the Paradox of the Self-Torturer, where we slide from "the difference between adjacent settings of the device is undetectable" to "there is no difference between adjacent settings of the device".

Sometimes, we confuse the idea that a small change cannot make a *definite* or *determinate* difference to the applicability of some qualitative category with the idea that a small change simply *cannot affect* the underlying property. For instance, we infer from the premise [Adding a single grain of sand cannot make a pile of sand definitely cross over from being a non-heap to being a heap] to the conclusion [Adding a single grain of sand definitely makes no difference to whether something is a heap]. Or we infer from [Turning the dial up by one setting does not determinately make one cross over from experiencing non-pain to experiencing pain] to [Turning the dial up by one setting makes no difference to painfulness].

A similar mistake occurs when we say, for instance, "Eating one potato chip will not make me fatter" (which we might use to justify eating another chip). That is false: eating one potato chip will add a very small but nonzero quantity of fat to your body.

3. *Confusion:* There is more than one type of confusion, but what I have in mind here is a *failure to distinguish* things that are (for purposes of the problem at hand) relevantly different. This includes the error of equivocation, in which one fails to distinguish two or more senses of a word or phrase.

A kind of equivocation occurs in Newcomb's paradox, in which we are invited to confuse two interpretations of the principle, "If an action makes it more likely that your goals will be achieved, then you thereby have a reason to perform that action." Here, the confusion would be between making something more likely in the sense of causing its physical probability to increase, and making something more likely in the sense of providing oneself evidence that the thing will occur.

Another conceptual confusion occurs in the two-envelope paradox, where we confuse a variable (more precisely: a symbol standing for an unknown quantity, whatever its value may be) with a number (more precisely: a symbol expressing a specific, known quantity). We thus erroneously attempt to perform an expected utility calculation on the variable as if it were a number.

4. *Binary thinking:* Often, we apply a discrete system of categories to a continuous reality, causing us to neglect the infinite variations of degree that the underlying reality may exhibit. This mistake is not limited (as the term "binary" might suggest) to cases where we insist on classifying everything into one of two categories; the error may also

occur when we insist on three categories, four categories, and so on, where the underlying reality is subject to continuous variation.

This mistake is at work in the Sorites Paradox, where we treat thoughts or sentences as being either satisfied or unsatisfied by any possible state of affairs, thus enabling us to ascribe to them unique propositional contents.

The same error occurs in the Surprise Quiz Paradox, where we are invited to reason about whether the students at a given point (*i*) believe or (*ii*) do not believe (alternately: (*i*) believe, (*ii*) disbelieve, or (*iii*) withhold judgment) that there will be a quiz the following day. The underlying reality is that individuals may have varying degrees of expectation, that is, one may have more or less confidence, that a quiz will occur the following day.

Binary (otherwise knowns as "black-and-white") thinking is very common in ordinary contexts, especially in political discourse. Suppose, for instance, that one person states that it is rational to fear Muslims due to the many cases of Islamic terrorism over the past few decades.[1] A second person replies that it is irrational to fear Muslims, because most Muslims are peaceful and pose no danger to others. This debate between the options "Muslims are dangerous" and "Muslims are safe" ignores the possibility that there exist different Muslims with varying degrees of dangerousness. The fact that some are dangerous is entirely consistent with the fact that others are peaceful.

A similar error occurs when we debate whether the drug laws "work" or "do not work", whether gun control laws "work" or "do not work", and the like, ignoring the possibility that the laws work to some degree but also fail to some degree.

5. *Oversimplification:* Binary thinking is a species of the broader category of oversimplification, in which we unduly limit the options considered. Another common species of oversimplification is that in which we consider some controversial principle, but we consider only the options of (*i*) endorsing the principle in its simplest, unqualified form, and (*ii*) rejecting the principle outright. In most cases, a superior

---

[1] As Michael Flynn famously stated in 2016, before he was chosen as national security advisor to President Trump (Gibbons-Neff 2016).

option is to refine the principle in a way that retains its underlying motivation while avoiding its most serious problems.

For instance, critics of the Principle of Indifference argue that we must reject the principle since it leads to paradoxes. But we need not choose between accepting the most naive reading of the Principle of Indifference and completely rejecting the Principle. We also have the option of adopting qualifications to the Principle, accepting it only for certain ranges of cases, and so on. Critics of the Principle of Indifference also err in taking an oversimplified view of what (for purposes of applying the Principle) counts as a *reason* for preferring one alternative over another. For instance, if there is no empirical evidence as to the color of a certain book, it is said that there is no reason to prefer the view that the book is non-green over the view that the book is green. This neglects the a priori reason for thinking the book is more likely non-green, namely, that non-green color-shades comprise a larger volume of the color solid than green shades.

6. *Inappropriate Idealization:* Sometimes, we invent idealized scenarios, or discuss real scenarios in an idealized way – that is, we abstract from physical limitations that we know to apply in the real world but that we consider irrelevant distractions from some central problem. And sometimes when we do this, we are wrong about what is an irrelevant distraction; sometimes the details from which we abstract are in fact essential to the problem.

Thus, in the Shooting Room paradox, we may initially feel that the finitude of the actual population of the Earth is an irrelevant distraction; we can simply assume an unlimited population. (Alternately, we may think that we can at least assume a *large enough* population that the probability that the shooting room will run out of victims is "negligible".) We likewise assume away the costs (in time, energy, and so on) of running the Shooting Room, which may seem like irrelevant distractions from the central, conceptual problem.

Idealization is a useful tool in some situations. Students of physics are sometimes asked to imagine objects sliding along frictionless planes, or falling in perfect vacua. Students of economics are sometimes asked to imagine perfectly competitive markets using infinitely divisible currency. This kind of idealization can enable one to better understand the most important principles operative in a given scenario, without irrelevant distractions. In these cases, the factors we abstract from are small in comparison with the factors retained in the analysis, and our reasoning provides an approximate picture of reality.

Matters are otherwise in the Shooting Room case: in that case, the unrealistic assumptions are essential to generating the paradox. Any possible way of incorporating the real physical limitations (for instance, any finite population size we may assume, however large) results in a very different prediction, entirely dissolving the paradox. So the idealizations do not give us an approximate picture of reality.

Inappropriate idealization occurs often in other areas of inquiry, though seldom leading to outright paradox. It often occurs, for example, when we reason about what the law should be in some area (drug laws, gun control laws, and so on) on the assumption that everyone will follow the law – that is, without taking account of the costs that will be produced by some individuals' non-compliance. It may also occur when we reason about policy without taking account of the possibility of corruption or incompetence by the individuals tasked with implementing policy. Sometimes, those matters are minor distractions; but other times, they are essential to the issue.[2]

7. *Inference from Partial Data:* It is well-known in epistemology that sometimes, we have evidence that, taken by itself, supports a given conclusion, and yet that same evidence, when taken together with some additional information, fails to support (or even undermines) that same conclusion. That is, it can be true that e_1 supports h, yet (e_1 & e_2) fails to support h. More generally, the degree to which e_1 supports h often differs from the degree to which (e_1 & e_2) supports h. In such cases, it is an error to infer h from e_1; we must base our opinion about h on our total relevant evidence, or the logically strongest set of information that we have relevant to h.

This principle is key to resolving the puzzles about self-locating belief. Thus, in the Sleeping Beauty paradox, the subject should base her credence in [The coin came up heads] on the evidence [I am awake now], rather than the logically weaker evidence [I am awakened at

---

[2] For more on inappropriate idealization, see Huemer 2016.

least once at some time]. In evaluating the Multiverse Argument, we should base our conclusion on the evidence [I exist in a life-sustaining universe] rather than merely [Some being exists in a life-sustaining universe].

I have tried to generalize from the specific mistakes in each of our ten paradoxes, to arrive at kinds of error that are common in a variety of circumstances. This gives us some reason to hope that the study of paradoxes can help us to think more clearly in general, not just about paradoxes.

12.2   Against Radical Revision

I turn to the first philosophical lesson vaguely suggested by our study of paradoxes. The truth about disputed matters is usually subtle and complex, not simple and obvious. That goes even for the truth about our tendency toward error. When we go wrong, it is typically not in the most simple, obvious way; there is some degree of subtlety to the mistakes we make.

So when we consider a paradox, or any other case of known mistaken reasoning, the most likely thing to have gone wrong is typically not that some principle regarded for centuries as a self-evident, necessary truth is flat-out wrong. For example, it probably is not that we were simply wrong to think contradictions can't be true, or wrong to think that any thing must either have or lack a given property. It probably is not going to turn out that one of the propositions generally regarded as among the most obvious and least controversial of all propositions is in error. It is much more likely, for example, that a paradox takes advantage of a hidden assumption that we have yet to explicitly identify, perhaps one that is generally true but that fails in special cases. Thus, paradox solutions that require us to give up classical logic are unpromising on their face. In general, as (I hope) we have seen in the preceding chapters, paradoxes can be solved without messing with logic. We don't, for example, need propositions that lack truth values or that are both true and false at once.

Sometimes we have a traditional intuition that is less central and obvious than the laws of logic but still strong and widespread, as in the case of the Principle of Indifference. Again, there should be some subtlety in our account of error: prima facie, we should be suspicious of the idea that (say) the Principle of Indifference is completely wrong and that there is nothing at all to this widespread intuition. It is much more likely that the Principle requires refinement and clarification. Most intellectual problems are best addressed with modest rather than radical revisions to our beliefs.

12.3   Reality Is Intelligible, with Difficulty

In his *Critique of Pure Reason*, Immanuel Kant presents four "antinomies of pure reason".[3] These are four cases in which, according to Kant, one can present compelling arguments for each of two incompatible metaphysical conclusions. For instance, in one of the antinomies, Kant argues first that the world must have a beginning in time, and then that the world cannot have a beginning in time. Kant's purpose in this, roughly speaking, is to criticize metaphysics as an attempt to understand objective reality. Reason, he held, can only be fruitfully applied within the realm of "appearances", not to "things in themselves".

I have not addressed Kant's antinomies, mostly because they are less clear and sharp than the paradoxes I have addressed, and they are of interest mainly to Kant scholars. My purpose in mentioning Kant's antinomies is as a foil for my own view of the paradoxes of philosophy. My own view is that objective reality, in general, is difficult but not impossible for human beings to grasp.

Begin with the point about *difficulty*. It is easy for human beings to go wrong: very often what seems obvious to us is false or confused, and we may persist in our errors for quite a long time. One reason for this is simply that we do not realize how error-prone we are; we thus tend to be highly overconfident in our initial impressions of things. This is something that you can learn by teaching college students, who frequently enter a class with firm but drastically oversimplified notions. College students, of course, are hardly the only examples; the lesson is also driven home by the study of the history of science and the history of philosophy,

---

[3] Kant [1781] 1998, pp. 470–95, B454–88.

in both of which one finds that nearly every theory that was ever seriously advanced was wrong. But the study of paradoxes is perhaps the most striking and entertaining way of driving home the point about our cognitive flaws. It also has the advantage that one cannot pass off the errors of which one learns as merely someone else's errors, since almost all of us are subject to the intellectual illusions that make up a good paradox. Recognizing how fallible we are can help us learn to counter our native overconfidence.

At the same time, we should not heed the counsel of skeptics and subjectivists: we should not give up on the project of understanding the world as it really is. The world is extremely complicated, subtle, and often mysterious, and the human mind is prone to many oversights, biases, and confusions. But the world is not *inconsistent*, nor the human mind *incorrigible*. It is possible, with work, to root out our confusions and, bit by bit, improve our understanding of the world. If there were a case to be made that reason is impotent, that case would perhaps be best made through considering the various paradoxes that have beset the human mind and to which the experts have yet to agree on a solution. The most satisfying way to counter such a case is to provide the solutions to the paradoxes.

References

Gibbons-Neff, Thomas. 2016. "'Fear of Muslims Is Rational': What Trump's New National Security Adviser Has Said Online", *Washington Post*, November 18, https://www.washingtonpost.com/news/checkpoint/wp/2016/11/18/trumps-new-national-security-adviser-has-said-some-incendiary-things-on-the-internet/, accessed June 3, 2017.

Huemer, Michael. 2016. "Confessions of a Utopophobe", *Social Philosophy and Policy* 33 (2016): 214–34.

Kant, Immanuel. [1781] 1998. *Critique of Pure Reason*, tr. and ed. Paul Guyer and Allen Wood. Cambridge: Cambridge University Press.

Index[1]

[1] Note: Page numbers followed by 'n' refer to notes.

Printed in Singapore by Markono Print Media Pte Ltd